2195

BJ
1275
.H49
2000

INEQUALITY AND CHRISTIAN ETHICS

Inequality and Christian Ethics provides a moral and empirical analysis of contemporary inequality. Drawing on Christian social ethics, political philosophy, and development economics, the book seeks to create an interdisciplinary conversation that illuminates not only the contemporary realities and trends of inequality, but their moral significance as well. It is necessary to examine and understand inequality in various forms – which the book maps out – including disparity in income, education, and health as well as differentials based on race, ethnicity, gender, and nationality. The book draws in particular on the theological ethics of Gustavo Gutiérrez and H. Richard Niebuhr to provide a Christian ethical approach to inequality and well-being. It considers the "capability approach" set forth by Amartya Sen, Nobel laureate in Economics. Sen's framework helps to add specificity to what the commitment to "equality before God" would demand in social and economic relations.

DOUGLAS A. HICKS is Assistant Professor of Leadership Studies and Religion at the University of Richmond, Virginia, and he teaches courses in international leadership, social movements, ethics, and leadership and religious values. An ordained minister in the Presbyterian Church, he has participated in seminars in South Africa, Kenya, India, Guatemala, and Mexico. His articles have appeared in *World Development*, *The Journal of Ecumenical Studies*, and *Sojourners* and he contributed to the CD-ROM *On Common Ground: World Religions in America*.

NEW STUDIES IN CHRISTIAN ETHICS 16

General editor
Robin Gill

Editorial board
Stephen R. L. Clark, Stanley Hauerwas,
Robin W. Lovin

Christian ethics has increasingly assumed a central place within academic theology. At the same time the growing power and ambiguity of modern science and the rising dissatisfaction within the social sciences about claims to value-neutrality have prompted renewed interest in ethics within the secular academic world. There is, therefore, a need for studies in Christian ethics which, as well as being concerned with the relevance of Christian ethics to the present day secular debate, are well informed about parallel discussions in recent philosophy, science or social science. New Studies in Christian Ethics aims to provide books that do this at the highest intellectual level and demonstrate that Christian ethics can make a distinctive contribution to this debate – either in moral substance or in terms of underlying moral justifications.

Other titles published in the series

1. KIERAN CRONIN
   Rights and Christian Ethics

2. IAN MCDONALD
   Biblical Interpretation and Christian Ethics

3. JAMES MACKEY
   Power and Christian Ethics

4. IAN S. MARKHAM
   Plurality and Christian Ethics

5. JEAN PORTER
   Moral Action and Christian Ethics

6. WILLIAM SCHWEIKER
   Responsibility and Christian Ethics

7. E. CLINTON GARDNER
   Justice and Christian Ethics

INEQUALITY AND CHRISTIAN ETHICS

DOUGLAS A. HICKS

University of Richmond, Virginia

Colorado Christian University
Library
180 S. Garrison
Lakewood, Colorado 80226

CAMBRIDGE
UNIVERSITY PRESS

PUBLISHED BY THE PRESS SYNDICATE OF THE UNIVERSITY OF CAMBRIDGE
The Pitt Building, Trumpington Street, Cambridge, United Kingdom

CAMBRIDGE UNIVERSITY PRESS
The Edinburgh Building, Cambridge CB2 2RU, UK   www.cup.cam.ac.uk
40 West 20th Street, New York, NY 10011–4211, USA   www.cup.org
10 Stamford Road, Oakleigh, Melbourne 3166, Australia
Ruiz de Alarcón 13, 28014 Madrid, Spain

© Douglas A. Hicks 2000

This book is in copyright. Subject to statutory exception
and to the provisions of relevant collective licensing agreements,
no reproduction of any part may take place without
the written permission of Cambridge University Press.

First published 2000

Printed in the United Kingdom at the University Press, Cambridge

Typeset in Baskerville 11/12.5pt   [CE]

A catalogue record for this book is available from the British Library

Library of Congress cataloguing in publication data

Hicks, Douglas A.
Inequality and Christian ethics / Douglas A. Hicks.
p. cm. (New Studies in Christian Ethics; 16)
Includes bibliograhical references and index.
ISBN 0 521 77253 2 (hardback)
ISBN 0 521 78754 8 (paperback)
1. Christian ethics. 2. Equality – Religious aspects – Christianity.
I. Title. II. Series.
BJ1275.H49 2000
241–dc21   99-087146 CIP

ISBN 0 521 77253 2 hardback
ISBN 0 521 78754 8 paperback

We measure what we value.

Paula Rayman[1]

[S]o long as no good, and then no single group of men and women, is dominant, so long as all value doesn't flow in one direction, we won't be counting and measuring all the time. Actual inequalities in this or that sphere will matter less than they do now; we will measure ourselves locally but won't need to fix our place in some larger and more general hierarchy. Or, more likely, some people will still need to do that and will look for some way of doing it, but enough of the rest of us will think this activity slightly ridiculous or beside the point.

Michael Walzer[2]

I do not mean for there to be relief for others and hardship for you, but rather it is a question of equality, with your present surplus going towards their lack. At another time, their surplus may be for your lack, so that there may be equality. As it is written, "The one who had much did not have too much, and the one who had little did not have too little."

2 Corinthians 8:13–15[3]

[1] Paula Rayman, "The New Economic Equation," presentation at the Center for the Study of Values in Public Life, Harvard Divinity School, November 19, 1996.
[2] Michael Walzer, "Response," in David Miller and Michael Walzer (eds.), *Pluralism, Justice, and Equality* (Oxford: Oxford University Press, 1995), p. 285.
[3] Author's translation; quoted biblical text is Exodus 16:18.

Contents

Figures and tables

Acknowledgment

Parts of chapter 2, chapter 10, and the appendices are reprinted, in modified form, from *World Development*, vol. 25, no. 8, Douglas A. Hicks, "The Inequality-Adjusted Human Development Index: A Constructive Proposal," pp. 1283–1298, copyright 1997, with permission from Elsevier Science.

General editor's preface

This is the sixteenth book in the series New Studies in Christian Ethics. The subject of inequality has concerned quite a number of theologians over the last few years. However, few if any of them show the sort of sophistication offered by Douglas Hicks in this book. In some respects *Inequality and Christian Ethics* is similar to the first book in the series, Kieran Cronin's *Rights and Christian Ethics*. The latter noticed that theologians often talk about "rights" but seldom show that they have a rigorous understanding of the detailed discussion of this issue in recent philosophy. Douglas Hicks has also noted a similar gap in the theological literature, although in this case in relation to the philosophical and economic discussion of equality and inequality.

There are further points of contact between Douglas Hicks's *Inequality and Christian Ethics* and other books in the series. Peter Sedgwick's *The Market Economy and Christian Ethics* is probably the closest. Both books offer a detailed account of socio-economics in the modern world, which is well informed and also careful not to claim too much in the name of Christian ethics. David Fergusson's *Community, Liberalism and Christian Ethics* offers a similar tension on the crucial issue of Christian distinctiveness in a pluralistic society, which differs significantly from the "ecclesial ethics" approach of theologians such as Stanley Hauerwas. Garth Hallett's *Priorities and Christian Ethics* shares Douglas Hicks's emphasis upon the needy and vulnerable: both are clearly motivated by a deep moral and theological perception of injustice in the world, as the opening pages of the present book make clear.

Having identified inequality as a subject which needs to be explored in greater depth, Douglas Hicks proceeds to offer a theological account of this issue which makes full use of the rival theories of John Rawls and Amartya Sen. It is finally Sen's understanding of "equality of basic capability" which he finds to be the more fruitful and which he believes can be better related to Christian ethics. From an explicitly secular perspective Sen has nonetheless long argued that moral perception is inextricably involved in an adequate understanding of equality and inequality in the world. An equality of basic capability involves qualitative issues and not simply a quantitative provision to satisfy basic needs. Douglas Hicks argues that, once this is acknowledged, Christian ethics can contribute at three distinctive levels. First, it provides a moral vision and justification for how inequality matters and why public response is needed. Then it can offer moral examples of Christians, such as Martin Luther King and Desmond Tutu, who have actively striven against inequality. And, thirdly, Christian ethics provides a particularly compelling moral call to action: at best, Christian communities can transform lives and behavior towards a greater equality of capability.

This is a lucid, scholarly, and highly committed book. It works closely with the two aims of the series, namely to promote monographs in Christian ethics which engage centrally with the present secular moral debate at the highest possible intellectual level and, secondly, to encourage contributors to demonstrate that Christian ethics can make a distinctive contribution to this debate.

I commend *Inequality and Christian Ethics* very highly indeed. It sets new standards for theologians discussing equality and inequality, as well as offering a thoughtful challenge to secularists who see the need for values and action beyond analysis in this crucial area.

ROBIN GILL

Preface

Recently I had the opportunity to visit South Africa, five years into its transition towards legal and political democracy. South Africa's present-day reality is marked by rich cultural diversity and hope amidst turmoil. Most striking to this observer, as I was editing *Inequality and Christian Ethics*, was the degree of social and economic inequality. As this book will emphasize, inequality can be indicated in various ways; flying into Cape Town at dusk, I could see below me a "map" of inequality contrasting well-lighted neighborhoods with others that were nearly or completely dark. These latter areas were part of vast shanty-towns and squatter settlements that have taken root around Cape Town in the past few years. One of the most beautiful cities in the world, Cape Town has suburbs as "modern" and affluent as any, complete with Audi dealerships and "cyber-cafes." Yet they exist just miles away from the absolute poverty of cardboard and metal shelters that characterize nearly every city of the developing world.

It is no wonder that violence, fear, and social division permeate South African society. It is not an overstatement to say that people in the suburbs *defend* themselves against their predominantly black neighbors – with fences and even barbed wire protecting houses, businesses, and schools. Carrying a gun has become commonplace. Magazines include prominent advertisements for security companies and alarm systems. Affluent people will only leave their vehicles in guarded parking lots, and even "common" cars have complex alarm systems that cost money to install and time to operate. A few car owners have gone as far as designing "flame throwing" mechanisms in order to deter or maim car-jackers. South Africa's transition toward democracy has laid bare the fact that social and economic inequality entails high costs for all people – citizens or foreigners, black, white, or "coloured," rich or poor.

By the numbers as well as by such narrative descriptions, South Africa experiences one of the highest levels of income-based inequality in the world. Yet the realities described above are just an exaggerated version of the phenomena that have also occurred in the United States, the United Kingdom, and in the world as a whole. The United States, by most accounts, suffers the highest level of income-based inequality in the developed countries – and it has increased significantly over the past three decades. The United Kingdom saw the steepest rise in inequality across the 1980s and into the 1990s. Many if not most readers of this book live in the United States or the United Kingdom; these facts make the book of particular interest to them.

In an era of globalization, rapid changes have allowed some people access to the entire world by means of the internet and air travel, while the majority do not ever leave their own country. When the world population is grouped together as one whole, the level of income inequality is as high as inequality in any single nation of the world. That is, global inequality stands at roughly the same level as exists in South Africa. This reality should be of concern to anyone who speaks of, or seeks to create, a global village or even a sense of global solidarity. If the world actually operated as one community, it would face the kind of social and economic pressures that plague South Africa. Many people, including Christians and other persons of faith, have expressed moral concern about such realities and trends of inequality. I hope that this book helps to clarify and promote discussions about the moral, economic, and policy-related dimensions of inequality, and their interrelation. Sharpened understandings, in turn, should lead to more determined personal and public responses.

Conspicuous on these pages are ideas appropriated from professors at Davidson College, Duke University, and Harvard

University: to them I owe the bulk of my intellectual debts and to them I offer my profound gratitude. At Davidson, Charles Ratliff moved me to consider the moral issues of economic distribution, posing the question (as only he could), "A rising tide may lift all boats, but what if you don't have a boat?" Clark Ross and Peter Hess provided me with the essential framework and tools of economic analysis. David Kaylor introduced me to liberation theology and critical biblical scholarship. Lois "Sandy" Kemp awakened my conscience and intellect to injustice and deprivation in Latin America, and she taught me the Spanish I needed to hear at first hand the stories of people in Central America, Mexico, Puerto Rico, and migrant worker camps of North Carolina.

Professors at Duke Divinity School helped me to develop the vision and skills required for constructing the "theologically informed approach" presented on the following pages. Mary McClintock Fulkerson taught me, in the spirit of "*Ecclesia reformata, semper reformanda*," to draw upon our shared faith tradition in order to address gender, race, and class inequalities. Frederick Herzog lived his theological passion and creativity. Without Thomas A. Langford I would be much less able "to think theologically." Thomas E. McCollough, who continues to provide good counsel and insight, encouraged me to invite others to join in morally serious conversation and action.

The professors with whom I learned and taught at Harvard sharpened my skills and vision. Harvey Cox, Cornel West, Diana Eck, John Rawls, Stephen Marglin, and Elisabeth Schüssler Fiorenza each contributed to my thinking on one or more dimensions of this project. From across the Charles River at Boston College, David Hollenbach, S.J., was a crucial model for developing a Christian ethical approach to economic life.

My greatest intellectual debts accrued during this project will be all-too apparent on the pages that follow. I am grateful to have had the opportunity to study with Amartya Sen, whose insights into ethics and economics pervade my own perspective. Much of the normative work I undertake is an effort to evaluate critically and to expand constructively the proposals offered by Professor Sen. If I have deepened a conversation between his "capability approach" and Christian social ethics, I will be pleased. His earning of the Nobel Prize in Economic Sciences is a tribute to his work in social choice and welfare economics, including his pioneering books and articles on the complexities of inequality.

I express profound appreciation to Ronald F. Thiemann, whose counsel, proposals, and support have been invaluable. In my view, Dean Thiemann embodies his vision of a person of faith who contributes to society by drawing upon the analytical skills and moral perspectives at his disposal. His framework for religion in public life has helped to shape not just this work but my wider intellectual project.

I would also like to express my appreciation to friends and colleagues who have read and discussed significant portions of this work, either in dissertation or book form: Robert B. Bennett, Jr., Joanne B. Ciulla, Brent B. Coffin, Richard A. Couto, Stephen J. Davis, Mark Engler, Eric Gregory, Cynthia McIntyre, Douglas F. Ottati, Brian Palmer, Robert L. Payton, Ellie Pierce, Terry L. Price, and Christopher Steck, S.J. Lawrence C. Metzelaar assisted me in the graphic presentation of the socioeconomic data. Thanks are due to Cindy Venturini, Raegan Williams, and Angela Mims for their research assistance at the University of Richmond. I express a special word of gratitude to Robert A. Johnson, Jr., of Union Theological Seminary in Virginia and the Office of Theology and Worship of the Presbyterian Church (USA), for his timely and thoughtful comments.

The arguments were improved by responses to my work at meetings sponsored by the Duke University Department of Religion, the American Academy of Religion, the Yale-Harvard-Boston College Ethics Colloquium, the Harvard Religion and Society Colloquium, the Religion, Values, and the Economy Forum sponsored by Harvard's Center for the Study of Values in Public Life, and the Leaders/Scholars Association. I benefited greatly from the welcome extended to me as an exchange scholar, during the 1997–98 year, by the Yale University graduate program in Religious Studies; I offer special thanks to Margaret Farley, Thomas Ogletree, and Gene Outka.

Substantial funding for dissertation research and writing was provided by two grants from the Mellon Foundation.

Faculty members at the Jepson School of Leadership Studies, at the University of Richmond, have been invaluable colleagues and conversation partners as we together seek to articulate and promote leadership as service, especially service to the most vulnerable citizens of our society and in the world as a whole. I hope that this work furthers the social and moral analysis needed to understand the human contexts that require effective and ethical leadership.

The parishioners of a number of communities of faith – especially Second Presbyterian Church of Indianapolis and Clarendon Hill Presbyterian Church of Somerville, Massachusetts – have enabled me to understand the equality before God as a form of communal practice and as a social vision. I express my gratitude to James D. Miller, William G. Enright, Joan B. Malick, Thomas W. Walker, Ray Bowden, and Patricia Budd Kepler for their ability to articulate the integration of faith commitments and intellectual inquiry.

I would like to state my appreciation to Kevin Taylor, Jan Chapman, and Michelle Williams at Cambridge University Press for their creative, constructive, and timely work in publishing this book.

Finally, I want to thank, for their support, Cathy and Michael Coscia, Judith Grant, Stuart Shapiro, Mary Malloy Dutkiewicz, Pat and Tom Kepler, Michael and Meg O'Leary, Stacy Marcus, Robert Johnson, Marianne Vermeer, and all of my family members – especially my parents Susan and Harry. Distributive justice and equality would mean little in a world without the friendship these wonderful people know how to share.

Abbreviations

ERP	*Economic Report of the President*
GDI	Gender-related development index
GDP	Gross domestic product
GNP	Gross national product
GWP	Gross world product
HDI	Human development index
HDR	*Human Development Report*
HPI	Human poverty index
IAHDI	Inequality-adjusted human development index
ILO	International Labour Organization
ISEW	Index of sustainable economic welfare
LIS	Luxembourg Income Study
MER	Market-based exchange rates
NCCB	National Conference of Catholic Bishops
NCES	National Center for Education Statistics
NGO	Non-governmental organization
OECD	Organization of Economic Cooperation and Development
PARE	Price adjustments of rates of exchange
PPP	Purchasing power parity
PQLI	Physical quality of life index
UN	United Nations
UNDP	United Nations Development Programme
UNESCO	United Nations Educational, Scientific and Cultural Organization
WA	*World Bank Atlas* method
WDR	*World Development Report*

PART ONE

Contextualizing inequality

CHAPTER I

Introduction: inequality matters

"Why is Inequality Back on the Agenda?" Economists Ravi Kanbur and Nora Lustig pose this question as the title of a recent essay.[1] Their own careful answer contributes to the growing chorus of international and domestic voices attending to inequality, its causes and its effects. While economic and political analyses have been at the center of this renewed public discussion, less prominent has been an explicit focus on the moral dimensions. How and why does inequality matter morally?

The stated purpose of the series, New Studies in Christian Ethics, is to engage a secular moral debate and to demonstrate the distinctive contribution of Christian ethics to that debate. To that end, this book considers the various dimensions of the public discourse on inequality. It offers a constructive approach that engages resources in Christian social ethics along with perspectives in political philosophy and development economics. The book seeks not only to contribute to the wider moral debate about inequality, but also to shed light on how moral values operate (and should operate) in all aspects of the discussions. It aims to understand and then move beyond the numbers, providing a moral framework for understanding and responding to them.

At the beginning, it is important to clarify the distinction between *poverty* and *inequality*: while poverty is a condition of

[1] Ravi Kanbur and Nora Lustig, "Why is Inequality Back on the Agenda?" Paper prepared for the Annual Bank Conference on Development Economics, World Bank, Washington, DC, April 28–30, 1999 (version: April 21, 1999).

people at the bottom end of a socioeconomic distribution, inequality is a phenomenon of a distribution as a whole. While poverty can be understood in either absolute or relative terms, inequality is necessarily a relational concept. Related empirically and conceptually, the two concepts are distinct. As one example of the difference between poverty and inequality, consider the context of the United States: while the official US poverty rate was roughly the same in 1996 as it was in 1968,[2] inequality of income expanded significantly over that period. (This is largely due to the fact that the "top" fifth of the population saw their incomes rise significantly, while the poorest fifth experienced little or no rise in real income.) The most explicit focus of this book is on the moral and social aspects of inequality.

In order to assess contemporary realities and recent trends, it is necessary to employ one or more measures of inequality. The choice of measure(s) is not without controversy, since no one indicator can fully capture the complexities of the issue. While various measures will be used, much of the analysis will employ a standard, summary measure of inequality called the *Gini coefficient*. The Gini coefficient for a population can vary from 0 to 1; values near "0" represent very low levels of inequality, and values near "1" represent high levels of inequality. Thus, if a Gini coefficient for a country increases significantly over time, as it has in the United States in the past three decades, it indicates rising inequality.[3]

This chapter introduces the contemporary state of, and the public debate over, inequality of various kinds and in different contexts. The chapter concludes with an outline of the argument and structure of the book. Perspectives from Christian social ethics can make a vital contribution to the wide public

---

[2] The official US poverty rate for all persons in 1996 was 13.7 percent, while in 1968 it was 12.8 percent (US Census Bureau, Historical Poverty Tables – Persons, table 2 <http://www.census.gov/hhes/poverty/histpov/hstpov2.html>). I do not mean to overlook important changes in the composition of the poor or the causes of changes in the poverty rate over this period; these are not, however, foci of my inquiry.

[3] The technical aspects and value-assumptions of the Gini coefficient are provided in appendix A.

debate. Toward that end, it is crucial to consider the multiple dimensions of contemporary realities and discussions of inequality.

CONTEMPORARY INEQUALITIES AND PUBLIC DISCOURSE: THE US CONTEXT

Over the decade of the 1990s, economic inequality has become increasingly prominent as an issue within American public discourse. Social scientists and commentators from a variety of perspectives have taken notice that since the early 1970s, inequality of income has increased across periods of economic boom and bust. By all measures, income inequality stands at its highest level in the postwar period. Overall US income inequality between 1968 and 1994, as measured by the Gini coefficient, increased by over 23 percent for families and by 18 percent for households.[4] By the mid 1990s, the top 20 percent of the household income distribution received nearly half of total national income, exceeding the income of the middle 60 percent. The share of the top 20 percent also amounted to approximately thirteen times the share of the poorest 20 percent.[5] The current income distribution in the United States is the worst of all developed nations.[6] These trends and figures of inequality have received significant attention in the mainstream press and in scholarly circles.[7]

[4] US Census Bureau, Historical Income Tables – Families, table F-4, "Gini Ratios for Families, by Race and Hispanic Origin of Householder: 1947 to 1997," <http://www.census.gov/hhes/income/histinc.fo4.html>, and US Census Bureau, Historical Income Tables – Households, table H-4, "Gini Ratios for Households, by Race and Hispanic Origin of Householder: 1967 to 1997," <http://www.census.gov/hhes/income/histinc.ho4.html>. See also Daniel H. Weinberg, "A Brief Look at Postwar US Income Inequality," *Current Population Reports – Household Economic Studies* P60–191, US Census Bureau, 1996, p. 1, based on Census Bureau data.

[5] Weinberg, "US Income Inequality," p. 2, based on Census Bureau data. In 1997, the highest fifth of households claimed 49.4 percent of total income, the middle three-fifths earned 47.1 percent, and the lowest fifth dropped to 3.6 percent (US Census Bureau, Historical Income Tables – Households, table H-2, "Share of Aggregate Income Received by Each Fifth and Top 5 Percent of Households (All Races): 1967 to 1997," <http://www.census.gov/hhes/income/histinc.ho2.html>).

[6] See my discussions in chapter 4.

[7] Some of the recent articles and opinion-editorials on various dimensions of economic inequality in the *New York Times* include Steven A. Holmes, "Income Disparity

Inequality has not always been such a focal issue of public discussion and debate in the United States. In 1958 John Kenneth Galbraith asserted in a widely read book that "as an economic and social concern, inequality has been declining in urgency." He went on to state that "liberals and conservatives alike" agreed that increased production, instead of redistribution, was an appropriate social goal that would lead to reduction in inequality.[8] This claim was widely associated with the sentiment that "a rising tide lifts all boats." Alongside the focus on the increase of production, Galbraith emphasized the need for aid programs aimed specifically at that small percentage of

Between Poorest and Richest Rises" (6/20/1996), A1, A18; Louis Uchitelle, "Strike Points to Inequality in 2-Tier Job Market" (8/8/1997), A22; Tamar Lewin, "Women Losing Ground to Men in Widening Income Difference" (9/15/1997), A1, A12; Steven A. Holmes, "New Reports Say Minorities Benefit in Fiscal Recovery" (9/30/1997), A1, A26; Richard W. Stevenson, "Black–White Economic Gap is Narrowing, White House Says" (2/10/1998), A16; "Black–White Income Inequalities" (editorial, 2/17/1998, with letters to the editor, 2/23/1998); Peter Passell, "Rich Nation, Poor Nation: Is Anyone Even Looking for a Cure?" (8/13/1998), D2; Louis Uchitelle, "The Have-Nots, at Least, Have Shelter in a Storm" (9/20/1998), BU4; Lester Thurow, "The Boom that Wasn't" (1/18/1999); Michael M. Weinstein, "How Low the Boom Can Go" (6/13/1999); and Sheryl Gay Stolberg, "Racial Divide Found in Maternal Mortality" (6/18/1999), A18. An important article in the *Washington Post* is James Lardner, "Deadly Disparities: Americans' Widening Gap in Incomes May Be Narrowing Our Lifespans" (8/16/1998), C1, C4. Notably, the *Wall Street Journal* has also addressed this phenomenon: Alan Murray, "Income Inequality Grows Amid Recovery" (7/1/1996), A1; Irving Kristol, "Inequality Without Class Conflict" (12/18/1997), A22.

An important Census Bureau Report is: Weinberg, "US Income Inequality." The problem is discussed in chapters within many recent *Economic Reports of the President* (US Council of Economic Advisors: U.S Government Printing Office): *ERP 1992*, chap. 4; *ERP 1995*, chap. 5; *ERP 1997*, chap. 5; *ERP 1998*, chap. 4; and *ERP 1999*, chap. 3.

A much fuller review and discussion of the scholarly debate about economic inequality in the United States is contained in chapter 4. It is worth noting here just a few scholars who have offered analyses accessible to a wide public audience: Richard B. Freeman, "Unequal Incomes: The Worrisome Distribution of the Fruits of American Growth," *Harvard Magazine* 100/3 (January–February 1998), 62–64; Richard B. Freeman, with responses by Ernesto Cortes, Jr., Heidi Hartmann, James Heckman, Paul Krugman, Michael Piore, Frances Fox Piven, and James Tobin, "The New Inequality," *Boston Review* 21/6 (December 1996–January 1997); and Sheldon Danziger and Peter Gottschalk, *America Unequal* (New York: Russell Sage/Harvard University Press, 1995). An examination of inequality of wealth in the United States is Edward N. Wolff, *Top Heavy: The Increasing Inequality of Wealth in America and What Can Be Done about It* (New York: New Press, 1995).

[8] Galbraith, *The Affluent Society* (New York: Mentor Books/Houghton Mifflin, 1958), p. 83.

people who would not benefit from growth. Such programs would comprise Lyndon Johnson's War on Poverty beginning in 1964. The combined emphasis on production and targeted programs led to the decline in public discussion on inequality as an issue of its own merit.

In the 1970s social analysts continued to focus on poverty rather than on inequality as the principal issue of public concern.[9] Sheldon Danziger and Peter Gottschalk introduce a 1993 edited volume in this way:

Conventional wisdom about income inequality in America is radically different in the early 1990s than it was ten to fifteen years ago. At that time, Alan Blinder (1980) began a review article on the distribution of economic well-being by noting that "the more things change, the more they remain the same." Blinder's central conclusion was "when we . . . consider the *distribution* of economic welfare – economic equality, as it is commonly called – the central stylized fact is one of *constancy*. As measured in the official data, income inequality was just about the same in 1977 . . . as it was in 1947." (p. 416) Henry Aaron (1978) put it even more colorfully by stating that following changes in the income distribution "was like watching the grass grow." (p. 17) . . . Inequality, in contrast to poverty, was not much discussed in Congress or in the media.[10]

---

[9] There are, of course, notable exceptions. Arthur Okun's classic work, *Equality and Efficiency: The Big Tradeoff* (Washington: The Brookings Institution, 1975), calls for significant attention to inequalities alongside a focus on growth of production. Various works of Sheldon Danziger and colleagues, as well as of Lester Thurow, have been centrally important from the late 1970s to the present. In the 1970s, see, for instance, Danziger and Eugene Smolensky, "Income Inequality: Problems of Measurement and Interpretation," in Maurice Zeitlin (ed.), *American Society, Inc.* (Chicago: Rand McNally, 1977), and Thurow, *Generating Inequality: Mechanisms of Distribution in the U.S. Economy* (New York: Basic Books, 1975). The theoretical examination of inequality was expanded in the 1970s, most notably by A. B. Atkinson and Amartya Sen. For important contributions, see in particular Atkinson, "On the Measurement of Inequality," *Journal of Economic Theory* 2 (1970), and Sen, *On Economic Inequality* (Oxford: Clarendon Press, 1973). A full bibliography of the theoretical contributions up to the present day is contained in an "expanded edition with a substantial annexe by James Foster and Amartya Sen" of Sen's *On Economic Inequality* (Oxford: Clarendon, 1997).

[10] Danziger and Gottschalk (eds.), introduction to *Uneven Tides: Rising Inequality in America* (New York: Russell Sage, 1993), p. 3. The authors cite Alan Blinder, "The Level and Distribution of Economic Well-Being," in Martin Feldstein (ed.), *The American Economy in Transition* (Chicago: University of Chicago Press, 1980), and Henry Aaron, *Politics and the Professors: The Great Society in Perspective* (Washington: The Brookings Institution, 1978).

As Danziger and Gottschalk go on to argue, postwar trends in inequality looked very different to most analysts in the 1990s.

While there is now, in fact, a near-consensus that overall income inequality in the United States has increased over the past twenty-five years, significant disagreement persists regarding the relative importance of the causes for this rise in income inequality. The most discussed causes include the following: changes in tax policy, a structural economic shift to service and high-tech sectors characterized by bipolar earnings distributions, increasing relative returns to higher education, the greater impact on the US economy of low-paid labor in the developing world, changing demographic and household composition of the population, and the emergence of so-called "winner-take-all markets" across a variety of sectors.[11]

CONTEMPORARY INEQUALITIES AND DEVELOPMENT DISCOURSE: INTERNATIONAL CONTEXTS

Parallel to this discussion of inequalities in the United States, scholars and policymakers have recently heightened their concern about severe inequalities in international contexts. Questions of global inequality and of "North–South development gaps" have long been an important and disputed part of public debates within the international development community – engaging scholars as well as officials within groups like United Nations agencies, the World Health Organization, the International Labour Organization, and even the World Bank and the International Monetary Fund. Yet the past decade, during which the United Nations Development Programme (UNDP) has published an annual *Human Development Report*, has been notable for increased interest in the relationship of development and inequality.[12] Discussions have focused on various

---

[11] For different discussions and perspectives, see Danziger and Gottschalk, *America Unequal*; *ERP 1997*, chapter 5; Lester Thurow, *The Future of Capitalism* (New York: W. Murrow, 1996); Freeman and respondents, "New Inequality"; and Robert H. Frank and Philip J. Cook, *The Winner-Take-All Society* (New York: Free Press, 1995).

[12] The United Nations Development Programme's annual *Human Development Report* (New York: Oxford University Press) was first published in 1990. The 1995 issue focuses specifically on gender-related inequalities of development. *HDR 1996* con-

dimensions of inequality, including gender- and race-related disparities, rural–urban gaps, and cross-national comparisons.

As just one striking illustration of global inequality, a 1996 calculation by the UNDP received significant public attention:

Today, the net worth of the 358 richest people, the dollar billionaires, is equal to the combined income of the poorest 45 percent of the world's population – 2.3 billion people. This of course is a comparison of wealth and income. But a contrast of wealth alone, if it were possible, would be even starker, since the wealth of the poorest people is generally much less than their income.[13]

This startling juxtaposition helped to shed public light on the magnitude of international disparities. That calculation was updated in the UNDP's *HDR 1999* to indicate that the wealth of the two hundred richest people alone exceeds the annual income of 41 percent of the world's population.[14] The *HDR 1999* added that the world's wealthiest three human beings hold assets that exceed the combined gross national product of the world's forty-three "least developed countries" – with a total population of 568 million people.[15]

INEQUALITIES AND THEIR MORAL SIGNIFICANCE

Public intellectuals have lined up with distinct interpretations about the moral and social significance of inequality. Conservative columnist George Will entitled a 1996 *Newsweek* essay, "Healthy Inequality," adding the byline, "Today's most discussed economic 'malady' is actually a recurring benign phenomenon." The rise in economic inequality evidenced since

tains significant discussion of trends and gaps of human development within countries. *HDR 1999* considers aspects of inequality in relation to "globalization." Chapter 3 below reviews and discusses the literature treating many dimensions and contexts of international inequalities, and chapter 10 examines initiatives related to inequality with the UNDP framework.

[13] *HDR 1996*, p. 13. See my discussion in chapter 3. See also James Gustave Speth, "Global Inequality: 358 Billionaires vs. 2.3 Billion People," *New Perspectives Quarterly* (fall 1996), and Barbara Crossette, "U.N. Survey Finds World Rich–Poor Gap Widening," *New York Times* (7/15/1996), A3.

[14] *HDR 1999*, p. 38. The data used for this UNDP calculation come from *Forbes Magazine*, 7/6/1998.

[15] Ibid., and author's calculations based on table 16, *HDR 1999*, pp. 197–200.

1974, Will contends, is the result of the most recent technological revolution, a shift which will come to benefit society as a
whole. But this social progress, like the Industrial Revolution,
brings with it necessary short-term social costs, including inequality, that are decried only by those who fail to appreciate its
longer-term benefits: "Such progress is, as usual, accompanied
by a chorus from laments of sentimentalists who consider it a
cosmic injustice that progress has a price. And the laments are
loudest from those who make a fetish of equality."[16] From
within the so-called "lamenting chorus," commentators who
are concerned with rising inequality question Will's views of
historical progression and inequality. In an article called, "Gulf
Crisis," Michael Walzer asserts that the rise in inequality has
brought with it long-term *perils* for societies like the United
States:

[I]nequality is dangerous for liberal democracy. And the dangers are
self-perpetuating: disparities of wealth make it difficult to organize
countervailing powers, and the absence of countervailing powers
makes for increasingly radical disparities. The long-term effect of this
process, the characteristic product of radical inequality, is tyranny in
everyday life: the arrogance of the wealthy, the humbling of the
poor.[17]

Walzer's concern is precisely one taken up in this book: what
are the wider social, civic, and political costs of excessive
socioeconomic inequalities?[18] What levels of which inequalities
are socially problematic or morally objectionable?

A response to the latter question requires the building of
normative claims about full and equal personhood and social
solidarity. Seen one way, accounts of moral equality make

---

[16] George Will, "Healthy Inequality," *Newsweek* (10/28/1996), p. 92.
[17] Michael Walzer, "Gulf Crisis," *The New Republic* (8/5/1996), p. 25.
[18] Stating the problem in this way suggests that inequality can be looked at as an
"external cost" or "externality" to the market system, that is, as an effect that is not
factored into decisions by individual economic actors but whose impact is felt by
persons within that society. Such an approach is suggested in Lester Thurow,
"Income Distribution as a Pure Public Good," *Quarterly Journal of Economics* 85 (May
1971), and Sheldon Danziger and Robert Haveman, "An Economic Concept of
Solidarity: Its Application to Poverty and Income Distribution Policy in the United
States," Research Series no. 37, International Institute for Labour Studies (Geneva:
IILS, 1978). The insights of these thinkers inform my discussion in chapter 8.

claims for prohibiting or constraining certain inequalities – those that obstruct an equal moral attention to all people – while allowing other inequalities to persist as a result of empirical differences in their attributes, experiences, and luck. Since the meanings of equality and inequality are open to serious debate and interpretation, it is important to consider philosophical and theological debates that could inform a constructive theological approach from Christian ethics.[19]

Issues related to inequality and equality, of course, are legion. Few of them can be treated in detail in one book. The consideration of equality and inequality will raise related questions of justice and injustice, well-being and deprivation, freedom and oppression, solidarity and envy. The focus on evaluating inequality raises, of course, the question of the causes of inequality and its trends. Some of the issues noted here will be addressed throughout the book; others will only get indirect treatment. Hence it is important to acknowledge the limited, though broad, scope of this project. The following section lays out the structure of the inquiry into inequality and Christian ethics.

THE STRUCTURE OF THE BOOK

Inequality and Christian Ethics is an interdisciplinary effort. Structuring the argument and analysis is no straightforward matter. There is a need to understand the empirical realities and trends of inequality as well as to provide a moral framework or approach of why and how they matter morally. The normative approach constructed in the book is called "a Christian ethical approach," though it gains significant insights from philosophers and social scientists who do not work within the Christian tradition. Further, the approach developed here seeks to be a part of a pluralistic conversation on matters moral,

---

[19] My overall approach thus begins with current socioeconomic realities, drawing on moral and theological visions and ideals in order properly to understand and respond to them. My methodology, which will be made clearer in the second half of this introduction, is thus similar to that of Karen Lebacqz in her *Justice in an Unjust World: Foundations for a Christian Approach to Justice* (Minneapolis: Augsburg, 1987).

social, and economic, and thus the framework must also describe the kind of public contribution it makes. The structure of the book plays an important role in getting the interdisciplinary project "right."

The book is arranged into three broad parts. The first part, "Contextualizing inequality," critically reviews the philosophical, economic, and empirical discussions about recent inequality, both in international contexts and within the United States. Though the Christian ethical approach is not explicitly developed until the second part, the analysis in the first part is framed in a way that is consistent with the normative perspective outlined after it. Finally, the third part, "Transforming discourse, persons, and societies," returns to the wider public debates, demonstrating various ways in which a Christian ethical approach can inform and contribute to discourse about inequality, development, and well-being. If the emphasis in part one is on inequality, and in part two it is on Christian ethics, then part three is the most explicit effort to draw inequality and Christian ethics together. Those chapters attempt to demonstrate how normative insights can be made explicit within debates that too often appear to be value-free. Substantively, the argument models how the values of a Christian ethical approach could be enacted in the public debate about inequality.

While various theological perspectives inform this book, this three-part structure follows the methodological concepts of liberation theology. The respective parts of the book correspond, in the terminology of Clodovis Boff, to the three "moments" of liberation theology: *socioanalytic mediation, hermeneutic mediation,* and *practical mediation.*[20] Reviewing each of these steps provides a fitting way to outline more specifically the content of each chapter of the book.

---

[20] Clodovis Boff, "Epistemology and Method in the Theology of Liberation," in Ignacio Ellacuría, S.J. and Jon Sobrino, S.J. (eds.), *Mysterium Liberationis: Fundamental Concepts of Liberation Theology* (Maryknoll, NY: Orbis, 1993), 57–85, esp. p. 74. These mediations have also been characterized, less precisely, as sequential steps in doing liberation theology: seeing, judging, and acting. I prefer to employ the language of the three mediations, since they are not exclusively or sufficiently characterized as seeing, judging, and acting.

Socioanalytical mediation involves employing the resources of social theory and social science to examine and to understand contemporary socioeconomic conditions. In this step, the chief aim is to uncover structures and situations that produce oppression of persons and groups. This step in liberation theology is a form of "reading the signs of the times," a concept of Catholic social teaching explicitly introduced in the Vatican II document, *Gaudium et Spes* (1965): "[T]he Church has always had the duty of scrutinizing the signs of the times and of interpreting them in the light of the gospel."[21]

Language of "reading the signs of the times" entails more than merely being aware of the latest cultural or social trends; it involves, rather, a critical, "eschatological" analysis of and response to current situations, including a call for transformation of various forms of injustice.[22] This language of

---

[21] Second Vatican Council, *Gaudium et Spes: Pastoral Constitution on the Church in the Modern World*, para. 4, in David J. O'Brien and Thomas A. Shannon (eds.), *Catholic Social Thought: The Documentary Heritage* (Maryknoll, NY: Orbis, 1992). This language of "reading the signs of the times" arises out of an extensive biblical and theological debate over how to understand human and divine action within history. Biblical texts that employ this language within an eschatological framework include 2 Esdras 8:63–9:6 (in the Apocrypha) and Matthew 16:1–4. Encouraged by John XXIII's papal encyclical, *Pacem in Terris* (1963), the Second Vatican Council employed this language to analyze and address social, economic, and political realities of the modern world. In *Gaudium et Spes*, the Council expressed an implication of reading the signs of the times that bears directly on this project: "[A]lthough rightful differences exist between men, the equal dignity of persons demands that a more humane and just condition of life be brought about. For excessive economic and social differences between the members of the one human family or population groups cause scandal, and militate against social justice, equity, the dignity of the human person, as well as social and international peace. Human institutions, both private and public, must labor to minister to the dignity and purpose of man. At the same time let them put up a stubborn fight against any kind of slavery, whether social or political, and safeguard the basic rights of man under every political system" (*Gaudium et Spes*, para. 29.). See also John XXIII, *Pacem in Terris: Peace on Earth*, in O'Brien and Shannon (eds.), *Catholic Social Thought*, paras. 39–45, 75–79, 126–129, 142–145.

[22] The international Catholic Synod of Bishops, in the introduction to their 1971 document, *Justice in the World*, further explains that "scrutinizing the 'signs of the times' and seeking to detect the meaning of emerging history" (para. 2) require the understanding of human action within God's "plan of liberation and salvation." The Bishops go on to make the following statement, which has sparked significant controversy within the Catholic Church: "Action on behalf of justice and participation in the transformation of the world fully appears to us as a *constitutive* dimension of the preaching of the Gospel, or in other words, of the Church's mission for the redemption of the human race and its liberation from every oppressive situation" (in

Catholic social thought has been appropriated by liberation theologians, consistent with more progressive strands in the official Catholic documents, to analyze socioeconomic conditions of deprivation and disparity. This book follows such a liberationist view of "reading the signs of the times."

Chapter 2, which examines contemporary debates in political philosophy and development economics, is a reading of some intellectual signs of the times. It provides a critical examination of discussions by which this Christian ethical approach to inequality is informed. In particular, the question of "Inequality of what?" frames how equality and inequality have been understood in scholarly debates. Chapter 3 and chapter 4 critically analyze contemporary socioeconomic inequalities within international and US domestic contexts, respectively. An emphasis here is to demonstrate that the problem of inequality is more complex than merely examining trends in income for a country's population. Rather, inequalities exist in various important spheres of life (including education and health), and they can be analyzed along lines of race, ethnicity, and gender as well. These two chapters trace the principal social and economic problems that the remainder of the book addresses.

The second part of the book corresponds to the *hermeneutic mediation* of liberation theology, "the specific moment by virtue of which a discourse is formally theological discourse."[23] This step involves drawing upon sources of theological authority, employing an approach consistent with the "preferential option for the poor" (discussed in chapters 7 and 8).[24] Boff suggests, for instance, that the reading of the Bible should be marked by certain traits, including a prioritization of "*application* over that of explanation," an emphasis on the "*transforming energy* of the biblical texts," "accentuat[ing], without reductionism, the social context of the message," and incorporating "popular" interpretations of texts.[25] The second step, then, entails a

---

O'Brien and Shannon [eds.], *Catholic Social Thought*, para. 6, italics added for emphasis.

[23] Boff, "Epistemology and Method," p. 79.

[24] Three theological sources noted by Boff are "the Bible of the poor," "the great Christian tradition," and "the social teaching of the church" (pp. 81–82).

[25] Boff, "Epistemology and Method," p. 80.

constructive reading of theological sources within the context of the realities examined through socioanalytical analysis in the first step. Boff describes the task this way: "Liberation theologians are never mere accumulators of theological materials. They are authentic architects of theology. Thus, they arm themselves with the necessary theoretical daring and a good dose of creative fantasy, in order to be in a position to deal with the unprecedented problems they find on the oppressed continents."[26]

In this spirit, chapters 6 and 7 offer "creative" readings of two theological accounts of equality and inequality, from Reformed theologian H. Richard Niebuhr and liberation theologian Gustavo Gutiérrez. Chapter 8 employs and extends the insights of these theological accounts, alongside various social scientific and philosophical perspectives, to fill out a Christian ethical approach to situations of inequality.

The third and final part of the book corresponds to the *practical mediation* of liberation theology. While this step contains various tasks, its principal one is to move the social analysis and theological reflection "back to action": "to action for justice, to the deed of love, to conversion, to church renewal, to the transformation of society."[27] This step can involve wide-ranging calls for social attention and social change as well as very specific proposals for public policy and social action.

The discussions and insights developed in chapters 9, 10, and 11 entail such a range. The problem of inequality is multi-faceted; so must be the response to it. Chapter 9 draws together and clarifies the kinds of moral contribution that the Christian ethical approach makes to public debate, and it goes on to delineate four particular "axes" that can focus and expand discourse about socioeconomic inequalities. Chapter 10 provides a specific proposal to incorporate a concern for inequalities more explicitly than has been done into debate about international development discourse. An "inequality adjustment" is proposed for the widely used "human development index." The concluding chapter recasts some of the major

---

[26] Ibid., p. 83. [27] Ibid.

insights and arguments of the book. More important, it explores the implications of the project for Christian ethics, the wider moral debate about evaluating and addressing inequalities, and actions and policies that would be consistent with this approach.

CHAPTER 2

Inequality of what?: interdisciplinary perspectives

"Inequality of what?" This question is answered, either implicitly or explicitly, by anyone discussing inequality. Because data on income are relatively easy to obtain, the discussion of inequality is often *reduced* to considering income alone. But there are various kinds of inequality that can be of interest to Christian ethics and the wider moral debate. For instance, questions of unequal access to the internet and telecommunications have gained prominence as these forms of technology are seen as important vehicles for social participation.[1] Other kinds of inequality related to wealth, political influence, education, or healthcare bear some relation to income-based disparity, but they are distinct realities.

Understanding inequality – and equality – becomes more complicated when more than one good is considered. Can equality of political participation be guaranteed, say, when income inequality is severe? Are we interested in examining the level of inequality of a few items (like income, political power, internet usage, ice-cream consumption), or in establishing equality of some less tangible "thing," like social participation, or moral worth, or dignity? Philosophers and social scientists have contributed various other "currencies" in which inequality

[1] The cover of the *HDR 1999* (New York: Oxford University Press, 1999) is a graph showing the disparity of internet access among the various regions of the world: "The internet is linking people in a new global network, but access is concentrated among people in rich countries. Organization for Economic Cooperation and Development (OECD) countries, with 19 percent of the world's population, account for 91 percent of users" (*HDR 1999*, inside cover). See also Katie Hafner, "Common Ground Elusive as Technology Have-Nots Meet Haves," *New York Times* (7/8/1999), E8. Within the US context, see David E. Sanger, "Big Racial Disparity Persists Among Users of the Internet," *New York Times* (7/9/1999), A12.

(and equality) can be considered: utility, opportunity, resources, "primary goods," "human capability," "basic needs," and so on.

Treatments of how inequality has been understood by political philosophers – including how they answer the question, "Inequality of what?", and its relative, "Equality of what?" – will lay important groundwork. The specific approaches of John Rawls (the most influential moral and political philosopher of contemporary times) and Amartya Sen (noted philosopher and 1998 Nobel laureate in economics) provide resources that can be employed constructively and critically in a Christian ethical approach.

Economics as a discipline has been notable in the twentieth century for its emphasis on productivity and efficiency as first-order concerns – and for relegating distributional questions, including inequality, to second-order ones. Yet a number of perspectives in development economics, including the basic needs approach and Sen's capability approach, have widened economic analysis beyond the "space" of income to look at other dimensions of human development. Critical explorations of that discussion will also help to answer the question, "Inequality of what?" and to provide insights for constructing a Christian ethical contribution.

SPECIFYING EQUALITY AND CONSTRUCTING PUBLIC DISCOURSE

Inequality can be seen in relation to equality in a variety of ways. In one sense, equality can be understood in terms of inequality: if the degree of inequality (for some good like income) is viewed as a continuum, then equality is one endpoint – the lowest degree of inequality. In other words, equality is the complete absence of inequality. From another perspective, equality is the more foundational concept; and inequality is the lack or denial of equality. However this relationship is construed, important insights into inequality can be gained by exploring the concept of equality.

Equality is described in a variety of ways – as a concept, a value, an idea, an ideal, a norm, a principle, a relationship, a claim, a tool. Seen as a group, these terms support the view that equality can be appropriated in many distinct ways.

In mathematical terms, equality is a simple concept. At base, equality indicates a particular "binary" relationship resulting from a comparison of two objects (or persons), a and b. More than two objects may be said to be equal, but to bring in a third object, c, requires comparing the objects as pairs: a and c, b and c, as well as a and b.[2]

This simple, abstract concept of equality has proved to be analytically illuminative and rhetorically powerful for thinkers from a wide variety of disciplines, including economics, political science, philosophy, theology, and other fields. As a central idea in the Western intellectual pantheon, equality has been invoked in any number of intellectual debates and social movements.[3] In contemporary discussions, equality sparks and informs lofty and technical academic debates as well as general and inclusive public discussions.[4]

Many theorists have sought to clarify the disparate usages of equality by providing analytical distinctions or typologies. Sidney Verba and Gary R. Orren suggest four binary distinctions that illuminate some of the "ambivalence" in contemporary usage of equality: equality of opportunity versus equality of

---

[2] The formal relationship of "equivalence" holds when three properties are met: *symmetry* (if a = b, then b = a), *reflexivity* (a = a), and *transitivity* (if a = b and b = c, then a=c). "Equivalence Relations" (entry #135, pp. 530–531), in Mathematical Society of Japan, *Encyclopedic Dictionary of Mathematics* (edited by Kiyosi Itô), second edn., vol. 1 (Cambridge, MA: MIT Press, 1968 [1960]).

[3] For a classic overview of the idea of equality in the modern West, see Sanford Lakoff, *Equality in Political Philosophy* (Cambridge, MA: Harvard University Press, 1964).

[4] The work of Sidney Verba and his collaborators is an important example of descriptive analysis of citizens' and leaders' views of equality as well as theoretical engagement with the concept of equality itself. See Verba and Gary R. Orren, *Equality in America: The View from the Top* (Cambridge, MA: Harvard University Press, 1985); Verba, Steven Kelman, Gary R. Orren, Ichiro Miyake, Joji Watanuki, Ikuo Kabashima, and G. Donald Ferree, Jr., *Elites and the Idea of Equality: A Comparison of Japan, Sweden, and the United States* (Cambridge, MA: Harvard University Press, 1987); and Verba, Kay Lehman Scholzman, and Henry E. Brady, *Voice and Equality: Civic Voluntarism in American Politics* (Cambridge, MA: Harvard University Press, 1995). The Public Broadcasting Network has posted a web page on "American Beliefs about Equality," including excerpts from historic documents and speeches, based on a "National Conversation Kit" assembled by the National Endowment for the Humanities. The URL is: <http://www.pbs.org/ampu/equality.html>.

result; political equality versus economic equality; ideal equality versus real (or actual) equality; and equality among individuals versus equality across groups.[5] These distinctions suggest the need for careful specification in any discussion of equality.[6]

Thus the "meaning" of equality is anything but straightforward. Equality (and inequality) matters can provoke sharp disagreements among a wide range of viewpoints. Yet at the same time, most policymakers, intellectuals, and citizens hold views on the "meaning" of equality. In debates about equality, there is arguably common ground on which to hold a conversation. When many intellectuals decry the contemporary context as one of "cultural" warfare among people who talk past each other, equality is a "site of commensurability" on which most of those in contemporary, pluralistic society could hold a conversation. This does not imply consensus about equality's "meaning(s)"; on the contrary, a site of commensurability is one in which even *disagreement* among views is intelligible. The very fact that people can contest others' moral arguments is a sign that there are basic, shared premises.[7]

The concept of equality thus provides a "site" for serious moral and policy-oriented debates. *Public discourse about the "meaning," relevance, and implications of moral equality is both a possible and a promising way to deepen a public conversation about socioeconomic inequality.* The Christian ethical approach constructed in part two of this book is intended to serve as one ("theologically informed") contribution to that public conversation.

THE GROUNDING AND SCOPE OF EQUALITY

Contemporary political philosophers and social theorists have engaged carefully the question of the "meaning" of moral and

---

[5] Verba and Orren, *Equality in America*, esp. pp. 5–20.

[6] My project attempts to shed light on each of these distinctions. I do not employ these distinctions explicitly, however, since I find Amartya Sen's emphasis on the question, "Equality of what?" to be a more illuminative approach.

[7] An important discussion of this point, precisely in an argument about the role of religiously informed moral perspectives in public life, is found in Ronald Thiemann, *Religion in Public Life: A Dilemma for Democracy* (Washington: Georgetown University Press, 1996), pp. 105–108.

social equality. This conversation, carried on predominantly in the language of political philosophy, has a number of dimensions that together shed significant light on any inquiry into inequality and well-being.

There is no consensus on the *grounding* of the moral claim of the equality of people. Many philosophers do not even attempt to engage this question, taking equality as a "self-evident" claim, at least in contemporary Western conversations. For those who do consider the grounds of equality, there is a broad recognition that no claim to human *merit* can be made, since according to any merit-based standard, humans are in fact significantly unequal. Instead, as Joel Feinberg traces, philosophers have turned to explanations along lines of human *worth* in the quest to find sufficient grounds for moral equality. But the concept of worth itself requires the naming of the characteristic or standard according to which humans have worth. Feinberg typologizes the various characteristics proposed by philosophers as "value characteristics" (such as "intrinsic pricelessness"), natural capacities (like rationality), natural vulnerabilities (such as "liability to pain and suffering"), or transcendental properties (like "human dignity"). Importantly, Feinberg asserts that none of these grounds can be convincing to those who begin as skeptics of the very idea of moral equality. It is not possible to "prove" moral equality by reference to any ground.

"Human worth" itself is best understood to name no property in the way that "strength" names strength and "redness" redness. In attributing human worth to everyone we may be ascribing no property or set of qualities, but rather expressing an attitude – the attitude of respect – toward the humanity in each man's person. That attitude follows naturally from regarding everyone from "the human point of view," but it is not grounded on anything more ultimate than itself, and it is not demonstrably justifiable.[8]

As will be discussed in chapters 6 and 7, the theological accounts of equality, while raising other questions, provide their own distinctive and coherent answers to the question of the standard of human worth. Feinberg rightly argues that the

[8] Joel Feinberg, *Social Philosophy* (Englewood Cliffs, NJ: Prentice-Hall, 1973), pp. 88–94; quote on p. 94.

grounds of Christian accounts of equality, like philosophical grounds, are not "demonstrably justifiable." At the same time, a theological belief or attitude of equality does refer to something "more ultimate than itself" – that is, God.[9] Consistent with Feinberg's discussion, the significance of theological accounts of equality is precisely an attitude towards other humans and the social order understood more collectively. It is necessary, of course, to trace the ways in which particular theological commitments specify how the socioeconomic order should be structured – tasks undertaken in succeeding chapters.

In addition to the question of the "grounding" of equality is the question of *scope*. Who is included in claims to equality? While the scope of earlier understandings of moral and social equality were often limited – to citizens in the Greek *polis*, to God's "elect" or to members in some Christian communities, to property-holding free males in early modern liberal societies – almost all contemporary moral theories extend equality universally to all humans.[10] This universal scope, of course, is an ideal that contrasts sharply with actual practices and forms of oppression, in which nationality, race, ethnicity, gender, sexual orientation, class, and/or age obstruct equality's scope in practice. In

---

9 The theological accounts of equality developed in chapters 6 and 7 make no attempt to *prove* that equality is grounded in God; rather, each of these accounts *presupposes* a theocentric worldview in which a creating and giving God provides life to all humans; an equal moral status of each proceeds from this starting point. These theological accounts are thus consistent with a *non-foundational* approach to theology, taking "on faith" certain realities (including God and an ongoing divine relationship with human persons and communities) without an epistemological or apologetic effort to prove them. Such a framework is developed by Ronald F. Thiemann in his *Revelation and Theology: The Gospel as Narrated Promise* (Notre Dame, IN: University of Notre Dame Press, 1985). Thiemann argues for a non-foundational approach in which "theological positions are to be judged not by a universal criterion beyond tradition or by an imagined consensus within the [faith] community but by the content-specific arguments which theologians offer in support of their positions" (p. 73). In this book, I trace the theological perspectives of H. Richard Niebuhr and Gustavo Gutiérrez in a way that is accessible to people from a variety of worldviews, without attempts to demonstrate an epistemological justification for their accounts of equality. The equality before God, then, is treated not as a proposition to be proved, but as an attitude and commitment to be understood and appropriated for social engagement.

10 For many of the related issues, see Stanley Benn, "Equality, Moral and Social," in *The Encyclopedia of Philosophy*, vol. III (New York and London: Macmillan and Free Press, 1967).

Elizabeth Anderson's terms, the very "point" of equality theorizing should be to provide a normative vision that can be linked to and employed by contemporary egalitarian movements on behalf of people excluded on the basis of these characteristics or attributes.[11]

Feinberg's discussion serves to demonstrate that neither the grounding of equality nor its universal scope is a fact to be proved. The more constructive point, however, is that the contemporary conversation about equality places the burden of proof on those who would argue against either moral equality or its universal scope. Of course, the relevance and application of any notion of moral equality for addressing social realities depend on particular answers to the question discussed next: "Equality of what?"

THE SPACE OF EQUALITY

It will be helpful to introduce a term for distinguishing among different theorists' treatments of equality and inequality: the concept of "space." A space is the context in which social and moral analysis is undertaken. The conceptual framework and language in which an analysis of equality or inequality is made fundamentally shapes the contours of the debate. The space in which theorizing is done and people are compared can be income, or utility, or "opportunity," or "human capability."[12] Being explicit about the space of social analysis is crucially important because it helps to clarify empirical and moral discussions of inequality.[13]

In his 1979 Tanner Lecture on Human Values, Sen asserts that contemporary moral theorists accept and employ the understanding of moral equality in distinct ways by focusing on

[11] Elizabeth S. Anderson, "What is the Point of Equality?" *Ethics* 109 (January 1999).
[12] The emphasis on distinguishing the "space" of social analysis follows the work of Amartya Sen – most notably his 1979 Tanner Lecture, "Equality of What?", in Sterling M. McMurrin (ed.), *The Tanner Lectures on Human Values*, vol. 1 (Cambridge: Cambridge University Press, 1980).
[13] The question of "Equality of what?" can be employed in either descriptive or normative exercises. As discussed below, Sen offers his own normative view of the space in which equality should be guaranteed, but descriptive analyses of particular usages of equality-language can be sharpened by posing this question as well.

different spaces. For each theory, the belief in the equality of persons requires *equal* moral and political attention. Each theory assumes an equality of *something*, but Sen's point is that this "something" is distinct for different moral theories. What is at issue is the proper *space* of moral and political attention.[14]

Sen's own proposal is to focus on the space of "capability and functionings."[15] For his part, John Rawls's theory of justice includes a strong presumption of an equality of "primary goods," requiring that inequalities in income and wealth, for example, be justified according to his stringent "difference principle," discussed below.[16] Ronald Dworkin promotes a position he calls an "equality of resources."[17] At base, utilitarians assume the equal value of an increase in each person's utility. Even a libertarian theorist such as Robert Nozick, whose theory is criticized for having inegalitarian implications for wealth and income, defends an equal endowment of rights for all people.[18] All these "ethics of social arrangements" contain some notion of equality, but equality operates in a different space for each.

It will be valuable to consider in more detail two of these positions – those of Rawls and Sen – in order to reveal more fully what is at stake in these debates about the space of equality and inequality – and the principal question, "Inequality of what?".

Rawls and primary goods

In the most influential book of contemporary political philosophy, John Rawls presents his two principles that together

[14] This argument is laid out in Sen's "Equality of What?" (1979/80). For refinements of his approach, see Sen, *Inequality Reexamined* (Cambridge, MA: Harvard University Press/Russell Sage, 1992), and "Capability and Well-Being," in Martha Nussbaum and Sen (eds.), *The Quality of Life* (Oxford: Clarendon Press, 1993).

[15] The most straightforward presentation of Sen's approach is offered in his essay, "Capability and Well-Being."

[16] See especially his classic work, *A Theory of Justice* (Cambridge, MA: Harvard University Press, 1971). Important refinements are offered in *Political Liberalism* (New York: Columbia University Press, 1993).

[17] Ronald Dworkin, "What is Equality?: Part II: Equality of Resources," *Philosophy and Public Affairs* 10 (1981).

[18] Robert Nozick, *Anarchy, State, and Utopia* (Oxford: Blackwell, 1974).

comprise *A Theory of Justice*. From a brief (and recent) statement of the two principles of justice-as-fairness, it is clear that equality is central to Rawls's approach:

a. Each person has an equal right to a fully adequate scheme of equal basic liberties which is compatible with a similar scheme of liberties for all.
b. Social and economic inequalities are to satisfy two conditions. First, they must be attached to offices and positions open to all under conditions of fair equality of opportunity; and second, they must be to the greatest benefit of the least advantaged members of society.[19]

The first principle is "lexicographically prior" to the second principle. This priority of the first principle is meant to guarantee, through the basic institutions of society, the "priority of liberty" – not just liberty in the abstract, but an equal "scheme" or basket of liberties which are given to every citizen. Rawls intends the basic structure to help to ensure not just these equal baskets, but the *fair value* of the basic political liberties. With this equality of a basket of liberties established, the theory moves to the first part of the second principle, the fair equality of opportunity. This sub-principle is meant to establish not merely *formal* equality of opportunity, but rather it seeks to guarantee that people with equal skills, talents, and initiative should have equal "life chances."[20] When these conditions are met, then the final sub-principle, the "difference principle," takes effect. The difference principle requires that any inequalities of income or wealth – within the ideal conditions described in the earlier principles – must be justified in terms of benefit to the least well-off citizens in a society.[21]

Thus at each step in the Rawlsian principles of justice, the presumption is equality in basic political, social, and economic matters; inequalities must be justified within the context of a carefully specified framework. The space in which Rawls discusses this theory of justice – and therefore questions of equality

---

[19] Rawls, *Political Liberalism*, p. 291.
[20] Rawls, *Theory of Justice*, p. 73.
[21] See especially ibid., pp. 75–80. While the second principle's second component (the "difference principle") is often taken out of the wider theoretical context, the Rawlsian account of justice needs to be seen as a whole.

and inequality – is that of "primary goods." Primary goods are described as "various social conditions and all-purpose means that are generally necessary to enable citizens adequately to develop and fully exercise their two moral powers [a capacity for a sense of justice and for a conception of the good], and to pursue their determinate conceptions of the good."[22] Particular primary goods include basic liberties, powers and opportunities, wealth and income, and the social bases of self-respect.[23] While these various goods comprise a motley set, Rawls sees primary goods as a workable space in which to make determinations of justice within a well-ordered society of democratic pluralism. Since people in contemporary societies should have the freedom to pursue a variety of ends, Rawls contends, the determination of (political) justice can only consider adequate *means* – like primary goods – to those ends. Equality and compelling justifications for inequality are determined in terms of primary goods.

Sen, capability, and functionings

Since his 1979 Tanner Lecture, Sen has advocated the equality of "basic capability" for all people. The normative emphasis in Sen's approach is for all to have the capability to function within their own societies. An equality of "basic capability" is what is demanded by moral equality. The focus on capability to function, as opposed to functioning itself, is a way for Sen to ensure that *freedom of choice* is part of his approach. Still, "functionings" – the "doings and beings" of a person within her or his society – are the most "primitive notion" of Sen's approach.[24] A "capability set" contains the alternative combinations of functionings from which people can choose.[25] Some functionings can be considered elementary – like being well-nourished, having basic shelter, escaping morbidity, breathing

---

[22] Rawls, "Principles of Justice" (mimeographed, Harvard University, 1994), p. 49; the two moral powers are defined in his *Political Liberalism*, p. 19 and pp. 103–104.
[23] Rawls, *Theory of Justice*, p. 83; see also his *Political Liberalism*, p. 181.
[24] Sen, "Capability and Well-Being," p. 31.
[25] Ibid.

unpolluted air, being disease-free, and so on. Others are more complex, such as having self-respect, preserving human dignity, taking part in the life of community, and appearing in public without shame.[26]

There is considerable flexibility in how one chooses to define various functionings and to weigh them amongst or against each other. Sen prefers not to specify the particular functionings that should be normatively valued as a part of capability. Sen's hesitancy to embrace an "objective normative account"[27] of capability seems to involve at least two different aspects. First, different societies and cultures value different functionings and capability. Second, even within particular societies, individuals (and groups) value different functionings and capability. Sen suggests in his writings that *reasoned deliberation* among people is one good way for a society to determine important functionings and their weights. Regardless of the depth of the agreement, the capability approach will leave room for choosing between various bundles of functionings. The particular, context-dependent functionings and freedoms to be included in the "basic capability," to be made equal, can be agreed upon through reasoned deliberation.[28]

Sen's critique of Rawls rests on the notion that the actual space in which moral deliberation should take place – and indeed, the space in which Rawls himself at points is admittedly interested – is one of capability to function. Rawls's reliance on primary goods places emphasis on the *means* to freedom and the *means* to well-being, and not those ends themselves. In contrast, capability and functionings are *ends*. Sen asserts that the ability of people to *convert means into desirable ends* varies to a significant degree. An important example (and practical application) of this point is the disparity in the "conversion" rate of men and

---

[26] See Sen, ibid. and *The Standard of Living* (Cambridge: Cambridge University Press, 1987), p. 104; Nussbaum and Sen, introduction to *Quality of Life*, p. 3.

[27] Sen, "Capability and Well-Being," p. 47. The suggestion for an "objective normative account" is taken from Martha Nussbaum, "Nature, Function, and Capability," *Oxford Studies in Ancient Philosophy* Supplementary Volume (1988). See also Nussbaum, "Non-Relative Virtues: An Aristotelian Approach," in Nussbaum and Sen (eds.), *The Quality of Life.*

[28] See Sen, *Commodities and Capabilities* (Amsterdam: North-Holland, 1985), p. 36 and pp. 57–59; see also "Capability and Well-Being," p. 48.

women: a number of social and biological factors, "related to pregnancy, neonatal care, conventional household roles, and so on," disadvantage women.[29] Sen's point is that *because of the variability in conversion rates, equality in the space of primary goods means unacceptable inequality in the capability to function.*

Rawls's response to this criticism is summarized as follows: "I have assumed throughout, and shall continue to assume, that while citizens do not have equal capacities, they do have, at least to the essential minimum degree, the moral, intellectual, and physical capacities that enable them to be fully cooperating members of society over a complete life."[30] Thus Rawls can say that when his two principles of justice are operational, no *injustice* is caused by differentials in conversion abilities.[31] From his perspective, then, his principles will be adequate to assure a just basic structure – although admittedly significant inequalities will exist.[32]

This examination of Rawls's and Sen's approaches to equality and the spaces of moral attention illuminates a number of important points. Both Rawls and Sen have demonstrated that equality as a concept must be carefully specified, within particular theoretical frameworks, in terms of particular goods. Both acknowledge that equality of any good requires considerations of, and sometimes tradeoffs with, equality of other goods and other social values – like freedom and efficiency. Rawls in particular makes explicit attention to a condition of pluralism a part of his theory; Sen emphasizes that reasoned deliberation toward agreement among various normative views will be necessary to determine what basic (and complex) functionings

---

[29] Sen, "Justice: Means vs. Freedoms," *Philosophy and Public Affairs* 19 (1990), p. 116.
[30] Rawls, *Political Liberalism*, p. 183.
[31] Ibid., p. 184.
[32] It should be added that Rawls has significantly hedged his bets by introducing an important caveat to his theory of justice. Responding to certain objections about the urgency of basic needs, Rawls allows for the possibility that his two principles could be *preceded* by a: "principle requiring that citizens' basic needs be met, at least insofar as their being met is necessary for citizens to understand and to be able fruitfully to exercise those rights and liberties [guaranteed in the first principle of justice]" (*Political Liberalism*, p. 7). This caveat serves to show that recent accounts of Rawls's theory of justice are interested in more than merely the means to pursue well-being and freedom, namely in the (basic) capability to function.

and capability will be valued. Further, Sen's discussion of means to achieve versus achievement – the "conversion rate" problem – suggests the importance of focusing on the spaces that most accurately reveal the desired moral and social outcomes. Rawls is correct that the measurement of some capabilities and functionings is difficult – a point Sen would not deny. Rawls would seem to agree with Sen, however, that were it possible to focus on equality (and inequality) within more intrinsically valuable spaces like basic social functionings, such an exercise would be a worthwhile enterprise. This is an important point for the purposes of this project, since one central task herein is to conceptualize and measure inequality of basic functionings related to income, health, and education.

EQUALITY AND INEQUALITY

The question "Equality of what?" helps to illuminate what spaces merit close attention by citizens and policymakers interested in guaranteeing the social conditions for moral equality. The social context(s) with which these moral theories are concerned include empirical inequalities according to various standards of talent, intelligence, beauty, need, and so forth. Policies based on "promoting equality" will leave significant social, economic, and political inequalities. Even if full equality is achieved in one space – whether it is basic capability, primary goods, or some other – people's different "conversion rates" and the elements of risk and luck will mean that inequalities in other goods will persist. Further, equality *over time* cannot be guaranteed even in the particular space in which moral and social attention is focused. In other words, to maintain equality even in one space, some mechanism within the social, political, or economic structure would need to operate continually.[33] To complicate further the question of equality, theorists like Rawls start from a presumption of

[33] Hence Rawls's language of a "just basic structure." In some theories of equality, such as Dworkin's, the emphasis is on equality of resources *over the course of an entire life*. In such theories, at any given time there will be some inequality of resources that are themselves not a sign of injustice. See Dworkin, "Equality of Resources."

equality but allow certain inequalities within the space of their moral theories. Indeed – as discussed above – much of the discussion of Rawls's theory entails the conditions under which inequalities of primary goods can be justified as legitimate.

In the distribution of any particular good, there is a spectrum from absolute equality, in which every person holds the same amount of the good, to absolute inequality, a situation in which some person or group of persons holds all of the good, while all others hold none of it. The distributions of most goods, of course, fall somewhere in between these two endpoints of the equality–inequality spectrum.

Catholic moral theologian Drew Christiansen, in his examination of recent Catholic social teaching, employs the term "relative equality."[34] A crucial question, of course, is the space in which relative equality is advocated. Christiansen helpfully suggests that as the discussion of equality and inequality moves from moral theory into empirical application and analysis, the central issue becomes not one of absolute equality in any social good, but rather the level of inequality that is morally acceptable in the distributions of various social goods. "Relative equality" can denote, in a normative sense, a situation in which inequalities are acceptable. In this vein, the normative perspectives offered by Sen and Rawls, for instance, call for stringent limits on inequalities of basic functionings or primary goods. This point leaves open the question of the just or tolerable levels of inequalities (considered below); it merely stresses that, within frameworks in which equality plays a substantive role, absolute equality is not necessarily required in any good.[35]

---

[34] Drew Christiansen, S.J., "On Relative Equality: Catholic Egalitarianism after Vatican II," *Theological Studies* 45 (1984). Christiansen, of course, is not alone in employing the term. For instance, in his book, *Equalities*, Douglas Rae takes up the issue of "relative equalities," and in particular the various criteria by which distributions could be ranked as more or less equal than other distributions (Cambridge, MA: Harvard University Press, 1989 [1981], chap. 6). While the issue of competing conceptions involved in ranking inequalities is not taken up explicitly in this project, surely this issue bears on the discussion. The implicit social welfare function involved in employing the Gini coefficient as a measure of inequality, for instance, is taken up in appendix A.

[35] It can be argued that a commitment to moral equality does require an absolute equality in political or legal spaces – such as one (adult) citizen, one vote, and an

This discussion of equality and inequality raises a number of complexities involved in applying a moral ideal such as equality to the social conditions of actual societies. Even when particular spaces are carefully specified, a commitment to moral equality would translate into absolute equality of any particular good only in exceptional circumstances. Rawls's discussion of primary goods and Sen's discussion of basic social functionings are moral arguments that articulate *social, political, and economic conditions under which particular inequalities are not so great as to impair any persons from being treated as moral equals.*

One related point regarding criticisms of the concept of equality deserves attention here. Some social theorists, borrowing from Marxist critiques of all moral theory, suggest that calls for moral equality can too easily coexist with situations of gross socioeconomic inequality. There is significant historical evidence to support this assertion.[36] Further, as will be considered in chapter 5, such a critique serves as a reminder that rhetoric of "equality before God" has too comfortably allowed or even legitimated gross this-worldly inequalities and injustices. Yet there is no reason why an account of moral equality cannot be combined with a critical analysis of the very social structure, indeed as a site of discourse for forging a just basic structure. The normative approach constructed in part two argues for the necessity of critical social examination and, when required, for transformative praxis on the part of persons, institutions, and governments.[37]

"equality under the law." While not in the purview of this project, I would support these particular understandings of absolute equality.

[36] For a discussion of "equality amidst inequality" in pre-modern thought, including Stoicism and pre-Reformation Christian thought, see Lakoff, *Equality in Political Philosophy,* chapter 2. With respect to the period of European colonization of Latin America, Tzvetan Todorov makes an important claim that Bartolomé de Las Casas helped to fuel cultural and economic colonialism, precisely because he asserted a fundamental equality – but in a European "space" – between Spaniards and indigenous people (*The Conquest of America: The Question of the Other* [New York: Harper Perennial, 1984 [1982]]). For a contrasting interpretation of Las Casas as a force for humanitarian defense of, and relationship with, indigenous people, see Gustavo Gutiérrez, *Las Casas: In Search of the Poor of Jesus Christ* (Maryknoll, NY: Orbis, 1993 [1992]). While I am sympathetic with Gutiérrez's account, Todorov rightly displays the potential dangers of claiming equality for coercive, if well-meaning, ends. I will argue below that such an account of equality is normatively mistaken.

[37] This is consistent with Nancy Fraser's call for transformative politics of both

The discussion thus far has considered questions of equality and inequality among persons *qua* persons. In Verba and Orren's terminology, these are questions of *individual* equality or inequality. Attention to *group* inequality requires the examination of differentials in the holdings (or distribution) of social goods for different groups of persons. For example, one can examine the differential in the average annual income between adult women and adult men for the United States in any given year. Such groups can be arranged – in a process of "disaggregation" – according to any number of criteria, including gender, race, ethnicity, class, age, nationality, height, and so on. Analysis of such inter-group inequality, of course, requires examining some variable, such as mean or median holdings. If the value of the variable is equal for the various groups, there is absolute inter-group equality; in other cases, the degree of inequality could be determined by the level of the differentials across that variable.[38] As chapter 9 asserts, if the characteristic (e.g., race or gender) is considered morally irrelevant to the holdings of a particular good-in-question (e.g., income or schooling), then there should be a presumption of absolute equality among group mean or median holdings. Statistically significant differentials (inequalities) should be addressed as possibly contrary to the social conditions required by moral equality.

EQUALITIES AND DIFFERENCES

How does this discussion about equality and inequality illuminate the debate over "equality and difference," and, more specifically, what is the relation of inequality to difference? The previous section suggests that a constructive response to this question can be made by examining the *space* in which inequality or difference is said to operate.

Feminist scholar Joan W. Scott argues that the so-called "equality-versus-difference debate" is misplaced. "Here a

---

recognition and redistribution (Fraser, *Justice Interruptus: Critical Reflections on the "Postsocialist" Condition* [New York: Routledge, 1997], pp. 23–31). For a further discussion of Fraser, see the following section of this chapter.

[38] The discussion of inequality comparisons in chapter 9 expands these points.

binary opposition has been created to offer a choice to feminists, of either endorsing 'equality' or its presumed antithesis 'difference.' In fact, the antithesis itself hides the interdependence of the two terms, for equality is not the elimination of difference, and difference does not preclude equality."[39] Scott rightly goes on to assert that the ideal of equality does not obliterate differences. Rather, she accepts Michael Walzer's contention that equality "aims at eliminating not all differences but a particular set of differences, and a different set in different times and places."[40] This language echoes the assertions, in the previous section, about inequalities and the social conditions for moral equality. In fact, *within any given space*, languages of inequality and of difference can be employed similarly or synonymously.

Yet language of "difference" is used in various ways, a fact that complicates this discussion. In order to trace further the relationship between inequality(ies) and difference(s), Nancy Fraser's "analytical distinction" between *redistribution* and *recognition* is helpful. Redistribution refers to questions of social arrangements and political economy, while recognition is concerned with cultural questions of symbol and identity. (Fraser's work emphasizes this analytical distinction in order to illuminate the *interrelationships* between concerns of political economy and cultural identity.) In this schema, inequality and inequalities are first terms of redistribution. Talk of differences can relate either to redistribution (as noted in the previous paragraph) or to recognition. "Difference" in the singular is most often employed in the latter sense – within discussions of recognition and identity.

Fraser, like Scott, decries creating a simple dichotomy by which equality and difference are opposed. In her discussion of political economy, she suggests that language of equality can, in fact, serve to focus social attention on socioeconomic inequalities that lead to forms of oppression of persons and groups.

---

[39] Joan Scott, "Deconstructing Equality-Versus-Difference," *Feminist Studies* 14 (1988), p. 38.
[40] Ibid., p. 44, quoting Michael Walzer, *Spheres of Justice: A Defense of Pluralism and Equality* (New York: Basic Books, 1983), p. xii.

Emphasis on equality can further redistributive ends without threatening goals related to cultural recognition and expressions of differences. The perils of difference language are the "essentializing" of characteristics that are socially constructed, and the loss of diversity *within* particular groups. Scott considers such dangers with respect to gender-related difference:

It is not sameness *or* identity between women and men that we want to claim but a more complicated historically variable diversity than is permitted by the opposition male/female, a diversity that is also differently expressed for different purposes in different contexts. In effect, the duality this opposition creates draws one line of difference, invests it with biological explanations, and then treats each side of the opposition as a unitary phenomenon. Everything in each category (male/female) is assumed to be the same; hence, differences within either category are suppressed . . . the sameness constructed on each side of the binary opposition hides the multiple play of differences and maintains their irrelevance and invisibility.[41]

Drawing on these feminist insights, the Christian ethical approach developed in part two focuses on differences rather than difference. When they are excessive, differences (inequalities) in basic social functionings will be shown to be incompatible with the social conditions of moral equality. When (and only when) these social conditions of equality become operative, then differences in less "basic" spaces can be seen as genuine expressions of human diversity and thus part of a social structure that enables the attainment of full personhood by its citizens.[42] On the other hand, without the social conditions of moral equality in place, differences (inequalities) are often

---

[41] Scott, "Deconstructing," pp. 44–45.

[42] Nancy Fraser makes a related claim in her critique of Iris Marion Young's approach to "justice and the politics of difference." Young's views are contained in *Justice and the Politics of Difference* (Princeton: Princeton University Press, 1990). Fraser notes that some forms of differences should be rejected as dehumanizing; others should be embraced as part of flourishing lives; and still other "differences" should be universalized (*Justice Interruptus*, pp. 202–204). My approach also bears similarities to the approach of Michael Walzer in *Spheres of Justice* – especially the assertion about separate spheres of life that have different criteria for distribution. As Susan Moller Okin argues, this "separate spheres" argument of Walzer can be accepted without necessarily endorsing his "shared meanings" argument, which interpreted narrowly can deny a plurality of meaning-making worldviews within a society's population. See Okin, "The Complex Inequalities of Gender," in David Miller and Michael Walzer (eds.), *Pluralism, Justice, and Equality* (Oxford: Oxford University Press, 1995).

expressions of injustice. Equality and difference is a false dichotomy; it is preferable to speak of basic equalities that enable genuine complex differences. Thus part two will expand the claim that *equality of basic capability is a necessary condition for the expression of genuine differences.*

THE DISTRIBUTIONAL QUESTION IN ECONOMIC ANALYSIS

One additional debate requires critical examination – both for contextualizing the empirical analysis of international and US inequality and for developing a Christian ethical approach to inequality. Notable in the current, standard, neo-classical economic framework is its *lack* of direct or first-order attention to matters of distribution or inequality. With a focus on levels of production and its growth, economic analysis considers distributional concerns usually only when they bear on efficiency concerns.[43] Yet by revisiting some of the foundational commitments and assumptions of economics, it is possible to address questions of inequality – particularly as they bear on individuals' welfare. Indeed, the towering economist A. B. Atkinson has noted (and applauded) a trend toward addressing inequality: Atkinson entitled his 1996 Presidential Address to the Royal Economic Society, "Bringing Income Distribution in from the Cold."[44] Through emphasis on basic needs, human development, and capability, other economists have moved even further, by addressing inequality of other kinds of goods.

Over the twentieth century, economic science narrowed its focus toward technical, mathematical problem-solving. Yet various economists have vociferously maintained that at bottom, economics must be concerned about questions of personal and social well-being and quality of life.[45] According

---

[43] For an overview of the way in which Pareto optimality and economic efficiency have come to dominate welfare economics (which is the most promising area of economics for taking on distributional issues), see Amartya Sen, *On Ethics and Economics* (Oxford: Blackwell, 1987), especially pp. 29–37.

[44] A. B. Atkinson, "Bringing Income Distribution in from the Cold," *The Economic Journal* 107 (March 1997).

[45] Among a variety of perspectives, some important works include Amartya Sen, "Capability and Well-Being"; Partha Dasgupta, *An Inquiry into Well-Being and Destitution* (Oxford: Clarendon Press, 1993); and the literature surrounding and including

to the founder of neo-classical economic thought, Alfred Marshall, human deprivation and its alleviation give "to economic
studies their chief and their highest interest."[46] Indeed, the
earlier rise of political economy as a branch of moral philosophy
suggests the central humane motivation for economics as a
discipline.

If the technical economic tools and the whole "economic
approach to human behavior"[47] can be seen to be in service of
wider, humane ends, the economic problems of all societies –
"developed" and "developing" alike – can be approached in
parallel fashion through questions about human well-being.
Amartya Sen makes the following claim:

The enhancement of living conditions must clearly be an essential – if
not *the* essential – object of the entire economic exercise and that
enhancement is an integral part of the concept of development. Even
though the logistic and engineering problems involved in enhancing
living conditions in the poor, developing countries might well be very
different from those in the rich, developed ones, there is much in
common in the respective exercise on the two sides of the divide.[48]

The specific problems faced, of course, will be context-dependent and therefore distinct; yet the well-being of people,

the United Nations Development Programme's annual *Human Development Report*
(New York: Oxford University Press, 1990–99).

[46] Alfred Marshall, introduction to *Principles of Economics*, eighth edn. (London:
Macmillan, 1920).

[47] This phrase is Gary Becker's, who received the Nobel Prize for his efforts to expand
the model of the "economic approach" to various forms of human behavior; his own
work and that of his students have extended this model to examine the family, sex,
religion, the legal justice system, among other aspects of life. See, among his other
works, *The Economic Approach to Human Behavior* (Chicago: University of Chicago Press,
1978). Much of this work has arguably lost focus on the humane motivation for
economics.

[48] Amartya Sen, "The Concept of Development," in H. Chenery and T. N. Srinivasan
(eds.), *The Handbook of Development Economics* (Oxford: Elsevier Science Publishers,
1988), p. 11. As was discussed in chapter 2, Amartya Sen's emphasis on delineating
the *space* of social analysis allows one to speak of *absolute* capabilities and functionings
that require the holding of particular baskets of commodities that are *relative* both to
one's society and to each person's biological and cultural background. See, for
instance, these works by Sen: *Inequality Reexamined*; "Poor, Relatively Speaking,"
Oxford Economic Papers 35 (1983); and "Capability and Well-Being." Partha Dasgupta
notes in the preface and introductory chapter to his massive work, *An Inquiry into
Well-Being and Destitution*, that while destitute people exist in all societies, destitution is
only endemic to certain societies. Yet he is seeking to examine a "common core" of
human conditions that affect people in whatever society they live in.

especially those facing deprivation, sets the context for economic inquiry.

Since development economics addresses societies with a high proportion of severe deprivation and destitution, it is no surprise that many economists in this sub-field prioritize questions of quality of life and living standards. Yet, like the wider discipline of which it is a part, even development economics has increasingly focused on the growth of production as the principal objective.[49] The improvement of living conditions has been valued most explicitly as a means to increase "human capital," an important input to the production process. Paul Streeten has noted an ironic result of this approach: "A well-nourished, healthy, educated, skilled, alert labor force is the most important productive asset. This has been widely recognized, though it is odd that Hondas, beer, and television sets are often accepted without questioning as consumption goods, while nutrition, education, and health services have to be justified on grounds of productivity."[50]

BASIC NEEDS, HUMAN DEVELOPMENT, AND INEQUALITY

In response to the dominant economic paradigm, various alternative approaches to development have been offered, such as the "basic needs" approach, Sen's "capability" approach, and the "human development" approach. As a way of expanding development discourse away from a limited focus on gross national product (GNP), gross domestic product (GDP), and growth thereof, a number of alternative measures for development and well-being have been offered. Among them are the physical quality of life index (PQLI), the human devel-

---

[49] For a helpful discussion, see Amartya Sen, "Development: Which Way Now?" *Economic Journal* 93 (December 1983). For a critical view of the whole notion of "development" as a process that necessarily involves the destruction of traditional cultures through the inseparable components of modernization, see Stephen Marglin, "Towards the Decolonization of the Mind," in F. A. Marglin and S. Marglin (eds.), *Dominating Knowledge: Development, Culture, and Resistance* (Oxford: Clarendon Press, 1990).

[50] Paul Streeten, "Human Development: Means and Ends," *American Economic Review* 84/2 (1994), p. 232.

opment index (HDI), and the index of sustainable economic welfare (ISEW).[51]

Such alternative economic approaches have sought, in distinct but arguably complementary ways, to pursue development that expands people's capacities and opportunities. Efficiency, production, and growth are not rejected as "bads," but neither are they accepted as intrinsic goods. Economic production is seen as a means to the wider human end(s) of development. The questions of personal and social well-being are raised explicitly in these approaches. In the language of the UNDP, one aim should be "to put people back at the center of development."[52]

The related distributional question – central to this book's inquiry – is, *"Which people?"* For the standard neoclassical framework, distributional questions enter as only instrumental, second-order ones, when distribution impacts on questions of human capital or savings rates, when relative well-being affects people's incentives and behavior, or when the relative holding of goods is seen to affect individuals' own well-being.[53] As A. B. Atkinson points out, even when "theory of distribution" is discussed in economics, it customarily refers not to questions of distribution among people but rather to the division of returns among the three factors of economic production: land, labor, and capital.[54]

The question of distribution among people arises more centrally in the so-called alternative approaches to development. Indeed, a central thrust of the basic needs approach is to

[51] A fuller examination of the "basic needs" approach, with references, is offered below. The HDI is treated in detail, and a proposal for adapting the index to account for inequality, is provided in chapter 10. On the PQLI, see M. D. Morris, *Measuring the Condition of the World's Poor: The Physical Quality of Life Index* (London: Frank Cass, 1979). The ISEW is described in H. Daly and J. B. Cobb, Jr., *For the Common Good: Redirecting the Economy Toward Community, the Environment, and a Sustainable Future* (Boston: Beacon Press, 1989).

[52] These perspectives are well-stated in the recent issues of the *Human Development Report*. See, for instance, *HDR 1999*.

[53] For instance, see Robert Frank, *Choosing the Right Pond: Human Behavior and the Quest for Status* (New York: Oxford University Press, 1985); Fred Hirsch, *Social Limits to Growth* (Cambridge, MA: Harvard University Press, 1976); and Richard Easterlin, "Does Economic Growth Improve the Human Lot? Some Empirical Evidence," in P. A. David and M. W. Reder (eds.), *Nations and Households in Economic Growth* (New York: Academic Press, 1973).

[54] Atkinson, "Bringing Income Distribution in from the Cold," p. 298.

prioritize that some essential needs be met for all persons in a society before focusing on less pressing needs (or wants) for a few.[55] While the rhetoric of the basic needs approach has been on eliminating absolute or abject poverty, its proponents acknowledge that, in the short term, meeting the objective will require intentional public action for redistribution. At the same time, they emphasize that on a global scale, the degree of redistribution needed would be small indeed.[56]

Being more specific about the relationship between the basic needs approach and matters of inequality depends on the definition of basic needs that is employed. While talk of basic needs has been influential in development discourse, it has also had polyvalent meanings. In the words of the late Mahbub ul Haq, "[I]t is amazing how two such innocent, five-letter words could mean so many different things to so many different people."[57] What are the needs that are considered basic, and how are they met?

The answer to this question is not straightforward. The concept of basic needs was first articulated in a 1976 document for the International Labour Organization, *Employment, Growth, and Basic Needs: A One-World Problem.* In that document, basic needs were seen to be "the minimum standard of living which a society should set for the poorest group of its people." As they were developed by the ILO at that time, basic needs included more than merely material minimum requirements, but also political and social participation and freedom of all people.[58] This relatively broad definition – beyond the mere provision of material commodities like food, shelter, and clothing – was

[55] P. Streeten et al., *First Things First: Meeting Basic Needs in the Developing Countries* (Oxford: Oxford University Press for the World Bank, 1981), p. 8.

[56] See, for instance, ibid., p. 4. On this point the authors of the *Human Development Reports* concur. For instance, the *HDR 1998* (p. 37) notes an estimate that "the total additional yearly investment required to achieve universal access to basic social services would be roughly $40 billion, 0.1% of world income, barely more than a rounding error. That covers the bill for basic education, health, nutrition, reproductive health, family planning and safe water and sanitation for all."

[57] Mahbub ul Haq, foreword to Streeten et al., *First Things First*, p. ix.

[58] Geneva: ILO, 1976. See also Stephen Knowles, "The Evolution of Basic Needs and Human Development," *Rivista Internazionale di Scienze Economiche e Commerciali* 40 (1993), pp. 518–519.

retained by Streeten in a 1977 article. Streeten stated at that time that the objective of the basic needs approach was "providing the opportunities for the full physical, mental and social development of the human personality."[59] From its earliest moments, then, the goals of the basic needs approach were stated very broadly in terms of the value of incorporating the most needy into full participation in their societies.

Yet both the philosophy and the strategic implementation of the basic needs approach quickly became problematic. Which needs are basic? Are these needs universal across societies? Within societies, do relative factors matter in determining the level of goods needed to meet particular needs – like shelter or clothing? Is it paternalistic (and therefore contrary to the neoclassical economic assumption that consumers themselves know what is best for them) for governments or other institutions to tell individuals what they need? Who would provide for such needs? How would their provision be funded?[60]

Faced with such problems, in its operation the basic needs approach came to be associated – fairly or unfairly – with the provision of a particular bundle of material goods and services for consumption by "needy" persons. That bundle of goods and services, however, should not be seen as an end in itself. Rather, they should enable all people "to achieve certain results, such as adequate standards of nutrition, health, shelter, water and sanitation, education, and other essentials."[61]

Understood within these wider human ends of development, there is clearly continuity between the basic needs approach and the "human development" approach, set forth and promoted by the UNDP since 1990 in annual *Human Development Reports*. The tenth *Report* (1999) begins by quoting the opening words of the first *Report* (1990, p. 1): "The real wealth of a nation

---

[59] Paul Streeten, "The Distinctive Features of a Basic Needs Approach to Development," *International Development Review* (1977), reprinted in *Development* 40 (1997), p. 50.

[60] For interesting discussions of these questions and related criticisms of the basic needs approach, see Knowles, "The Evolution of Basic Needs," especially pp. 519–521 and 534–537; and Van B. Weigel, "The Basic Needs Approach: Overcoming the Poverty of *Homo oeconomicus*," *World Development* 14/12 (December 1986), especially pp. 1423–1425.

[61] Streeten et al., *First Things First*, p. 3.

is its people. And the purpose of development is to create an enabling environment for people to enjoy long, healthy, and creative lives. This simple but powerful truth is too often forgotten in the pursuit of material and financial wealth." The UNDP, in the effort to receive widespread public attention for its *Reports*, emphasized the newness of the human development approach, and therefore played up its distinction from other perspectives, including basic needs.[62] As Knowles points out adeptly, this effort may have contributed to the limited characterization of the basic needs approach as promoting merely a particular bundle of goods and services.[63]

Alongside the continuities between basic needs and human development is one area in which the two approaches differ, at least in their rhetoric. While the basic needs approach has had developing countries as its focus, the UNDP has made a concerted effort to devise ways to evaluate development at all levels and in all countries of the world. While this is not to say that deprivation and poverty are not important for the *Human Development Reports* – surely they are – there is a more explicit attempt for universal extension of development strategies. As Streeten says, "[a] pure basic needs approach would give zero weight to meeting the needs of those above the basic needs line, until the basic needs of all were met."[64] The UNDP has broadened the purview of human development.

What the basic needs and human development approaches share most prominently – and admirably – is the call to shift evaluation of development away from the space of income to incorporate other important aspects of life. Even with their different emphases, in practice each approach recognizes the need to balance universal concern with concern for those least advantaged – in terms of income, health, education, and other spheres of life essential to social participation. Both approaches

---

[62] The continuity can be seen in the centrality in both efforts of economists including Mahbub ul Haq, Paul Streeten, Frances Stewart, and others.
[63] Knowles, "The Evolution of Basic Needs," p. 527.
[64] Streeten et al., *First Things First*, p. 55. Streeten goes on to consider approvingly a mixed or moderated strategy that attends to others' condition and the overall economy alongside meeting basic needs. Such recognition moves toward the position articulated by a human development approach.

leave room to address distributional questions – inequality of income and wealth, educational attainment, access to health-care, and the like. Yet more work needs to be done if there is normative concern for direct attention to inequality.

The complexities of basic needs and human development can be significantly clarified by employment of the language of capability and functionings, as considered earlier in the chapter. Following Sen's terminology, whatever approach to develop-ment and well-being is employed, the emphasis should be on the "space" that is most intrinsically valuable and thus of the most direct moral concern. In the question of basic needs and human development, what is important are functionings like "having adequate income," "being well educated," and "being in good health." Certainly goods like money, textbooks, and nutritious food are necessary for achieving these functionings, but different people will require different amounts of these goods in order to reach their potential and to function well. Thus, as much as possible, in empirical analysis and in norma-tive theorizing, capability and functionings should be empha-sized over commodities. When this insight is recognized, the discrepancies between the basic needs and human development approaches are attenuated.

The emphasis on capability and functionings, further, helps to bring together the interdisciplinary insights drawn in this chapter. Responses to the question, "Inequality of what?", should focus as explicitly as possible on intrinsic moral con-cerns. The "capability approach" has been suggested as one framework that enables moral, social, and economic analysis to capture multiple dimensions of human development and well-being. While it is difficult to assess people's actual functioning in all spheres of life, it is possible, at least, to widen the frame beyond income and wealth and to examine goods related to education, health, and other important dimensions. In descrip-tive or moral terms, there is no simple answer to "Inequality of what?" But the chapter has suggested various ways to clarify the complexities.

CHAPTER 3

International contexts of inequality

CONTEXTUALIZING AN EMPIRICAL EXAMINATION OF SOCIOECONOMIC INEQUALITY

People motivated by moral and religious commitments seek to act faithfully and effectively in the face of the "signs of the times." In order for such efforts to be well placed, of course, analysis and understanding is needed of the social realities that persons, societies, and creation as a whole, face. Religiously motivated actors have been criticized for acting with passion – but without sophistication – regarding contemporary social issues. When economic systems in particular are in question, Christian ethical perspectives are often discounted for being naïve and/or utopian – and not only by social scientists.[1] It is incumbent upon *all* people who wish to engage in public debate about social and economic questions to understand the complexity, ambiguity, and indeed the potential urgency of the contemporary situation.

To examine empirical levels and trends of inequality is principally a descriptive-analytical task – undertaken in order

---

[1] Of course, such criticism can come from people benefiting from the *status quo* who prefer not to hear from "naysayers" of any perspective, or it can arise from those who simply do not believe that religious perspectives have anything distinctive and/or rational to offer to public debate in contemporary societies. In this book I attempt to address each of these criticisms. My argument as a whole is an effort by example to reject the latter type of criticism. See especially the discussion of theological perspectives in public discourse, in chapter 5. My objection to the former type is less direct. In addition to the moral force of my arguments, I would also assert that the promotion of social arrangements in which all people have a genuine stake as equals can be in the (enlightened and prudential) interest of *all* persons within those societies.

to understand the signs of the times. Yet description, of course, reflects conscious choices that frame a particular picture of contemporary socioeconomic reality.[2] Rather than deny this implicit value-dimension of this descriptive analysis, it is important to acknowledge that there is no other way in which to proceed with an empirical analysis. Further, as was demonstrated by reference to discussions in political philosophy and development economics, there are normative reasons for widening economic and policy-oriented debate beyond the sphere of income to include various dimensions of well-being. To that end, inequalities can be examined in other spheres of life, including education and health.

The various kinds of inequality can be analyzed at international and national levels (among others). As was discussed in the opening chapter, the question of inequality has recently been raised both within the international development community and in US domestic public discourse. Yet the severity, trends, and the social meanings of such inequalities differ according to their context.

Globalization in its various meanings and manifestations has served to widen the scope of economic issues from the national to the international level – though at both levels, economic problems are shared disproportionately. Globalization has made two types of international concerns relevant and important to consider, despite the difficulties of these inquiries. First, cross-country comparisons of inequality are increasingly relevant, since people now have increasing access to the cultural expressions, social relations, and economic data of other countries with which to compare their own country. (For instance, how does inequality in the United States compare with that in the United Kingdom?) Second, international and even global economic distributions are increasingly relevant as well, since technology makes it more and more possible for people to view themselves as members of transnational groupings like the European Union, or even as "global citizens."[3] It is important

[2] See, for example, Amartya Sen, "Description as Choice," *Oxford Economic Papers* 32 (1980).

[3] For an interesting argument for seeing oneself as a "citizen of the world," and for

to note that globalization is not a phenomenon of proportional influence of cultures on one another. As many scholars have maintained, globalization entails the increasing expression of Western, predominantly American commercial values across various former cultural divisions.[4] At the same time, economic and technological advances – if harnessed properly – can open up opportunities for even marginalized people to become global participants. The perils and promise of globalization make inequality a crucial consideration.[5]

INCOME INEQUALITY: THE GLOBAL LEVEL

Examining inequality at the global level yields striking results but also requires the tackling of serious methodological problems. In addition to it being increasingly important, in a globalizing era, to understand the world's income distribution, it also creates a wide context that informs the regional and national analyses that follow.

Recent *Human Development Reports* have highlighted some of the most severe inequalities in the world distributions of income and wealth. Some of the more graphic comparisons among the

---

situating nationalism within a view of "cosmopolitanism," see Martha Nussbaum (with respondents), *For Love of Country: Debating the Limits of Patriotism* (Boston: Beacon Press, 1996).

[4] For one widely discussed account of this aspect of globalization, see Benjamin Barber, *Jihad Versus McWorld* (New York: Times Books, 1995). Three other perspectives that illuminate the negative effects of globalization are offered in a special issue on "The Global Economy" in *Current History: A Journal of Contemporary World Affairs* 96/613 (November 1997): Blanca Heredia, "Prosper or Perish?: Development in the Age of Global Capital"; Douglas Watson, "Indigenous Peoples and the Global Economy"; and Thomas M. Callaghy, "Globalization and Marginalization: Debt and the International Underclass." The remaining essays in this issue offer important insights into the complexities of globalization.

[5] See *HDR 1997*, chapter 4, and all of *HDR 1999*, for discussions of globalization and the various ways that inequality is discussed in relation to human development. In addition see James Gustave Speth, "Global Inequality"; and Andrew Glyn (with responses by William Greider, Geoffrey Garrett, Rachel McCulloch, Thomas Palley, and Dani Rodrik), "Egalitarianism in a Global Economy," *Boston Review* 22/6 (December 1997–January 1998). Glyn's central contention, debated by the various authors, is that the principal barriers to equality and justice remain domestic ones, not international ones. See also Bread for the World Institute, *Hunger in a Global Economy: Hunger 1998 (Eighth Annual Report on the State of World Hunger)* (Silver Spring, MD: BFWI, 1998).

"super-rich" and the poorest millions of human beings were provided in chapter 1. *HDR 1999* includes this wider view of international income distribution: "Today, global inequalities in income and living standards have reached grotesque proportions. The gap in per capita income (GNP) between the countries with the richest fifth of the world's people and those with the poorest fifth widened from 30 to 1 in 1960, to 60 to 1 in 1990, to 74 to 1 in 1995."[6]

A 1993 *Special Issue* of the United Nations, *Trends in International Distribution of Gross World Product*,[7] reveals both the severity of the global income distribution and the complexities of its determination. Because of the different methods of converting national income figures to a common currency – conventionally, into US dollars – the levels of total and per-capita global growth, as well as the trends in the global income distribution, are disputable. Yet by all measures, over the period 1970–89, real gross world product (GWP: the total value of the end goods and services produced throughout the world in a year) increased by at least 90 percent. Given an increasing global population during that period, *per capita* real GWP still rose by 35 to 40 percent.[8] That is, by the most conservative measures, average *production* per human being increased by at least 35 or 40 percent. Seen by itself, this increase is a most positive result.

How was the income from this increased global production distributed? The UN *Special Issue* determines GWP according to four alternative conversion methods.[9] For each determination

---

[6] *HDR 1999*, pp. 104–105. Note that these figures class people first by their countries. As discussed below, this is a conservative way to measure global inequality.

[7] United Nations Department for Economic and Social Information and Policy Analysis – Statistical Division, *Trends in International Distribution of Gross World Product* (New York: United Nations, 1993) National Accounts Statistics *Special Issue* series x, no. 18.

[8] UN, *Special Issue*, pp. 20–22, esp. table 1.

[9] These various methods are described in detail in UN *Special Issue*, chapter 1, pp. 7–17. They include: market-based exchange rates (MER), the *World Bank Atlas* method (WA), purchasing power parity (PPP), and price adjustments of exchange rates (PARE). It should be noted that the *Human Development Reports* employ the purchasing power parities method, since they argue that it is the method most consistent with its task of comparing the holdings of basic goods and services that play a vital role in the provision of the basic capability to function within society.

of the GWP, the authors calculate a *Gini coefficient*, an important indicator of inequality.[10] According to two methods, inequality in the GWP increased by at least 9 percent over the period 1970–89. According to a third method, global inequality increased by 4.2 percent. By the final method, though, there was no significant change in inequality.[11]

It is important to note that this UN *Special Issue* employs nation-based data to calculate Gini coefficients. Individual-level data are thus first classed according to country and only then, as a second step, combined to arrive at the inequality figures for GWP. There are two important, related points here. First, inequalities within nations are not addressed in this study – the global-level figure is calculated as if every person within each respective country had exactly equal incomes – the mean national per capita income figure.[12] Second, the consequent indices of inequality indicate less inequality than if the world population were aggregated only once – at the global level. If people were classed in a single step, according to their (personal, familial, or household) share of GWP, a higher index of inequality would be attained.[13]

One further point will serve as context for the discussions, below, of regional and national inequalities: Even with this problem of an intermediate (national) level of aggregation of data, which underestimates inequality, the Gini coefficient for global income distribution is at least as high as that measure calculated for the population of any nation in the world.[14] That

---

[10] The Gini coefficient as a measure of distributional inequality is discussed in detail in appendix A.

[11] The two methods that estimate an increase of over 9 percent in the Gini index are the MER and WA methods; the PPP method yields a 4.2 percent rise, and the PARE yields no significant change.

[12] This point is noted in passing on p. 25 of the UN *Special Issue*.

[13] These points may be seen more clearly with the background of appendix A.

[14] In numeric terms, the Gini indices for the 1970–89 period according to the MER, WA, and PARE techniques range from 0.67 to 0.73. The PPP estimates, which only cover a set of 117 countries that tends to underestimate actual global inequality (see p. 26 of the UN *Special Issue*), fall in the range of 0.55 to 0.58. According to Deininger and Squire's comprehensive data set on income inequality, estimates of the Gini coefficient for Brazil have ranged from 0.53 to 0.62, and South Africa's index has been estimated at 0.62 (Klaus Deininger and Lyn Squire, "A New Data Set Measuring Income Inequality," *The World Bank Economic Review* 10/3 [1996], table 1, pp. 574–577). *World Development Report 1998/99* (Oxford: Oxford University Press,

is to say that the degree of global income inequality is at least as severe as the worst national inequalities. The countries with a comparable level of income inequality include Brazil and South Africa, each of which has experienced social unrest related to inequality – violence, crime, street children – as "first-world" and "third-world" conditions coexist. At the global level, during the 1970s and 1980s, that level of inequality did not decline, and by most measures, it increased.

INCOME INEQUALITY: REGIONAL PATTERNS AND COMPARISONS

While the global-level examination reveals a complex yet serious situation of inequality, region-by-region comparisons of income inequality indicate that the degree of inequality differs widely. The relationship of growth and inequality is seen to be indeterminate – though the most *equitable* growth strategies have had the most significant long-term success in terms of production.

Before assessing the inequalities within regions themselves, it is important to note the ways in which global output has changed in distribution across regions.[15] As shown in figure 3.1, the respective shares of GWP produced by major regions of the world shifted significantly over the period of the 1970s and 1980s. The proportion of world product in North America and in Sub-Saharan Africa (whose share was already disturbingly meager) dropped seriously by all measures between 1970 and 1989. The share produced by Latin America held basically the same. Most significant was the increase in the proportion of world product attributed to Asia, with an increase estimated between 35 and 60 percent. Most of the increase occurred in South-eastern and Eastern Asia (including Japan).[16] Thus as

1999), estimates Brazil's Gini coefficient at 0.601, South Africa's at 0.584, and Sierra Leone's at 0.629 (table 5, pp. 198–199).

[15] Note that in this case, the "units" of analysis are the regions, and the range is the entire world. In the paragraphs below, the units are households or individuals, and the range is each particular region, or countries grouped by region.

[16] As noted in the citation to figure 3.1, the analysis of this paragraph draws from table A.6 of the UN *Special Issue*.

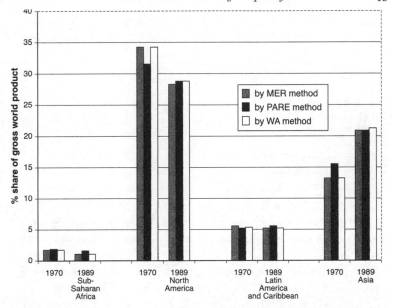

Figure 3.1. Change in share of gross world product, for selected regions, 1970–1989. (Source: United Nations, *Trends in International Distribution, Special Issue* 1993, table A.6, pp. 313–331, and author's calculations.)

the analysis next turns to see how each particular regional "pie" has been distributed, it is important to keep in mind that the absolute and relative sizes of these regional pies have also changed notably within the expanding world "kitchen."

Most economies in Asia are far more egalitarian in terms of income than are the economies of Latin America. Industrial countries, including the nations in the OECD (Organization for Economic Cooperation and Development), as a group fall closer to the Asian levels of inequality than to the Latin American levels. While there is significant variation among each regional grouping, table 3.1 indicates the general regional situation by way of the income ratios of the richest quintile of persons to the poorest quintile in each region.

These general indicators, of course, do not hold for all countries in any particular region. In Latin America, income is much more equitably distributed in Costa Rica or Cuba than in Brazil or Guatemala. In the "developed world," income is

Table 3.1. *Income ratios of richest quintile to poorest quintile, by region*

Region	Ratio
Latin America and the Caribbean	18.7
North America	8.7
East Asia and the Pacific	7.1
Eastern Europe	6.6
European Union	6.3
South Asia	4.4

Source: Human Development Report 1977, Annexe table A2.1, p. 56.

more equitably distributed in Sweden than in the United States. Asia is arguably the most complicated region or set of regions to assess, as it can be misleading to consider China and Japan together economically, or even to see India as a unified economic whole. Indeed, China and India are each important cases on their own. Each country's population numbers over one billion, and together they comprise well over a third of the world's human beings.[17] Thus it is significant to note that China's and India's respective Gini coefficients are located in the respectable 0.30–0.35 range.[18] Of course, to note these moderate levels of inequality is not to state that the overall economic situation in either China or India is good. While not the poorest nations in the world, growth of production is needed in both countries to assure that a decent standard of living can be enjoyed by most citizens.

While regional groupings are helpful in demonstrating that different types of development strategies and institutional arrangements have resulted in very different degrees of income inequality, some general statements can be made about regional *trends* in inequality. In their review of reliable income inequality

[17] See Barbara Crossette, "In Days, India, Chasing China, Will Have a Billion People," *New York Times* (8/5/1999), A10.

[18] See Deininger and Squire, "New Data Set," table 1, p. 575. Recent World Bank data place India's Gini coefficient at 0.297 but put China's at 41.5 (*WDR 1998/99*, table 5, pp. 198–199). For overviews of the overall development situation in China and India, see the *HDR 1997*, pp. 49–52. For a recent and important analysis of India, see Jean Drèze and Amartya Sen, *India: Social Development and Economic Opportunity* (Oxford: Clarendon Press, 1995). As Drèze and Sen note, inequality within the different states of India varies widely.

estimates, Deininger and Squire present decade-specific averages of Gini coefficients for various regions. Methodological factors admittedly limit their inquiry,[19] but their results, shown graphically in figure 3.2 provide a helpful overview of regional levels and trends.

Most evident is the 16 percent increase in the average of Gini coefficients in Eastern Europe in the 1990s, a rise confirmed by the UNDP.[20] In addition, Latin America showed some decline (of 8 percent) in its average Gini coefficient between the 1960s and 1970s, before steadying at high levels in the 1980s and 1990s. In Sub-Saharan Africa, for which inequality data are most scarce and unreliable among the major regions, inequality fluctuates, dropping 13 percent from the 1960s until the 1980s but rebounding by over half of that amount in the 1990s. The Middle East and North Africa, East Asia, South Asia, and the "industrial countries" as aggregate groupings show little fluctuation over this period.

INCOME INEQUALITY: CROSS-NATIONAL TRENDS AND COMPARISONS

The fact that inequality within regions has changed only marginally over recent decades should not mask the fact that substantial changes in inequality have occurred within particular countries. In Asia, inequality between 1960 and 1990 decreased in Hong Kong, India, Malaysia, Singapore, and Taiwan. In contrast, the situation worsened in Bangladesh and Thailand.[21] In Latin America, the region with the most serious inequality problems, the UNDP reports that the state of income inequality improved in Colombia, Costa Rica, and Uruguay, and it worsened in Argentina, Bolivia, Brazil, Peru, and Venezuela.[22] The comparison and contrast between Asian and Latin American income-based inequalities will be further explored in relation to other socioeconomic inequalities later in this chapter.

---

[19] Though they include observations from 108 countries, they note that trends in regional averages of the Gini coefficient may be significantly impacted on "by the fact that not all economies have observations for all decades" ("New Data Set," table 5, p. 584).

[20] *HDR 1996*, p. 17.   [21] Ibid.   [22] Ibid.

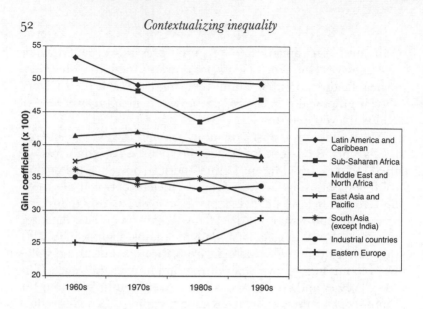

Figure 3.2. Changes in averages of Gini coefficients, by region and decade. (Source: Deininger and Squire, "New Data Set," table 5, p. 584.)

Trends in and the states of income inequality in the industrial countries[23] are similarly complex. The widely used Luxembourg Income Study (LIS), which grew out of an academic meeting of US American and European scholars in 1982, has enabled careful comparative and intertemporal studies of income inequality among the countries of the OECD – predominantly from North America and Europe (though it has now expanded to include twenty-eight countries).

For the period ranging from the late 1970s through the 1980s, the LIS study finds that the degree of inequality differed

---

[23] The grouping "industrial countries," of course, is not technically a regional or geographic grouping. The *Human Development Reports*, for instance, oppose "industrial countries" and "developing countries"; these *Reports* also include Eastern Europe and the Commonwealth of Independent States in the "industrial countries" grouping. For instance, see *HDR 1997*, pp. 244–245. In contrast, the discussion of this section, and figure 3.2, do not include these countries within the industrial countries. As noted in the text, the following paragraphs will focus on a subset of countries within the OECD, which in the periods covered by the analysis, did not include Poland, Hungary, or the Czech Republic, as it now does.

significantly for OECD countries. The Scandinavian and Benelux countries and (West) Germany had the lowest levels of income inequality, while the United States, Ireland, and Switzerland experienced the highest levels.[24]

The most serious increase in inequality occurred in the United Kingdom, where rises in the Gini coefficient have been alternately estimated at 13 percent (from 1979 to 1986)[25] and at 33 percent (1979 to 1990).[26] The next most significant increase in inequality occurred in the United States, a case considered in detail in the next chapter. Overall, inequality also rose, but by lesser degrees, in Sweden, Japan, Australia, (West) Germany, and Belgium. Few significant changes occurred in Norway, Austria, the Netherlands, Ireland, Canada, Finland, or France. Only Portugal and Italy are credited with decreases in inequality over the 1980s.[27] The most recent inequality measures available for the World Bank are given in table 3.2.

These sections on global, regional, and national inequalities have sought to present a critical overview of one aspect of the socioeconomic signs of the times: trends and states of the inequality of *income*. The broad region that has experienced the most dramatic growth of the past thirty to forty years, Asia, has also tended to do well in terms of constraining income disparity. Within regions and at different levels of development, individual countries vary significantly. Among the Western European and North American countries, distinct socioeconomic and political arrangements have led to a range of inequality outcomes. Income inequality is thus neither a necessary nor an immutable socioeconomic reality, and it is not strongly correlated with economic success or growth.

---

[24] A. B. Atkinson, Lee Rainwater, and Timothy Smeeding, *The Income Distribution in OECD Countries: Evidence from the Luxembourg Income Study*, OECD Social Policy Studies no. 18 (Paris: OECD, 1995), chap. 4, esp. pp. 44–46 and p. 58.

[25] Ibid., table 4.8, p. 49.

[26] Ibid., table 5.23, p. 75.

[27] Ibid., chaps. 4 and 5, esp. p. 80. Similar, but slightly different results are presented in *HDR 1999*, reporting findings of Peter Gottschalk and Timothy M. Smeeding, "Cross-National Comparisons of Earnings and Income Inequality," *Journal of Economic Literature* 35/2 (1997).

INEQUALITIES IN EDUCATION AND HEALTH/LONGEVITY: WHY MOVE BEYOND INCOME INEQUALITY?

The discussion thus far has focused on inequalities *of income*. Income-based figures are the most readily available data in most instances. Thus despite the problems of converting data into a common money-currency, income is the default space for most economic discussions. Yet, of course, many other socio-economic goods exist. While money can be used to buy many things, it is sometimes not sufficient, or even relevant, for gaining access to certain goods. Non-money barriers can block people from obtaining social goods. For instance, people with adequate incomes can be denied access to education or health-care because of their gender, race, or religion. Facing their own matrix of personal and institutional factors (including opportunity and discrimination), all people must "convert" goods like income into other goods like education and health, or more complex goods like social participation, self-respect, and so on. This conversion is not the same for everyone – if it were, then the problem of social inequality would be significantly simpler than it actually is.[28]

Because people are empirically different and face different social opportunities, distributions in one space do not usually translate into the same distribution in other spaces. Examining multiple spaces thus promises to provide additional information for judging social and personal well-being. This raises the question, of course, of "Which spaces?" – also discussed in chapter 2. Answers to this question reflect the normative interests of the theorist and/or citizens. On a practical level, of course, the choice of spaces to be considered is constrained by the availability of data. It might be desirable to examine inequality in landholding or in the burden of household chores, but in each of these spaces, inequality would be difficult to

---

[28] On this question of various spaces of analysis, people's varying "conversion rates" among them, and the implications for moral theories, see the work of Sen, in particular *Inequality Reexamined* and "Capability and Well-Being." Refer to the discussion in chapter 2, above.

Table 3.2. *Inequality measures for selected OECD countries*

Country	Year	Gini coefficient (× 100)
Belgium	1992	25.0
Sweden	1992	25.0
Norway	1991	25.2
Finland	1991	25.6
(West) Germany	1989	28.1
Italy	1991	31.2
Canada	1994	31.5
The Netherlands	1991	31.5
United Kingdom	1986	32.6
France	1989	32.7
Australia	1989	33.7
Ireland	1987	35.9
Switzerland	1982	36.1
United States	1994	40.1

Source: World Development Report 1998/99, table 5, pp. 198–199.

determine because "intra-household" or "intra-family" data are not readily available. Basic individual-level data are available for education and health, however, and based on these data, the level of inequality can be calculated. Thus the remainder of this international examination is to consider inequalities in education and health/longevity as a way of broadening this critical overview of inequality.

INTERNATIONAL TRENDS IN EDUCATION AND
HEALTH/LONGEVITY

Like the discussion of inequalities of income, the examination of education and health/longevity begins by considering the overall states and trends within these spheres. In aggregate terms, over the period 1960–94, various indicators of "educational attainment per capita" and "health per capita" generally improved, for the world as a whole and by most measures, for all regions. The adult literacy rate for the developing countries rose from 43 percent in 1970 to 64 percent in 1994. With the adult literacy rate in industrial countries listed at 98.5 percent, the world adult literacy rate stood at 77.1 percent. The gross enrollment ratio for school-age children has also risen in recent decades in the developing world.[29]

The developing world as a whole has "narrowed the gaps" with industrial countries in terms of both education and health/longevity. While life expectancy in the developed countries was 67 percent of that in industrial countries in 1960, it had risen to 84 percent of the industrial countries' figure in 1994. Progress has been made as well on daily calorie supply per capita, under-five mortality, and adult literacy.[30] Thus as a whole, significant progress has been realized in health and in education during the period of rapid development.

Yet this type of reporting does not examine as directly as is possible how these benefits are distributed within the developing world. To be sure, aggregate increases in factors like life expectancy could be strongly related to improvements for the least healthy persons in a population. But this is not necessarily the case, as improvements in the longevity of the healthiest, even with no improvement at the bottom end of the life-span distribution, also improve life expectancy figures. Figures like under-five mortality reflect the situation of those at the bottom of health distributions, though such figures do not address relative inequality as much as absolute deprivation. The adult literacy rate is only a primitive distributional indicator; each person either possesses the good "literacy" or does not possess it. Surely health-based and education-based indicators that convey more information about inequality can be devised – such is the task of the remainder of the chapter.

---

[29] *HDR 1997*, table 47, pp. 224–225. All regions have shown improvement in adult literacy rate and in gross enrollment ratio, with the exception of Sub-Saharan Africa, whose enrollment ratio remained unchanged between 1980 and 1994.
[30] Ibid.

CONCEPTUALIZING GINI COEFFICIENTS FOR EDUCATION
AND HEALTH/LONGEVITY[31]

As is described and illustrated in appendix A, a Gini coefficient can be determined for any good for which the share held by each person (in a group or society) can be known. This section discusses the construction of Gini coefficients in education and in health/longevity that will provide a more direct indication of inequalities in these dimensions. It is important to consider these conceptualizations because they are also suggestive of the social-relational component of goods in the educational and health dimensions.

In the sphere of income, each person holds some share of the total of the good income (for any given year). Analogously, in the sphere of education, every person holds some quantity of the good called "schooling"; adults have attained, or possess, up to twelve, or more, years of schooling or formal education. It is possible to conceptualize a "stock" of educational attainment, which is reflected in the total number of years of schooling for that population. Each person holds some share of that total educational attainment. Given the right data, people can be placed in order according to their years of schooling. Consequently a Gini coefficient of educational inequality can be calculated.

The relevant data for educational attainment (assuming that schooling is a good proxy for education) are thus the years of schooling attained in one's lifetime. The quality of schooling is not the same even within countries. This is a serious limitation, and if quality were accounted for, the distributional "in-equality" of education would surely increase (since students with greater years of schooling probably receive better-quality schooling along the way). But as there is no easy way to incorporate quality, educational attainment in years of

---

[31] My constructive work on Gini coefficients within spheres of education and health/longevity is reprinted, in a modified form, from *World Development*, vol. 25, no. 8, Douglas A. Hicks, "The Inequality-Adjusted Human Development Index: A Constructive Proposal," pp. 1283–1298, copyright 1997, with permission from Elsevier Science.

schooling must be considered to be a conservative way to measure educational inequality.[32]

Analogously, though perhaps less intuitively, it is possible to talk about longevity achievement, or life-span achievement. The "good" here is years of life lived. Longer life spans are preferred to shorter life spans.[33] One's age in years at death indicates, in fact, one's ultimate life-span attainment. The distribution in age at death thus reflects the inequality of life spans. (Of course, people do not know precisely what their "ultimate stock" is, until their death.) Seen in this way, there is significant life-span inequality, ranging from infants who die at birth or before one year, to persons who die at ages over a hundred years. It bears noting that in some least developed countries, like Ethiopia and Somalia, the *median* age at death is under five years old; while in other developing countries like Sri Lanka, it is above seventy years.[34] Within particular societies, recent age-at-death statistics are the best measure available for determining life-span attainment and its distribution.[35]

As is the case for income, the distributional measures for education and longevity say nothing directly about the mean attainment level. The increased achievement of a person at the high end of the distribution would increase the level of inequality. There is a dual effect of such a change: first, inequality increases; but second, the achievement level – both for one individual and in the aggregate – has increased. As a well-educated person gets more schooling without changing anyone

[32] V. Ahuja and D. Filmer note the same problem, and draw the same conclusion ("Educational Attainment in Developing Countries: New Estimates and Projections Disaggregated by Gender," Background Paper for the *World Development Report 1995* [Washington: The World Bank, 1995]).

[33] This is a normative claim, but it is the same type of claim required in employing the simpler indicator of life expectancy.

[34] World Bank, *World Development Report 1993* (New York: Oxford University Press, 1993), table A.3, pp. 200–201.

[35] There is a significant inter-temporal problem with treating longevity outcomes, for only when people die do we obtain their ultimate life-span achievement, and it is the ultimate figure in which we are interested. A person who dies in 1985 at age eighty-five has survived through conditions that were very different than, say, those of a five year old who also dies in 1985. The death statistics for the year 1985, then, are the outcome measures for people whose life spans varied in duration. These problems are arguably no more severe than problems of estimating life expectancies (looking into the future) based on present-day life tables.

else's level of schooling, there results an increase in aggregate educational figures[36] alongside a more unequal distribution of educational attainment. This reflects a trade-off between increased aggregate attainment and decreased inequality. Valuing distribution versus aggregation is a normative exercise – which will be considered further in chapters 9 and 10.

GINI COEFFICIENTS FOR INCOME, EDUCATION, AND HEALTH/LONGEVITY: EMPIRICAL RESULTS

Gini coefficients in the dimensions of education, health/longevity, and income are reported for a data set of twenty developing countries in table 3.3. The technical issues and data sources for these calculations are discussed in appendix B. These twenty countries were chosen because reliable, comparable distributional results could be obtained for these countries in all three spheres in question and for a roughly common period – the mid–late 1980s. Most of these countries are from Asia or Latin America, and thus some regional comparison is possible.

The most notable outcome of these calculations is that the ranking of countries by each of the three Gini indices is quite distinct. However, in terms of inequality of income, education, or health/longevity, Latin American nations dominate the bottom half of the countries when ranked (from least to most inequality). Guatemala in particular has the dubious distinction of a placing next to worst in inequality levels in income, education, and health/longevity. Asian countries like the Republic of Korea and Sri Lanka fare very well in all three distributions. Costa Rica and Malaysia each have moderately successful records in all three dimensions.

The situations of Zimbabwe and Bangladesh highlight another point. Bangladesh, with the lowest per capita income of this set of countries, fares best in the index of income inequality. Zimbabwe, with less than 1 percent of its population completing secondary education, and less than 5 percent moving beyond

---

[36] The literacy rate, presumably, would not change. But educational enrollment, and more significantly for this study, total years of schooling, would both increase.

Table 3.3. *Gini coefficients and rankings in income, education, and health / longevity*

Country	Educ. Gini	Educ. Rank	Age Gini	Age Rank	Inc. Gini	Inc. Rank
Zimbabwe	0.322	1	0.472	17	0.542	16
South Korea	0.332	2	0.209	2	0.329	3
Chile	0.332	3	0.223	3	0.533	15
Sri Lanka	0.332	4	0.311	7	0.290	2
Thailand	0.346	5	0.267	5	0.420	6
Philippines	0.355	6	0.447	16	0.391	4
Costa Rica	0.357	7	0.288	6	0.442	9
Hong Kong	0.359	8	0.146	1	0.392	5
Malaysia	0.360	9	0.269	4	0.463	10
Panama	0.366	10	0.321	8	0.543	17
Colombia	0.383	11	0.341	10	0.492	14
Mexico	0.385	12	0.377	12	0.486	13
Peru	0.400	13	0.511	18	0.437	8
Nicaragua	0.420	14	0.379	13	0.481	11
Venezuela	0.427	15	0.353	11	0.423	7
Honduras	0.455	16	0.392	14	0.565	18
Brazil	0.462	17	0.339	9	0.604	20
Dominican Rep.	0.477	18	0.447	15	0.483	12
Guatemala	0.549	19	0.576	19	0.569	19
Bangladesh	0.649	20	0.626	20	0.275	1

Sources: Calculations by author based on UN and World Bank data sets from 1983 to 1992, as discussed in appendix B.

primary school, boasts the least inequality of education. Unfortunately, each of these cases reflects the relatively equal distribution of deprivation.[37]

Finally, a few observations can be made from the correlations between the Gini coefficients in the three dimensions. The correlation between the Gini coefficient for income and that for life span is 0.053. The correlation between the Gini indices for income and education is 0.002. The only significant correlation

---

[37] It is important to note, however, that the Zimbabwe case entails another encouraging factor. As the *HDR 1995* notes, Zimbabwe (along with Sri Lanka which also fares well here) has made significant efforts to lessen female illiteracy. Efforts toward the equal education of women, *ceteris paribus*, would correspond to a more equal distribution of education in any society.

exists between the respective Gini coefficients for education and life span – with a value of 0.718. These results taken together are a reminder that levels of inequalities in some spheres of life are not necessarily related to inequalities in other spheres. In this particular study, inequality in education and longevity, however, are positively and relatively strongly correlated.

The importance of this section on inequalities of education and health/longevity is fourfold. First, it is an argument by example that inequality calculations can be conceptualized and calculated in spheres besides income. Second, the empirical results show that additional information is gained by incorporating other spheres besides income, since inequalities of education and health/longevity are not highly correlated with income inequality. Third, the results reveal that significant inequalities exist in education and health/longevity. Despite observations contained even in the *Human Development Report* that the variables of education and health "are naturally distributed much less unequally than is income,"[38] the Gini coefficients for all three spheres fall in roughly the same range. Fourth, this empirical examination has revealed that while national rankings differ across the different dimensions, regional performance between Asia and Latin America is telling. In general, Asian countries experience less income inequality, less educational inequality, and less health/longevity inequality than Latin American countries.

CONCLUSIONS

The empirical findings reveal that the severity of income inequality is not uniform across societies. These figures of

[38] See *HDR 1993*, p. 101. Paul Streeten echoes the call for emphasizing inequality in income more than in life expectancy or in literacy. He writes that "high incomes of some can cause relative deprivation in others. This is not true for human indicators. If anything the benefits in the health and education of anybody benefit the whole community" ("Human Development," pp. 235–236). This is not necessarily the case. There are positive externalities associated with good health and educational background. But these goods can be used selfishly just as income is; education or health, like income, can be used to exploit others. Thus it is not clear that the education and health of some always benefit the community as a whole, or more specifically, those at the bottom of socioeconomic distributions.

inequality cannot be readily accounted for by any single model of development, such as one in which each society must experience and then pass through stages of severe inequality.[39] The cross-regional comparisons in particular demonstrate that significant and rapid growth of production can occur in societies of relative socioeconomic equality. James Gustave Speth, administrator of the UNDP, makes an even stronger claim:

Indeed, our study [*HDR 1996*] shows that, since 1960, no country has been able to follow a course of lopsided development – where economic growth is not matched by human development or vice versa – for more than a decade without falling into crisis. During the past three decades, every country that was able to combine and sustain rapid growth did so by investing first in schools, skills and health while keeping the income gap from growing too wide.[40]

The financial crises of the late 1990s notwithstanding, countries of Asia and the Pacific Rim have managed to achieve both growth and relatively equal socioeconomic distributions. Studies have also indicated that genuine human development is most likely to occur in situations in which there is cooperation between public services and private sector growth – thus creating the social and economic conditions for growth, relative income equality, and the universal provision of basic social services.[41]

The international examination of inequalities further reveals that there are significant inequalities within and across societies in health and education, but that they do not necessarily correlate with income inequality. Each type of inequality must

[39] Such is the argument illustrated by the Kuznets hypothesis, which suggests that developing societies would need to endure inequality for some period in order to achieve further development. The results of this chapter add support to the arguments against the "need" for such inequality. For a critical discussion that questions the empirical validity of the Kuznets curve and, rather, calls for growth along with special attention to raising the income and wealth of the poor, see Klaus Deininger and Lyn Squire, "New Ways of Looking at Old Issues: Inequality and Growth," *Journal of Development Economics* 57/2 (December 1998).

[40] Speth, "Global Inequality," p. 33.

[41] See the important article by Sudhir Anand and Martin Ravallion, "Human Development in Poor Countries: On the Role of Private Incomes and Public Services," *Journal of Economic Perspectives* 7/1 (1993), which focuses in particular on the development strategies and successes of Sri Lanka in relation to the discussion of Amartya Sen's "capability" approach and the UNDP's "human development" approach.

be examined on its own terms. Substantial aggregate progress has been made in narrowing the global "North–South gap" in these socioeconomic spheres, though again, Asian countries in general have done better than their Latin American counterparts in establishing relative equality in education and health. Indeed, the investment in human development and "human capital" in Asian countries created assets that these nations can draw upon to withstand or even overcome temporary crises in the financial sector.[42]

Each country has its own opportunity to address and constrain socioeconomic inequalities. Costa Rica and Guatemala, a few hundred miles apart in Central America (though admittedly with very different political and historical circumstances), have adopted divergent development strategies. Costa Rica's political and economic initiatives have enabled it to enjoy levels of well-being – and political stability – that its Central American neighbors have not. Among industrialized countries, the United Kingdom and the United States experience levels of income and healthcare inequalities that are not tolerated in the social-welfare states of the Scandinavian and Benelux countries. These cross-national differences suggest that, among other factors, social policies play a major role in irritating or alleviating inequalities.

[42] I have asserted this point vis-à-vis the 1998 "Asian crisis" and Amartya Sen's emphasis on developing human capability (and not just incomes) in Douglas A. Hicks, "A Human Face for Economics," *Journal of Commerce* (10/27/1998).

CHAPTER 4

Inequalities in the United States

At least two factors can be credited for the reemergence, within contemporary public discourse, of debate about domestic US inequality. Most often cited, and emphasized in chapter 1, are the trends that reveal steady increases in income and wealth inequality since the early 1970s. In contrast to the first quarter century of the postwar period (1945–70), in which substantial real income gains were experienced by all economic levels and demographic groups, the past three decades have yielded only a small rise in median income for the population as a whole, while a disproportionate share of income and wealth gains have gone to the "top" 10 percent of the population. Further, analysts have asserted that many of these small gains can be attributed to rising work hours experienced particularly by women in the workforce.[1]

A second factor also bears consideration. In an era of globalization, analysts and citizens increasingly have seen that, among "developed" nations, the United States experiences the highest level of income inequality. Stated differently: nations with similar levels of "human development" – most with lower per-capita incomes but with competitive or superior educational and health indicators – experience significantly less income inequality. For the world as a whole, the United States' degree of income inequality is surpassed by only the most unequal developing nations, including most Latin American nations,

---

[1] See, for instance, Danziger and Gottschalk, *America Unequal*, and Juliet Schor, *The Overworked American: The Unexpected Decline of Leisure* (New York: Basic Books, 1992). See also Louis Uchitelle, "More Work, Less Play Make Jack Look Better Off," *New York Times* (10/5/1997), WK4.

Thailand, and South Africa.[2] Comparisons among nations can be problematic since they differ in terms of degree of homogeneity, limitations on economic and other kinds of freedom, and so on. Yet such factors contextualize and nuance – but do not remove the significance of – cross-national comparisons.

As with the analysis of international contexts of inequality, a focus on the United States will depend on answering the question, "Inequality of what?" Not only is it fruitful to look at the spheres of income, education, and health, but it is also important to consider inequalities across lines of sex and race/ethnicity.

US INCOME INEQUALITY – COMPARATIVE PERSPECTIVE

In terms of the real income (GDP) per capita of each nation of the world, only Luxembourg and tiny Brunei Darussalam fare better than the United States.[3] Indeed, by all *aggregate* measures of income, the US economy is placed near the top of international comparisons. In contrast, *distributional* comparisons place the United States nearer the bottom. When the ratio of the per-capita income of the poorest fifth (or quintile) of the population to the per-capita income of the whole population is calculated, the United States is among the group of nations whose ratio – at 0.20 – is less than 0.25. While the worst ratios exist in countries like Brazil and Guatemala, the United States is one of a handful of industrial countries that fall beneath this 0.25 (or 1:4) threshold. In contrast, other developed nations like Japan and Sweden have ratios of 0.37 and 0.36, respectively.[4]

The Luxembourg Income Study (LIS) has enabled more careful distributional comparison among the OECD countries than was previously possible. The LIS methodology includes

[2] Crossette, "U.N. Survey," and author's calculations from *HDR* data. Further discussion and figures are presented in the present chapter.

[3] *HDR 1999*, table 1, pp. 134–137. According to these comparative figures, given in purchasing-power-parity adjusted dollars for 1994, the United States' real GDP per capita was $29,010, Luxembourg's is $30,863, and Brunei Darussalam's was $29,773.

[4] *HDR 1996*, table 1.1, p. 13, and author's calculations from *HDR 1999*, table 1, pp. 134–137 and from table 5, pp. 149–150. The United Kingdom, Switzerland, and Australia also fall beneath the 0.25 threshold. See also Crossette, "U.N. Survey."

parallel adjustments within all countries for household size and definitions of income.[5] According to results from the LIS study, comparisons (for the mid–late 1980s) indicate that the United States' distribution was unambiguously more unequal than all countries in the study except Italy, Ireland, and Switzerland – and no definitive comparison could be made with these three nations.[6] According to two important summary measures – the Gini coefficient and the ratio of the incomes of people at the tenth percentile and the ninetieth percentile, the United States contained the highest level of income inequality of all the OECD nations in the study.[7] As discussed in the previous chapter (and shown in table 3.2, page 55), the most recent available data continue to show the United States with the highest Gini coefficient of income inequality among industrialized countries.

A note about comparative *trends* can also be made. The LIS analysis confirms the general phenomenon, discussed below, of rising income inequality in the United States over the period of the 1970s and 1980s. Rising inequality occurred in most developed countries over that period. Yet, over the 1980s, in no industrial country except the United Kingdom was rising inequality more striking than in the United States.

US INCOME INEQUALITY – INTERTEMPORAL TRENDS

The factors involved in examining trends in income inequality in the United States are complex. Yet seen in various ways and controlling a variety of factors, almost all analysts agree that income inequality dropped substantially from the end of World War II until the late 1960s. Then, after its nadir, inequality rose across the 1970s, 1980s, and early 1990s. While there is significant debate about the trend since 1992 – debate that is fueled by

[5] The methodology of the LIS study cited here is described in detail in Atkinson, Rainwater, and Smeeding, *Income Distribution in OECD Countries*, chapter 2.

[6] According to a Lorenz-curve comparison, the US income distribution was thus unambiguously more unequal than Australia, Belgium, Canada, (West) Germany, Luxembourg, Norway, Sweden, and the United Kingdom (ibid., table 4.3 and figure 4.3, p. 44). See appendix A for a discussion of Lorenz dominance.

[7] Ibid., table 4.4, p. 46 and table 4.5, p. 47.

a methodological change in Census Bureau data, political considerations, and the lack of time to clarify the current situation – no party claims that there has been substantial improvement in the income distribution. Most evidence suggests that the *rise* in income and earnings inequalities have subsided – that there has been a levelling off.[8] Indeed, most analysts concur that the economic and sociological forces that have contributed to this inequality have not subsided. They dispute, however, the relative importance of the causes noted in chapter 1.

The basic trends in inequality of income for the United States are shown in figure 4.1, which indicates the Gini coefficient for US families since 1947.[9] The general trends for the population as a whole reveal falling income inequality until the late 1960s; beginning with 1969, inequality increases in a remarkably steady way at least until 1993.[10] Over the post-1970 period, inequality *within* racial/ethnic groups has also increased. While inequality among whites has remained slightly below the overall US figure, inequality among blacks and inequality among Hispanics have both increased above overall US inequality. A viable explanation for these latter groups is that while some African Americans and Latinos/Latinas have experienced significant economic progress into middle or upper income levels, others have stagnated, and thus wider within-group gulfs have been created.[11]

---

[8] The strongest positive claim can be found in the *ERP 1997*, which notes that "although these results [a rise in real household income growth by the lowest quintile between 1993 and 1995] are encouraging, it is too soon to tell whether the longer term trends of increasing inequality have been reversed" (p. 165). The *ERP 1999* adds further support for the claim that the strong labor market of the 1990s' recovery has begun to benefit "disadvantaged groups" including low-wage workers, less educated workers, blacks and Hispanics, immigrants, and single mothers. See especially pp. 41–42 and 103–116.

[9] US Census Bureau, Historical Income Tables – Families, table F-4, <http://www.census.gov/hhes/income/histinc/f04.html>.

[10] A complicating factor for the 1992–94 period is a change in survey methodology by the Current Population Surveys, in particular a change in the upper-end categories of reported income. These survey changes are attributed with about a third of the rise in the Gini coefficient between 1992 and 1993. See Weinberg, "US Income Inequality," p. 1 of text and n. 3.

[11] For a discussion, see *ERP 1998*, pp. 125–127.

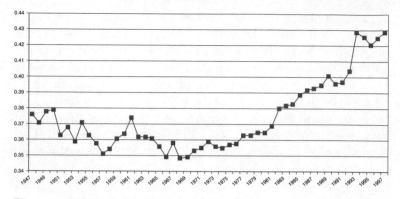

Figure 4.1. US inequality of income, by families: Gini coefficient, 1947–1997. (Note: A change in methodology makes figures after 1992 not strictly comparable with 1992 and earlier. Source: US Census Bureau, Historical Income Tables – Families, table F-4, <http://www.census.gov/hhes/income/histinc.fo4.html>.)

There are a number of complicating factors that need to be considered. First, the data shown in this figure reflect rising inequality in *family* incomes; by Census Bureau definition, the category "families" does not include single-person households or unrelated individuals who live together. In addition, the Census Bureau's definition of income does not include government noncash transfers or benefits, nor does it adjust for taxes.[12] Census Bureau analysis indicates that the former factor – transfer benefits – has a moderate impact toward lesser inequality, while the overall redistributive effect of taxes has only slight impact. When these factors are incorporated, the degree of rise in inequality is lessened modestly, but the general trends indicated in figure 4.1 remain.[13]

---

[12] The Census Bureau's technical definition of income and the survey methodology for its determination are described in "Definitions of Income and Poverty Terms – Income," <http://www.census.gov/hhes/income/defs/income.html>.

[13] Weinberg, "US Income Inequality," pp. 3–4 of text and nn. 10–11; see also Danziger and Gottschalk, *America Unequal*, chapter 3 and *ERP 1997*, chapter 5, especially box 5–4. Even this slight impact towards equality is questioned; Edward M. Gramlich, Richard Kasten, and Frank Sammartino argue that over the 1980s, tax and transfer policies actually "worsened the disparity by a noticeable amount" ("Growing Inequality in the 1980s: The Role of Federal Taxes and Cash Transfers," in Danziger and Gottschalk [eds.], *Uneven Tides*, p. 245).

Of the various sources that comprise total income (for persons, households, or families), *earnings* from work contribute a significant share. A notable trend in the distribution of earnings of individuals in the labor market is that inequalities have increased both *across* levels of educational attainment and *within* groups of persons with similar educational background.[14] The former phenomenon indicates that the "earnings premium" for a four-year college degree has increased significantly over the past thirty years. This can be seen by the fact that the ratio of college to high-school median earnings for all workers of ages twenty-five to twenty-nine increased significantly from 1970 to 1995. For men, that ratio increased from 1.24 in 1970 to 1.52 in 1995; for women, it rose from 1.68 to 1.91. While the sex-based differences in this ratio will be further discussed below, the significant point here is that for both men and women, the relative value of a college degree has risen dramatically since 1970.[15]

US INEQUALITIES IN EDUCATION AND HEALTH/LONGEVITY

When the US population is considered as a whole, the trends in inequality in education and in health/longevity are considerably more encouraging than are the recent trends in income inequality. In order to calculate Gini coefficients in education and health/longevity, data were obtained for educational attainment of the adult population and for age at death, for selected years since 1940.[16] As can be seen in figure 4.2, the Gini coefficients for education and longevity have both decreased steadily over the past fifty years. (The most recent data points for mortality suggest a possible leveling off, or even a slight rise, in the Gini coefficient for health/longevity – but there is not sufficient information to take this as a significant shift.) The Gini coefficient for education fell from a high of

---

[14] *ERP 1997*, pp. 170–175.
[15] These data are taken from the National Center for Education Statistics, *The Condition of Education 1997*, NCES 97–388 (Washington: 1997), p. 120.
[16] The technical and data notes of this calculation are presented in appendix B.

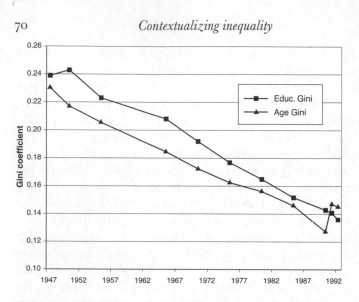

Figure 4.2. US inequality of education and health/longevity: Gini coefficients, 1947–1992. (Source: Calculations by author as described in appendix B.)

0.243 (in 1950) to 0.127 (1996); the figure for health/longevity fell from 0.231 (1947) to 0.128 (1990).

These positive overall trends can be attributed in significant part to a reduction of the most severe forms of deprivation in these spheres. In education, the percentage of the population (of age twenty-five and over) whose educational attainment is eight years or less dropped dramatically, from 50 percent in 1947 to 8 percent in 1996.[17] Similarly, in health/longevity, 9.5 percent of people who died in 1947 were under age five; that figure had dropped below 2 percent by 1992.[18]

It is important to note that these data cannot capture all aspects of inequality in education or health/longevity.[19] Yet, as

[17] Author's calculations from Census Bureau data; see appendix B for a description of the data set.
[18] Author's calculations from US Department of Health and Human Services; see appendix B for further details of the data set.
[19] For instance, as noted above, examining years of schooling cannot reveal directly issues of the differential quality of education. The data set on education is limited at the upper end as well, as people with baccalaureate and higher degrees are classed together in this overall calculation. The age-at-death statistics do not address directly the quality of health that people at any age experience.

general indicators, these Gini-coefficient figures are suggestive about the inequalities of *basic* education and *basic* health in the postwar United States.

As a way of comparing the broad trends among various socioeconomic spheres, figure 4.3 juxtaposes Gini coefficients for income, educational attainment, and life-span attainment. The values for each Gini coefficient of a given year are expressed as a proportion of their 1970 value. The 1970 date was chosen as a baseline because it falls near the nadir of income inequality. The figure shows that from 1947 to 1970, inequality was decreasing in all three spheres. At the point at which income inequality began to rise again, educational and life-span inequalities continued their remarkably steady decrease into the present decade.[20]

These overall trends, of course, are significant in themselves. They serve to show the limits of the view that "economic inequality" narrowly understood has increased since the late 1960s. Inequalities in income and in wealth have in fact risen, while inequalities in some other basic socioeconomic goods have decreased. But these findings do not reveal the entire picture: As the remainder of the chapter will demonstrate, significant differentials (some of which are increasing) persist along lines of sex and race/ethnicity.

INEQUALITIES ALONG LINES OF RACE/ETHNICITY AND
SEX: DISAGGREGATING DATA FOR INCOME, EDUCATION,
AND HEALTH/LONGEVITY

As a complement to examining inequalities among the entire population, it is also possible, and potentially illuminating, to consider "differentials" among the median (or the mean) for different groupings of people. People can be grouped, or classed, in a variety of ways; the remainder of this chapter

---

[20] There are significant intertemporal or "time-lag" problems, when comparing these three spheres. While the income figure reflects income for the given year, the age at death and educational attainment figures indicate long-term, indeed life-long, factors more directly. Stated differently, the income figure can shift dramatically for particular persons from one year to the next; educational attainment for any person cannot change more than one year in any year.

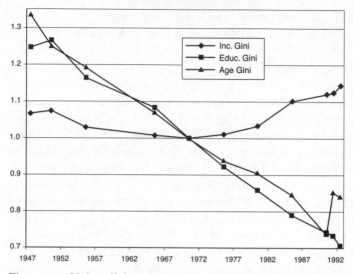

Figure 4.3. Gini coefficients in income, education, and health/longevity, US, as a proportion of the value in 1970. (Source: Calculations by author as described in appendix B.)

examines differentials by race/ethnicity and sex.[21] By proceeding with roughly analogous analyses, the data results and discussion will indicate that the inequalities faced by African Americans, on the one hand, and by women, on the other, are notably distinct.

US DIFFERENTIALS BY RACE/ETHNICITY

Income

In 1997 the US median household income for all races was $37,005. For households headed by whites, the figure was $38,972; for black-headed households, $25,050; and for

---

[21] In the section on earnings inequality, above, differentials were discussed for people grouped by educational attainment, that is, by high school graduates and by college graduates. In this section those education "classes" will be employed further within the discussions of race/ethnicity and sex.

Hispanic-headed households, $26,628.[22] Thus the respective ratios of Hispanic and black household median incomes were each just under two-thirds of the median figure for white households. The trends in real median household income for these three groups are indicated in figure 4.4; the trends in the ratios relating these three indicators are indicated in figure 4.5.

All three racial/ethnic groups experienced aggregate trends consistent with business cycles over this thirty-year period. Real median income rose only modestly for whites and blacks, with little or no absolute gain for Hispanics since the early 1970s. Figure 4.5 also shows that the ratio of black/white median household income has remained roughly constant, around 0.6, over the past thirty years. More precise examination reveals that the period of the late 1960s involved a peak, while the ratio in the 1980s was a trough; improvement can be seen across the 1990s. The four most recent observations, 1994–97, reflect a more favorable ratio than the 1970 figure. As figure 4.5 indicates, the general trend for Hispanics has been a relative loss vis-à-vis blacks and whites. A number of factors, including increased immigration from Latin American countries, have been posited for the worsening relative economic position of this group.[23]

---

[22] U.S Census Bureau, Historical Income Tables – Households, table H-5, <http:// www.census.gov/hhes/income/histinc/h05.html>. Note that in this case I am employing household-based data, because it is as readily available as family-based data for the post-1968 period, and it is arguably more illuminative. Households are classed by the "race or Hispanic origin" of the householder. In this case and in the use of much Census Bureau data, there is a small overlap of the groups "White" and "Black" with Hispanic. That is, people may self-identify as both White and Hispanic, or as Black and Hispanic. The proportion of the population that fits more than one of these categories is relatively small, and the general trends are not significantly affected by this overlap. I employ in this chapter the categories "white," "black," and "Hispanic" to be consistent with Census Bureau language and survey methodology. By following the lead of the Census Bureau, I do not mean to trivialize the significant ethical issue here about the (self-)identification of groups – in my wider discussions I employ the terms "African American" and "Latino/Latina," although neither of these terms is universally accepted.

[23] See also Danziger and Gottschalk, *America Unequal*, pp. 73–74. For an overview of the issues, see Carey Goldberg, "Hispanic Households Struggle as Poorest of the Poor in US," *New York Times* (1/30/1997), A1, A16.

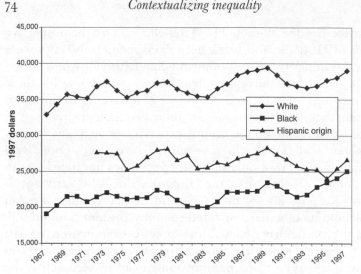

Figure 4.4. Median real household income, by race of householder, US, 1967–1997. (Source: US Census Bureau, Historical Tables – Households, table H-5, <http://www.census.gov/hhes/income/histinc.h05.html>.)

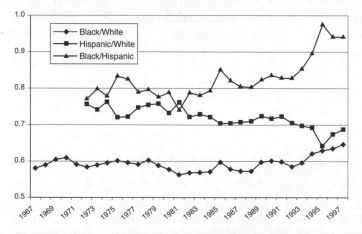

Figure 4.5. Ratios of median household income, by race of householder, US, 1967–1997. (Source: US Census Bureau, Historical Income Tables – Households, table H-5, <http://www.census.gov/hhes/income/histinc.h05.html>.)

Education

The data for people of Hispanic origin indicate slight progress in the 1970s in both the high-school and college figures, while across the 1980s and 1990s there has been no improvement. According to analysis by the National Center for Education Statistics, though, there was a significant rise in the percentage of Hispanics who graduated from high school to complete either one year, or four or more years, of college education.[24]

The trends for African Americans are two-sided. There has been significant progress in high-school and college attendance and graduation, but especially at the post-secondary level, wide gaps remain between whites and African Americans. At the high-school level, there has been notable progress in the proportion of the population to complete four or more years; in fact, the white and black figures are now effectively equal for the 25–29-year-old cohort. However, in terms of completion of four years of college, the progress has not been nearly as significant. In fact, seen in one way, the "time-lag" in years between whites' and blacks' respective college completion figures is twenty-nine years, the highest it has been in the postwar period. A comparison of the progress of blacks vis-à-vis whites in high school and college completion is given in tables 4.1 and 4.2. This "time-lag" figure indicates the number of years between whites' and blacks' respective attainment of an educational completion percentage. That is, the time-lag figure answers the question: "How many years has it taken the black attainment rate to reach that of whites?" These indicators are different from merely examining the *absolute* difference in the educational attainment rate of whites and blacks; the time-lag figures account for the increasing difficulty of marginal improvements in attainment rates. It is easier to move the high school education rate from 60 to 70 percent than to raise it from 70 to 80 percent of a population. These time-lag figures reveal that while significant progress has been made in reducing the black–white differential in high-school graduation, the time-lag

[24] NCES, *Condition of Education 1997*, p. 94.

Table 4.1. *"Time-lag" in high-school education, by race: percentage of US 25–29-year olds completing high school*

Percentage completing high school	Year for whites	Year for blacks	Lag (years)
71.0	1964	1975	11
76.6	1969	1980	11
80.6	1972	1985	13
81.7	1973	1990	17
86.5	1994	1995	1
87.6	1997	1998	1

Source: US Census Bureau Historical Tables – Educational Attainment, table A-2, <http://www.census.gov/population/socdemo/education/tablea-02.txt>.

in college completion has actually increased over recent decades.

These education figures merit careful attention for another reason. According to various sources and calculations based on Census Bureau figures, the "premium" of higher income due to a college education has increased for all groups of Americans in the past three decades. Economic and technological shifts in the economy have thus raised the financial reward to those who obtain a bachelor's degree – or at least an associate's degree.[25] In order for African Americans to increase their relative income position, progress on the college completion differential will be required; significant impact in the income sphere should follow.

Health and longevity

In the dimension of health and longevity, significant differentials by race persist in the United States. Life expectancies of black women and men in 1992 were roughly the same as the life

---

[25] In a discussion of the benefits of a strong economy and labor market, the *ERP 1999* notes that "less educated workers" have begun to experience improvement alongside those with more education, including an increase in the real median wage for male high-school graduates over the mid 1990s and even a recent rise in the median real wage of male high-school "dropouts." See *ERP 1999*, pp. 105–107.

Table 4.2. *"Time-lag" in college education, by race: percentage of US 25–29-year olds completing college*

Percentage completing college	Year for whites	Year for blacks	Lag (years)
10.7	1950 (est.)	1975	25
11.6	1957	1980	23
11.5	1957	1985	28
13.4	1965	1990	25
15.3	1966	1995	29
15.8	1969	1998	29

Source: US Census Bureau Historical Tables – Educational Attainment, table A-2, <http://www.census.gov/population/socdemo/education/tablea-02.txt>.

expectancies that whites faced in the 1940s and 1950s.[26] In terms of infant mortality, the rate for blacks in 1992 was equal to the rate for whites in 1971. The infant mortality rate for both black and white children has dropped by more than half over the postwar period, but the lag between whites and blacks actually increased over the 1980–92 period. The time-lag in infant mortality is shown in table 4.3.

The race-based differentials in health/longevity can be stated more vividly and starkly. In his 1993 article, "The Economics of Life and Death," Amartya Sen notes that for men and women between the ages of thirty-five and fifty-four, blacks were over two and a quarter times more likely to die than whites. When death rates were adjusted for income, the figure for blacks remained over one and a half times that of whites. Sen notes in the same article that black men in Harlem were less likely to reach the age of sixty-five than were men in Sri Lanka.[27]

---

[26] These data are indicated in US Department of Health and Human Services, *Vital Statistics of the United States 1992* (Hyattsville, MD: US Department of Health and Human Services, 1996), vol. II, pt. A, table 6–4, pp. 16, 18. Life expectancy at birth for black women was 73.9 years in 1992; for white women it was 74.2 in 1959–61 and 72.1 in 1949–51. For black men, life expectancy at birth was 65.0 years in 1992; for white males it was 66.3 in 1949–51 and 62.8 in 1939–41.

[27] Amartya Sen, "The Economics of Life and Death," *Scientific American* 268/5 (May 1993), pp. 44, 46.

Table 4.3. *"Time-lag" in infant mortality rates, by race of child*

Rate	Year for whites	Year for blacks	Lag (years)
41.7	1940	1965	25
32.6	1945	1970	25
26.2	1950	1975	25
21.4	1965	1980	15
18.2	1969	1985	16
17.0	1971	1990	19
16.8	1971	1992	21

Notes: Rates = deaths under age 1 year, per 1,000 births; 1992 rate is by race of mother.
Source: US Dept. of Health & Human Services, *Vital Statistics of the United States 1992*, vol. II, pt. A, table 2-2, p. 3.

US DIFFERENTIALS BY SEX

Income

Many of the examinations of disaggregated data can be made along lines of sex in the same way as they were made along lines of race and ethnicity. However, some of the disaggregations are not possible. Most notably, families and households can readily be classed according to race/ethnicity (of the householder), but not along lines of sex.[28] Figures exist for female-headed households with no husband present (which comprise some 90 percent of single-parent households) but these data can only address one important dimension of sex-related differentials in income. Along lines of sex, the intra-household or intra-family distribution is not easily revealed through any form of data. When food is scarce, who will get what portions? When time is scarce, who will have to perform the household chores? Studies from economics of development and other sub-fields reveal that in many (or most) cases, women and girls do not fare equitably vis-à-vis men and boys.[29] Yet it is difficult, if not impossible to

[28] Mixed-race families and households are not fully classified in race-based disaggregations by householder, but the significance of this issue is not taken to have a large empirical impact.
[29] The intra-household distribution problem is helpfully described by Amartya Sen as

obtain an accurate picture of socioeconomic distributions of goods which can be shared within families or households.

Although this distribution problem at the household and family levels remains, comparisons made for individuals do shed some light on sex-based differentials in income. As shown in table 4.4, for all people aged twenty-five and older who are year-round, full-time workers, the median income of women is only 0.72 times the median income of men. Interestingly, this proportion holds constant when sub-grouping persons by educational attainment. As a consequence, while there are significant income differentials between women's and men's median figures, women and men who are full-time, year-round workers receive the same *proportionate* gains on a college degree. This can be readily seen in table 4.4 in the college/high-school ratio of median incomes for males and for females.[30]

Education

Inequalities in secondary and college educational attainment themselves do not plague women in the same way that they obstruct the socioeconomic progress of African Americans and Latinos/Latinas. For the adult population, the percentages of women and men completing four years of high school has been

"cooperative conflict," in which some degree of cooperation occurs but in which women most often receive a lesser share of the distribution. Amartya Sen, "Gender and Cooperative Conflict," in Irene Tinker (ed.), *Persistent Inequalities* (New York: Oxford University Press, 1990). Sen critiques the most well-known economic analysis of intra-family distribution, Gary Becker's, according to which the "breadwinner" is seen to be purely self-interest maximizing outside the family and purely altruistic within the family (Sen, "Economics and the Family," *Asian Development Review* 1 [1983]).

[30] When part-timers are included in the data set, then women's premium is significantly higher – the ratio of college/high-school median income is 1.97 for women, and 1.65 for men. (Author's calculations from data in US Census Bureau, detailed tables for *Current Population Report* P20–513, "Educational Attainment in the United States, March 1995," table 8, pp. 42–43.) It should be noted that the Census Bureau's total income figures include income from all sources; earnings (from wages and salaries in the labor market) comprise a significant fraction of total income. As discussed above, in terms of *earnings* alone, while the premium for a college education has risen steadily since 1970 for both men and women, that premium is higher for women than for men when all workers are included – just as is the case for the total-income premium (*ERP 1997*, pp. 169–170; NCES, *Condition of Education 1997*, p. 120).

Table 4.4. *Median incomes, persons 25 and older, year-round, full-time workers, by sex, 1998*

	Median income ($)		Ratio of incomes: women/men
	Men	Women	
Highest education level			
All levels	38,759	28,005	0.72
High school	31,215	22,067	0.71
College	48,616	35,379	0.73
Professional	85,011	61,051	0.72
Ratio of incomes			
College/high school	1.56	1.60	

Source: US Census Bureau, detailed tables for *Current Population Report* P20-513, table 8, pp. 42–50.

roughly equal throughout the postwar period. The percentage of adults (over twenty-five) with at least a bachelor's degree is greater for men than women (26.5 and 22.4 percent, respectively, in 1998).[31] Yet for the 25–29-year-old age group, the percentage of women completing college has outpaced the figure for men since 1980. In 1998, that figure was 29.0 percent for women, and 25.6 percent for men, in the 25–29 cohort.[32] Indeed, most recently analysts have begun to consider the causes and implications of the reality that women significantly outnumber men in college.[33]

Health and longevity

Men's and women's life expectancies have generally and steadily risen in the past fifty years; female life expectancy at birth (rising from 65.2 years in 1940 to 78.9 in 1995) has continued ahead of the corresponding male figure (increasing from 60.8

---

[31] US Census Bureau, detailed tables for *Current Population Report* P20–513, "Educational Attainment in the United States, March 1998," table 1, pp. 1–7.
[32] Ibid.
[33] Tamar Lewin, "American Colleges Begin to Ask, Where Have All the Men Gone?" *New York Times* (12/6/1998).

years in 1940 to 72.5 in 1995).[34] The positive differential in life expectancy for females – which occurs in all developed countries and in most developing countries – has risen in the United States over the postwar period.[35]

One troubling issue, infant mortality, was treated above along lines of race, because African Americans and other minorities suffer relatively high rates (see table 4.3). Surely infant mortality is a women's basic health concern as well, as it relates directly to the overall healthcare, prenatal care, and birthing conditions faced by women. The overall US infant mortality rate, at 7 per 1,000 live births in 1997, is lower (better) in twenty-four other countries in the world, including Ireland, South Korea, and the Czech Republic. In terms of maternal mortality rate, the United States ranks seventeenth in the world.[36] With arguably the most advanced medical care in the world available in the United States, such statistics are troubling indeed.

CONCLUSIONS

The examination of US inequalities in the postwar period demonstrates that for the population as a whole, income inequality has increased since the early 1970s while the most severe inequalities in education and health/longevity have gradually but steadily decreased. Household income for African Americans as a share of white household income continues to lag about 40 percent behind, a ratio that has changed little over the past thirty years, but which showed signs of improvement in the mid–late 1990s. African Americans as a group have made significant progress vis-à-vis whites in high school education, but their college-level attainment figures continue to lag over twenty years behind whites' attainment. This latter finding is particularly disturbing because the economic returns on a

[34] US Department of Health and Human Services, *Monthly Vital Statistics Report*, vol. 45, no. 11, suppl. 2, 1997, table 5, p. 19.
[35] For an important study of the ratio of females and males (which is related to but distinct from life expectancy) as an important indicator of the relative treatment of women and girls, see Amartya Sen, "More Than 100 Million Women are Missing," *New York Review of Books* (12/20/1990).
[36] *HDR 1999*, table 8, pp. 168–171.

college education are rising rapidly. And basic health figures, like life expectancy and infant mortality rates, reveal continuing, severe differentials between African Americans and whites. Latinos and Latinas (or Hispanics) lag behind whites and African Americans in most socioeconomic indicators. Further exploration of issues affecting this reality, including the complexities of immigration, discrimination, and even the classification of people as "Hispanic" or "non-Hispanic," merit attention beyond the scope of this chapter.

The mosaic of male–female differentials in the United States is distinct from that of differentials of race and ethnicity. In the health sphere, women's basic health outcomes are good, outpacing men in life expectancy by acceptable proportions. However, troubling infant mortality rates continue for disadvantaged women. In the sphere of education, a higher proportion of young-adult females have completed high school and college than the respective group of males. To be sure, the gender breakdown of college majors and post-baccalaureate fields of specialization continues to locate men in more lucrative fields – a problem that merits attention beyond the scope of basic educational equality examined in the chapter. Household and family aggregations of data make it difficult to evaluate intra-household inequalities; it is evident that women lag seriously behind men in labor-market earnings and in total income. While the causes of labor-market differentials range from overt discrimination to questions of continuity and experience in the workforce, solutions will need to address the very structure of gender roles in family, work, and community contexts.

The empirical results of this chapter are wide-ranging and they demonstrate some of the complexity of inequality in the United States in relation to race/ethnicity and sex for three spheres of life. These findings relate to a number of social issues of broad public concern. What to make of these empirical realities, of course, is a question that draws the inquiry back towards the normative goals of the book. Thus the task of the next chapters is to develop an approach for understanding socioeconomic inequalities in moral context.

PART TWO

Constructing a Christian ethical approach

CHAPTER 5

Christian ethics and theology in a pluralistic society

What does Christian ethics have to say in the wider public debate about inequality? Should theologically informed perspectives be involved in a discussion that is clearly political, social, and economic? Does Christian ethics have anything distinctive to contribute? Why should, or should not, people of faith care about the inequalities described in the previous chapters?

In considering these questions, one must shift the inquiry from the empirical analysis of inequality to analyze, from a Christian ethical perspective, how such inequalities matter morally and theologically. It is conceivable for Christians to read the previous chapters and then respond that Christian faith has little direct relevance to those issues – and that conversely, inequalities have little relevance for Christian faith and practice. Indeed, the Christian commitment to the equality before God has often operated as a "spiritual truth" while offering little impetus to move Christians to denounce even severe forms of social inequality – including slavery.

How Christians interpret the "meaning" of equality is closely related to a wider theological question: what kind of involvement should Christians have in the "world's problems"? Some theologians and ethicists maintain that Christians have been sidetracked from their principal task of worshiping God by trying to "make the world turn out right." Others disagree and promote various forms of "world-transformative Christianity."[1]

---

[1] This phrase is from Nicholas Wolterstorff, *Until Justice and Peace Embrace* (Grand Rapids, MI: Eerdmans, 1983). Here I employ it broadly to include a number of perspectives, including an engaged Reformed theological ethic (whether of Wolter-

Finally, there is a philosophical (and sociological) question that Christian perspectives should consider if they are to engage in a wide public debate on inequality. In a contemporary society marked by religious and cultural pluralism – such as the United States, the United Kingdom, or even "the global village" – how should religiously informed convictions be expressed in public discourse? Is there "room" in public life for Christians – and Jews, Muslims, Sikhs, and Buddhists – to invoke explicitly religious or theological language and symbols?

CHRISTIAN ACCOUNTS OF THE EQUALITY BEFORE GOD: HOW "RELEVANT" ARE THEY?

Christian thinkers over time have disagreed on the social relevance of what can be termed "equality before God." Indeed, many Christian accounts have lessened or even denied altogether the moral and political force of the equality before God – interpreting it primarily as a description of some "spiritual" or "otherworldly" order that is distinct from contemporary, actual societies. Yet in some form or another, strands or sub-traditions of Christian "egalitarianism" have also operated.

Elisabeth Schüssler Fiorenza argues that struggles between more egalitarian communities and practices, on the one hand, and more hierarchical ones, on the other, have endured throughout Jewish and Christian histories. In her biblical scholarship she has shown how those conflicts, often embodied in struggles of women for participation and leadership in their communities and societies, are inscribed in canonical Christian texts. Reconstructing texts of the Christian New Testament from a feminist theological perspective, Schüssler Fiorenza demonstrates the potential for promoting current social arrangements based on a vision of "a discipleship of equals." At the same time, Schüssler Fiorenza notes that since the beginnings of the Jesus movement, egalitarians have been opposed by efforts to canonize patriarchal texts and to establish andro-

storff or H. Richard Niebuhr), liberation theology, and the Catholic social thought of magisterial encyclicals, among others.

centric traditions.[2] These latter views have "spiritualized" the relevance of equality by relegating it to an other-worldly eschatological reality. Such accounts could acknowledge some egalitarian practices within the early Christian communities themselves while arguing that these practices waned as eschatological expectancy dissipated.[3]

Attempts to "spiritualize" the belief in equality were made not only through appeals to an other-worldly eschatology, but also by reference to a "paradise lost." Augustine emphasizes this latter viewpoint, acknowledging that all people are created equal in the image of God and they are thus loved equally by God. Yet because of the "fall" of humankind, in the "city of man" social equality loses out to the necessity of social roles and hierarchy, which are seen to exist according to God's purposes.[4] Citing Augustine as a prime example, Kathryn Tanner critically describes this understanding of equality vis-à-vis the social order as follows:

Human beings were all created equal; thus before the fall, in a pre-lapsarian state of nature, no human being ruled over another. The import of this point for the present is blocked, however, by saying that this equality and the social relations proper to it were taken away with the onset of sin. Social relations that human beings enjoyed before the fall may be restored by God's grace, but implications of this restoration for the present are prohibited since such a restoration is not to be expected now. Restoration is perhaps a future state or a state after death. The association of an equality that has been restored with a graced state may indeed permit it to have some extension in the world now, but it is commonly only a limited one.[5]

While the Augustinian view of equality enjoys a privileged place in contemporary understandings of medieval Christianity, perspectives like Schüssler Fiorenza's constructively demonstrate that struggles between more other-worldly and more this-

---

[2] Elisabeth Schüssler Fiorenza, *In Memory of Her: A Feminist Theological Reconstruction of Christian Origins* (New York: Crossroad, 1983). See especially chapter 2.

[3] Lakoff, *Equality in Political Philosophy*, p. 21.

[4] Augustine of Hippo, *The City of God*, chap. 19, in Whitney J. Oates (ed.), *The Basic Writings of Saint Augustine* (New York: Random House, 1948).

[5] Kathryn Tanner, *The Politics of God: Christian Theologies and Social Justice* (Minneapolis: Fortress Press, 1992), pp. 171–172. See also Lakoff, *Equality in Political Philosophy*, pp. 21–22.

worldly egalitarian orientations persisted. Egalitarian practices and communities existed throughout the medieval period. Monastic orders provided social spaces in which women or men could enact equality in their everyday realities. Social movements and uprisings such as the Peasants' Revolt of 1381 in England (among many others) were influenced by a variety of Christian egalitarian beliefs.[6]

By many accounts, the Reformation played a crucial role in increasing the possibility for the belief in equality to have fuller societal relevance (even though Luther himself famously rejected the kind of peasant revolt that had been promoted by medieval egalitarians in England).[7,8] For instance, Sanford Lakoff makes this statement:

[I]t is in the writings of three prominent Protestant spokesmen [Luther, Calvin, and Müntzer] that we may first discern systematic statements of egalitarian doctrines shortly to emerge in explicit political terms. . . . The religious Reformers are united by a sense of the need to make the ultimate beliefs of the Christian immediate standards for understanding and conduct. Under the stimulus of this practical concern equality becomes a pressing issue. It can no longer

[6] See Brian Bird, *Rebel Before His Time: A Study of John Ball and the English Peasants' Revolt of 1381* (Worthing, England: Churchman Publishing, 1987).

[7] In this account I am following the interpretation of Sanford Lakoff, among others, stressing that the pre-modern accounts of Aristotle, Plato, and the Stoics – as well as the dominant Christian account typified by Augustine – alike maintained a dualism between ultimate equality and operative inequality. Such a simple interpretation could be complexified, of course, by pursuing the question of "[In]equality of what?" Aquinas in such a view is seen as drawing from Aristotelian and patristic Christian strands, and thus maintaining this dualism from both sources. For an interesting argument that Aquinas preferred "complementarity" over any democratic notion of equality in his writings, see Paul J. Weithman, "Complementarity and Equality in the Political Thought of Aquinas," conference paper, Society of Christian Ethics Annual Meeting, Atlanta, January 1998.

[8] According to Schüssler Fiorenza's emphasis on reconstruction, accounts of the Reformation should not be presented in a way that denies the egalitarian social struggles in the medieval period – or in the Reformation itself. The claim about the increased relevance of the belief in equality to the social order must also acknowledge the debates about the historical effects of the Protestant Reformation. As a prime example, the impact of the Reformation on women's social status and freedom is under fierce debate. Many scholars argue that with the Reformation came the normalization of the patriarchal, nuclear family and the decreased possibility for alternative social arrangements like women's monastic orders. See Lyndal Roper, *The Holy Household: Women and Morals in Reformation Augsburg* (Oxford and New York: Oxford University Press, 1991).

be assigned to heaven, or to a primitive Eden, or even to some indwelling soul-stuff. For tactical as well as creedal reasons, the Reformers were driven to argue against the justification of inequality that sustained church and society alike, even though some were concerned to deny the implications of their doctrines which seemed to promote more far-reaching effects than they themselves had in mind.[9]

The connection between Reformation views of equality and modern, liberal views of equality is complex, and certainly disputable. Yet clearly there is some degree of logical, and perhaps historical, relation between liberal and Christian views of equality in the political sphere. At a minimum, Christian-influenced deist theological claims undergird the central liberal statements of equality in documents like the American Declaration of Independence. Some scholars have asserted strong ideological linkages between particular Christian and particular liberal appropriations of equality.[10]

Alexis de Tocqueville wrote that "Christianity, which has declared all men equal in the sight of God, cannot hesitate to acknowledge all citizens equal before the law." Tocqueville went on, however, to admit that in practice, Christianity had "become entangled with those institutions democracy over-throws";[11] the French *ancien régime* is just one historic example among many in which Christian beliefs of equality coexisted with inegalitarian political and economic systems.

Thus within the Christian tradition the "meaning" of equality is disputed and disputable – much as it is in the wider public debate. The "dispute" or discussion over equality and inequality should be settled on moral grounds. (After all, if the "meaning" of equality were determined by the use of power or coercion, a form of excessive inequality would already be operating.) When they are not "spiritualized" or reduced to

9 Lakoff, *Equality in Political Philosophy*, p. 25.
10 For one view relating the thought of Luther and Rousseau on equality, see Joshua Mitchell, "The Equality of All under the One in Luther and Rousseau: Thoughts on Christianity and Political Theory," *The Journal of Religion* 72 (1992). Robin Lovin carefully traces the relations and distinctions between covenant and contract views of equality in his essay, "Equality and Covenant Theology," *Journal of Law and Religion* 2/2 (1984).
11 Alexis de Tocqueville, *Democracy in America* (New York: Harper Perennial, 1969 [1840]), pp. 16–17.

secular accounts, theologically informed perspectives should have a role in those moral discussions.[12] Stated positively, theologically informed accounts of the equality before God, such as H. Richard Niebuhr's and Gustavo Gutiérrez's, provide substantive and distinctive resources for understanding the moral significance of inequality.

CHRISTIAN ENGAGEMENT WITH THE WORLD

Some theological perspectives acknowledge that God intends all people to be treated as moral equals before God and within human communities, and yet they maintain that the proper way to live as Christians in the world is not to spend much time or effort addressing socioeconomic inequality – or at least not directly. One current and well-stated perspective deserves particular attention – that of Stanley Hauerwas.

David Fergusson has employed the term "ecclesially specific ethics" to describe Hauerwas's theological and ethical approach.[13] Hauerwas argues that Christians act faithfully to

---

[12] Lovin's examination of equality within Puritan covenant theology is one historical examination that makes a similar claim. While Lovin does not explicitly name the contemporary normative relevance of his examination, his work is suggestive for ordering public life. For instance: "In a community which structures equal participation and presumes that even its settled moral judgments may be mistaken, priority may be given to providing all persons with the material, educational, and experiential resources they need to participate in public life" ("Equality and Covenant Theology," p. 261).

[13] David Fergusson, *Community, Liberalism and Christian Ethics* (Cambridge: Cambridge University Press, 1998), p. 47 and chap. 3. Fergusson usually employs the term "ecclesial ethics" (see his n. 1, p. 48), but I prefer to follow his use of "ecclesially specific ethics" because it is more descriptive of the distinctiveness of the position held by Hauerwas, James McClendon, and John Howard Yoder, among others. Scholars have typically classified Hauerwas as a "sectarian" and/or as a "communitarian" – yet Hauerwas rejects both terms. He advocates "not a rejection of the world or a withdrawal ethic" but rather an ethic that "serve[s] the world on [Christians'] own terms" (*A Community of Character: Toward a Constructive Christian Social Ethic* [Notre Dame, IN: University of Notre Dame Press, 1981], p. 10). He denies the charge that he is a "communitarian" in an effort to emphasize that the "community" is not necessarily a moral good, and in fact can be dangerous: "Thus, I fear all appeals for community as an end in itself. For communities formed by the alienated selves who are created by liberalism too quickly can become a kind of fascism. No one should want community as an end in and of itself, but one should want to be part of communities because the forms of cooperation offered by them provide for the achievement of goods otherwise unavailable – such as the worship of God"

God not by supporting contemporary political and economic structures – or trying to improve them on their own terms. The wider world's impersonal and violent systems implicitly or explicitly deny God: within them people do not treat each other as God has called them to do. In an effort to try to fix social problems, Christian churches too often act as if they were social service agencies, therapy clinics, or dating clubs. Even when efforts to address genuine problems like severe inequality are well intentioned, Christians undoubtedly end up compromising themselves and acting like all other people in contemporary liberalism.

Rather than becoming easily and uncritically engaged in contemporary social, economic, and political problems – which for Hauerwas is bound to be unfruitful and morally dangerous – Christians should provide a model or foretaste of God's peaceable kingdom within the Christian church. "The first task of the church is to be the church," this position asserts.[14] While his position has been misappropriated to defend the moral superiority of Christians and their communities, Hauerwas emphatically denies such a claim. Hauerwas does defend Christian distinctiveness – not because of superiority but because of the need to follow the particular call of Christian discipleship in a world that, in his view, denies God.[15]

The moral character that the ecclesially specific ethic envisions as possible within Christian communities cannot be realized within a society that fails to acknowledge God as God. For Hauerwas, a Christian ethical approach to inequality that promotes efforts to transform public discourse, persons, and society as a whole runs serious risks of being ignored or co-opted. It cannot succeed in a world in which people do not possess the virtues to realize and sustain it. In contemporary

---

(*Dispatches from the Front: Theological Engagements with the Secular* [Durham, NC: Duke University Press, 1994], p. 158).

[14] "The primary social task of the church is to be itself – that is, a people who have been formed by a story that provides them with the skills for negotiating the danger of this existence, trusting in God's promise of redemption" (Hauerwas, *Community of Character*, p. 10).

[15] See, for instance, *The Peaceable Kingdom: A Primer in Christian Ethics* (Notre Dame, IN: University of Notre Dame Press, 1983), p. 60.

liberal society, dominated by self-interest and radical individualism, excessive socioeconomic inequality is an inextricable
dimension. Hauerwas would probably go so far as to say that
contemporary political, social, and economic structures could
not exist without the very kinds of inequality that are critically
viewed in this book.

David Fergusson offers a careful reading of Hauerwas's ethic
that is quite sympathetic with the aims of Hauerwas's project.
Fergusson thoughtfully treats the charge that the ecclesially
specific perspective is "sectarian," noting that Hauerwas (and
others like James McClendon) do not mean to abandon the
world, but rather to make the "proper contribution" (albeit an
indirect one) through modeling Christian community and promoting Christian virtue.[16] At the same time, Fergusson shows
that Hauerwas overstates the distinctiveness of the Christian
church in contemporary society. Hauerwas tends to idealize
what happens (or could happen) within the church, and he
discounts the potential of people and perspectives outside the
Christian community to be moral. To discount the rest of
society either as incapable of such virtue (whether by seeing
"the world" as godless or purely egoistic) is to miss the rich
cultural, moral, and religious diversity of people within
"liberal" societies. As Hauerwas would also acknowledge,
Christians can and should learn moral lessons from various
persons and communities.[17]

In a different vein, the ecclesially specific ethic does not pay
adequate attention to the historical linkages between Christian
theological-ethical claims, on the one hand, and modern
"liberal" beliefs, on the other. Hauerwas "disjoin[s] to an
unnecessary degree the liberal discourse of 'innate human
dignity' with Christian recognition of the claim of God upon
each human person."[18] While there is indeed a distinctive
Christian contribution to be made, there is enough continuity

---

[16] See Fergusson, *Community, Liberalism and Christian Ethics*, pp. 64–67, esp. p. 65.
[17] Indeed, in practice Hauerwas draws on an impressive and eclectic group of sources
to put forward his own normative framework.
[18] Fergusson, *Community, Liberalism and Christian Ethics*, p. 73.

for pluralistic discourse and even pragmatic cooperative action to take place.

Surely Hauerwas is correct that an ethical approach to inequality such as the one constructed in this book requires people to practice the virtues that Christian churches, at their best, develop in their members. But this emphasis on virtue need not overstate the moral distinctiveness of the Christian community. In Fergusson's words:

[T]he church should seek to maintain its homogeneity as a moral community while acknowledging its stake in the peaceful maintenance of a pluralist society. It should expect to meet both the hostility and hospitality of alternative moral arguments since it offers a distinctive vision but one which is not lacking in connection with other convictions and aspirations.[19]

The point of Christian distinctiveness is not distinctiveness for its own sake. Rather, Christians are called to be faithful to God by worshiping and acting in the world consistent with their theological and moral understandings. Distinctiveness is called for when other people (outside or inside the Christian community) are not acting in a way that is consistent with such a vision of the world. If many citizens are acting for goodness and justice in a society, there is no moral necessity to emphasize one's distinctiveness from them (though Christian and other forms of religious ritual will surely seem peculiar to many "modern" people). On the contrary, there is reason to celebrate that good and right actions are being undertaken. In societies in which injustice and violence predominate, there will be good theological reason to act distinctively, but only toward the more important end of acting faithfully.

THEOLOGICAL PERSPECTIVES IN PUBLIC DISCOURSE,
ACCORDING TO POLITICAL LIBERALISM

What form might such thinking and action take in a pluralistic society? As Ronald Thiemann has demonstrated in his *Religion in Public Life: A Dilemma for Democracy*, "political liberalism" has

---

[19] Ibid., pp. 172–173.

dominated recent discussion of the potential contribution of theological views to public discourse.[20] While keeping in mind the cautions that thinkers like Stanley Hauerwas have issued, a number of scholars, including Thiemann, have developed frameworks in which Christian ethical perspectives can maintain their distinctiveness and integrity but still engage in public debates. Articulating an acceptable arrangement requires critical revision of standard liberal accounts of the role of religion in public life. While the substantive content of a Christian ethical approach to inequality is developed in the following three chapters, it is worth describing in some detail a philosophical framework for the distinctive contribution that that approach makes in the wider moral discussion.

Some liberal theorists have asserted that the public sphere is one in which citizens engage one another *qua* citizens, and in which they should be unhindered by the "particularities" or "encumbrances" – such as religious commitments – that citizens do not share in common. John Rawls among others emphasizes that historically, political liberalism arose as a response to the bloody post-Reformation wars of religion. In contemporary times, only a few liberal theorists emphasize the fear that religiously based conflict could lead to serious violence and bloodshed in societies like the United States – although reference to religiously motivated terrorism (like violence tied to the radical arm of the anti-abortion movement or the bombing of the World Trade Center) are occasionally invoked.[21] More often but less dramatically, religion is portrayed as a complicating factor for a public, political sphere in which citizens should speak openly, respectfully, and intelligibly to one another. Still, in most liberal models of the public sphere, religion is first of all a problem, a source of conflict and disagreement.

A standard, well-stated view of these issues is Rawls's account

---

[20] Thiemann, *Religion in Public Life*. See also Paul Weithman, "Introduction: Religion and the Liberalism of Reasoned Respect," in Weithman (ed.), *Religion and Contemporary Liberalism* (Notre Dame, IN: University of Notre Dame Press, 1997).

[21] Weithman labels Charles Larmore and Robert Audi as two liberals who continue to see the dangers of sectarian strife as the chief alternative to political liberalism. Weithman, "Introduction," p. 3.

of "public reason" within political liberalism.[22] According to Rawls, citizens should exercise the virtue of mutual respect and the duty of civility by communicating to all citizens in language that is held in common within their given social-historical context. This task involves speaking to one another in terms and forms of reasoning that are "free and public" – making one's justifications to other citizens in terms they will understand. The employment of public reason will thus help to ensure that citizens are treated as free and equal. In his 1993 book, *Political Liberalism*, Rawls makes the following point about justifying "the basic structure and its public policies" in terms of public reason: "[I]n making these justifications we are to appeal only to presently accepted general beliefs and forms of reasoning found in common sense, and the methods and conclusions of science when these are not controversial."[23] He goes on to say that he "means that in discussing constitutional essentials and matters of basic justice we are not to appeal to comprehensive religious or philosophical doctrines – to what we as individuals or members of associations see as the whole truth."[24] Rawls asserts that it is possible to arrive at a "free-standing," limited, political conception of justice that can remain conceptually independent from any particular "comprehensive vision of the good." Indeed, to arrive at such a workable, free-standing conception of justice – supported by an "overlapping consensus" of people holding their respective comprehensive visions – is a principal task for Rawls. A consequence is that much content of people's comprehensive doctrines is excluded from the public sphere. For Rawls, this is necessary in order to ensure that there be a non-coercive public sphere that is characterized by "reasonable pluralism and the burdens of judgment."[25] It is simply not possible, in a pluralistic

---

[22] The Rawlsian discussion is developed in the chapter on "The Idea of Public Reason" (lecture VI) in Rawls's *Political Liberalism* and in his article, "The Idea of Public Reason Revisited," *University of Chicago Law Review* 64 (1997).

[23] Rawls, *Political Liberalism*, p. 224.   [24] Ibid.

[25] Rawls is thus interested in more than mere political stability, which a balance of political powers alone could guarantee. He is seeking, rather, a political public sphere in which citizens treat each other with civility, respect, and a spirit of reciprocity.

democracy, to allow all comprehensive visions into the public sphere and still achieve mutual respect and civility.

In this 1993 discussion of public reason, Rawls acknowledges that when societies are not "well-ordered," appeals to religious convictions may be morally defensible in exceptional cases – in particular if such appeals are made "for the sake of public reason itself."[26] Rawls refers to the abolitionist and civil rights struggles as examples in which theologically based arguments were made in order to promote basic justice, constitutional essentials, and a better-ordered society. While in these earlier US societies theologically based arguments made a distinctive and positive contribution to establishing basic justice, Rawls leaves open the question of whether public reason in the contemporary US context is "complete" – that is, whether on its own it offers "a reasonable answer for all or nearly all fundamental questions."[27] The answer to this question largely determines the room that Rawls's exceptions to public reason provide for theologically informed moral perspectives.[28]

Rawls's more recent (1997) article on this subject, "The Idea of Public Reason Revisited," expands the room for appeals to theological doctrines in the contemporary public sphere. Rawls helpfully distinguishes the ways in which appeals to theology might be morally distinct for judges, government officials, and citizens. Rawls would object to *judges*, for instance, who justify decisions based on theological principles. He argues that it is least problematic for *citizens* – who "ideally . . . think of themselves as if they were legislators"[29] – engaged in public, political debate to employ theological language. According to Rawls's recent "wide view of public political culture," it would be acceptable for theological language to be invoked in the public sphere, along these lines: "[R]easonable comprehensive doctrines, religious or nonreligious, may be introduced in public political discussion at any time, provided that in due course

---

[26] Rawls, *Political Liberalism*, p. 251.   [27] Ibid., p. 244.
[28] See discussions of Rawls's consideration of the abolitionist and civil rights cases in Thiemann, *Religion in Public Life*, pp. 85–88, and David Hollenbach, S.J., "Public Reason/Private Religion?: A Response to Paul Weithman," *Journal of Religious Ethics* 22/1 (spring 1994), pp. 305–306.
[29] Rawls, "Public Reason Revisited," p. 769.

proper political reasons – and not reasons given solely by comprehensive doctrines – are presented that are sufficient to support whatever the comprehensive doctrines introduced are said to support."[30]

This revised view enables a more expansive role of religion in public discourse. Yet while Rawls's "wide view of public political culture" allows theological language in the public sphere, there remains the moral imperative to support one's views in terms of public reason. This position continues to reflect the liberal understanding of *precluding* religion from the public sphere unless it can be tied to certain publicly accepted language. This places a moral burden of justification on those speaking theologically. In contrast, the position outlined below allows more space for all participants in public discourse to choose the language(s) in which they communicate their views.

Rawls's account of public reason within political liberalism illuminates important dimensions of the question of theological reasoning in public discourse. He rightly notes that in contemporary societies like the United States, there exist a wide number of religious, philosophical, and other "comprehensive visions of the good" that make fundamentally distinct claims about what is true and good in the world. Rawls seeks to conceive of public conversation about matters of basic justice in which representatives of no comprehensive vision are able to use coercion or deception to realize their own proposals. By Rawls's own account, he seeks to move beyond mere political or social stability to promote the most promising scheme for social unity that is possible in a situation of reasonable pluralism. Further, Rawls's emphasis on the ways in which religious communities in the past have employed such coercion to oppress religious minorities or to dehumanize particular groups is also an important word of caution.

While these are commendable aspects of the Rawlsian approach, there are at least three serious problems with his public reason and the limitations it places on theological language in public discourse. Each of the criticisms offered

---

[30] Ibid., pp. 783–784.

below results from disagreement about the best way to achieve social unity and a non-coercive public sphere, given reasonable pluralism.

The first problem with the Rawlsian account of political liberalism is the nature of public reason itself that Rawls proposes: what precisely constitutes public reason? Seeking to describe political liberalism and not a comprehensive liberalism, Rawls asserts that an overlapping consensus is achieved based upon the socially situated values that are shared by citizens within particular societies. These values include such items as "the values of equal political and civil liberty; equality of opportunity; the values of social equality and economic reciprocity" and "the common good." These values should comprise the sources of appeal within public conversation that is conducted according to public reason. But it is not altogether clear what any of these values mean without further specification. Rawls himself would not contest this point. An argument can be advanced that a theologically informed account can thicken the understandings of the "liberal value" of equality – and that this is just one among many moral perspectives contributing to public discourse. Rawls would maintain that such theological resources are not necessary in the public. His claim rides on whether in contemporary society public reason is "complete," in his own language. It is possible to maintain that, *contra* Rawls, on particular issues of basic distributive justice the resources of common political values and public reason are not sufficient (or "complete") for arriving at workable, ethical solutions.

Also problematic in Rawls's account of public reason is his apparent uncritical acceptance of the concepts of "common sense" and "noncontroversial science": public justifications are to be made not merely by "appeal[ing] only to presently accepted general beliefs" but also to "forms of reasoning found in common sense, and the methods and conclusions of science when these are not controversial."[31] Such a notion of common sense, rather than adding precision to an account of public

---

[31] Rawls, *Political Liberalism*, p. 224.

reason, begs more questions than it answers. And while beyond the scope of this book, it appears odd that a political philosopher interested in non-coercion would be willing to accept rather uncritically the methods and conclusions of "noncontroversial" science. Surely in the contemporary world, scientific forms of reasoning have as great a potential as religious ideas do to effect illegitimate coercion.

The second problem with Rawls's account of political liberalism is his distinction between the public, political sphere and the so-called "background culture" of civil society, the domain in which people congregate within universities, religious organizations, labor unions, and civic and professional associations. In the background culture, which Rawls calls "non-public," reason is not fully "public." That is, language within the background culture is only "public with respect to [the members of given groups] but it is non-public with respect to political society and to citizens generally."[32] Rawls rightly notes, however, that the "reason" of the background culture is "social, and certainly not private." Thus "[t]he public vs. nonpublic distinction is not the distinction between public and private."[33] The problem lies in the very attempt to distinguish between the kinds of discussions and activities that take place within universities, civic and professional organizations, and religious institutions – as "nonpublic" – and those discussions that take place as part of public policy discussions – which are "public." The issue here is more than the "meaning" of the term "public" – though Rawls's use of the term is quite narrow. Rather, what is at stake is the *integral relationship* among the kinds of discourse that take place in universities, religious institutions, associations and in policymaking discussions. The conversations that occur within these various settings, and within the various forms of media, should be seen as together comprising the discourse of the public sphere broadly understood. In David Hollenbach's terms,

[B]y seeking to neatly divide politics from culture and by calling the former public and the latter nonpublic, [Rawls] overlooks the con-

---

[32] Ibid., p. 220.   [33] Ibid., p. 220 of text and n. 7.

stant symbiosis and mutual influence between the two spheres. If this symbiosis were taken into account, it would make sense to regard religious communities, as well as universities, professional associations, labor unions, and so on, as helping to form the public reason by which a democratic polity seeks to achieve common action by its citizens.[34]

As Hollenbach's remark suggests, to remove the artificial boundaries between policymaking discourse and "cultural" discourse is inevitably to include theological language, as well as various other languages, into a wider public sphere. It is still possible to propose some "conditions of publicity" for maintaining orderly, meaningful public discourse. The important point here is that no particular form of discourse would be excluded from the start.

This leads to the third problem with the Rawlsian position, related to the first two. Empirically, theological perspectives and religious practices inform a significant proportion of the population. An account of political liberalism that excludes theological language (or begrudgingly admits it with provisos) unnecessarily impoverishes the resources for discourse in the public sphere. Even if public reason were somehow "complete," and if civil society (or the "background culture") could be neatly distinguished from a public, political sphere – the assumptions challenged in the two prior criticisms – asking citizens to compartmentalize their lives in this way is not only burdensome; it may be impossible.[35]

It is important to note that in a vision of a wider public sphere, other, "non-religious" resources from civil society would also be welcomed in public discourse. For example, the

---

34 Hollenbach, "Public Reason/Private Religion?," p. 307. Of course, Hollenbach's use of the term "public reason" is distinct from Rawls's own usage of the term. Based on my criticisms of the very term "public reason," I do not employ it constructively, preferring to use the term "public discourse" in a way that emphasizes disagreement as well as communication. See also Thiemann, *Religion in Public Life*, esp. p. 152. Rawls seeks to address this problem in his 1997 essay ("Public Reason Revisited") by using language of the "public political *culture*," but the distinction from the background culture still exists.

35 This critique bears an affinity with the critiques of Rawls by Michael Sandel, in his *Liberalism and the Limits of Justice* (Cambridge: Cambridge University Press, 1982). See also Sandel's *Democracy's Discontent: America in Search of a Public Philosophy* (Cambridge, MA: Belknap/Harvard University Press, 1996).

exercise of the "literary imagination" in public life called for by Martha Nussbaum would expand public discourse in a way that could promote justice and well-being. Indeed, the forms of "poetic judging" and "sympathetic imagining" she proposes to counter narrow, technical forms of economic reasoning are keen examples of moral contributions that a wide public sphere could embrace.[36]

While still maintaining Rawls's strong interest in mutual respect and civility, it is possible to expand the public sphere to enable the constructive contribution of theologically informed and other moral perspectives. The following section considers how theologically informed and other moral perspectives can participate in public life while meeting the aims of Rawls's own project.

"CONDITIONS OF PUBLICITY" AND THEOLOGICAL PERSPECTIVES

A thick public sphere, in which there is room for the contribution of various moral perspectives communicated in diverse moral languages, faces dangers of cacophony and conflict that political liberalism seeks to avoid. Yet for the reasons outlined above, those so-called risks are worth taking in order to gain the benefit of fuller moral resources for solving matters of public import. Further, and at least as important, such an arrangement would allow people to share their deepest moral (and theological) commitments with one another in public life.

Thiemann's "conditions of publicity" offer some moral guidelines for assisting a pluralistic democracy to avoid needless conflict and coercion. Thiemann suggests that three norms — public accessibility, mutual respect, and moral integrity — can serve as moral guides for public conversation. He stresses that these norms are value-based concepts that function positively; they do not seek to preclude, whether legally or otherwise, arguments from the public sphere that are protected by the guarantees of free speech. In Thiemann's words:

[36] Martha Nussbaum, *Poetic Justice: The Literary Imagination in Public Life* (Boston: Beacon Press, 1995).

[W]e should seek to define those virtues of citizenship that we seek to instill in all participants in our pluralistic democracy. These virtues will suggest conditions of publicity that should guide citizens in their efforts to sift through the many arguments they will hear and make in a pluralistic conversation. Conditions of publicity should function not as threshold requirements but as norms of plausibility, that is, as criteria that democratic citizens should employ to evaluate arguments in the public domain.[37]

One important implication is that as a group, religiously informed perspectives are not excluded because of their language, sources of appeal, or for any other reason. Rather, each argument that is presented in public, whether religiously based or not, is evaluated according to the norms of publicity. Thus, as Thiemann states succinctly, "The question is not whether religious arguments qualify as genuinely public, but what kind of religious arguments so qualify."[38]

Public accessibility

The first norm is concerned with "the broad accessibility of public arguments." While rejecting the Rawlsian notion of public reason, Thiemann concurs that making the premises and warrants of all arguments open to inspection by other citizens is of high value: "Opponents who *understand* one another's reasons may not be *persuaded* by them, but they are more likely to remain in communal solidarity with one another than opponents who believe they are being deceived or manipulated."[39] In presenting his account of public accessibility, Thiemann asserts that the fundamental orienting convictions of religious worldviews can be made "accessible to public inquiry and critique." Theological ideas must be understood with attention to the communities, traditions, and narratives in which those ideas have arisen. While "ecclesially specific" ethical approaches would tend to argue that theological language and concepts do not have public "meanings" outside those contexts, Thiemann suggests that they in fact can. Theological concepts,

[37] Thiemann, *Religion in Public Life*, p. 135. See also pp. 140, 173.
[38] Ibid., p. 150.   [39] Ibid., pp. 135–136.

however, take on *distinct* meanings in different contexts; Thiemann employs the example of how the "neighbor-love"
modeled in the parable of the Good Samaritan (from the
Christian New Testament) must be constructively appropriated
as "fairness and concern for the vulnerable" if it is to have
public value in contemporary debates about social issues like
universal healthcare.[40] If sufficient attention is paid to the
narratives and communities out of which concepts arise, constructive work can apply these concepts into wider public
discussions.

A crucial assumption of this position is that it is possible to
make publicly accessible the premises, warrants, and sources for
theologically informed moral arguments. Perspectives can be
public even though the sources of authority invoked are not
universally shared as authoritative. Accessibility does not
require shared sources of authority, but it requires that these
sources be identified and described publicly. There is in this
position a certain confidence, or faith, that the very communication of perspectives can in itself be illuminative or even
persuasive.

Mutual respect

Like advocates of political liberalism, Thiemann emphasizes
mutual respect as a virtue required in a pluralistic society in
which moral and policy-based disagreements are inevitable. Yet
mutual respect as a norm does not require speaking to each
other in terms of public reason; rather, it requires an open
attitude and disposition towards citizens from different worldviews: "Citizens who manifest the virtue of mutual respect
acknowledge the moral agency of those with whom they disagree and thereby treat their arguments as grounded not simply
in personal preference or self-interest but in genuine moral
conviction."[41] Another requirement of mutual respect is the
refusal to employ methods of coercion in the public sphere.
Thiemann rightly acknowledges and laments that there is

[40] Ibid., pp. 155–156.   [41] Ibid., p. 136.

"considerable historical evidence" that various religious beliefs have been employed to justify social coercion.[42] (This perspective was echoed in the earlier treatment of how the commitment to equality has not been fully enacted in social, political, or economic realities.) While there is thus reason for careful attention to the power of religion in public life for good or for ill, there is no reason why those who appeal to religious concepts cannot uphold the norm of mutual respect. People of faith can make truth claims without denouncing others' claims to truth or insight. In Thiemann's words: "Communities of faith must come to recognize the compatibility between deep and abiding commitment to the truth claims of one's tradition and an openness to and respect for the claims of another tradition. Truth claiming and an acceptance of religious pluralism are not inconsistent."[43]

The norm of mutual respect, then, enables people to draw upon the moral resources at their disposal, religious and otherwise, in order to address social and policy issues. At the same time, all persons are called to respect the agency of all other participants to do likewise. This view makes no claim that all moral/policy debates will be easily resolved (or resolved at all), but it does suggest that inviting a wide range of moral perspectives into a discourse guided by mutual respect will be more likely to produce positive outcomes.[44]

---

[42] Ibid., p. 159.   [43] Ibid., p. 161.

[44] A related articulation and application of this vision is made by the Latin American Bishops in their 1979 Council at Puebla. In the Puebla *Final Document*, the Bishops include a chapter entitled, "Church Collaboration with the Builders of a Pluralistic Society in Latin America" and another chapter on "Church Activity on Behalf of Persons in National and International Society" (Latin American Episcopate, *Final Document*, in John Eagleson and Philip Scharper [eds.], *Puebla and Beyond* [Maryknoll, NY: Orbis, 1979], paras. 1206–1293).

In these chapters the Latin American Bishops acknowledge that they "live in a pluralistic society where [they] find differing religions, philosophical conceptions, ideologies, and value systems" (para. 1210). As a way of participating in this pluralistic reality, they propose three "doctrinal criteria," which merit quoting in full:

a. We do not claim any privilege for the Church. We respect the rights of all people and the sincerity of all conviction, having complete respect for the autonomy of terrestrial realities.

b. However, we demand for the Church the right to bear witness to its message and to use its prophetic word of annunciation and denunciation in an evangelical Christian vision.

Moral integrity – and the space for dissent

The norm of moral integrity describes a number of qualities about persons and groups who communicate their perspectives in public discourse. Drawing from the work of Amy Gutmann and Dennis Thompson,[45] Thiemann labels these qualities as *consistency of speech, consistency between speech and action*, and *integrity of principle*. People (whether citizens or officials) advocating a particular position should do so on consistent moral grounds, without altering their view or justification according to the audience or constituency. Consistency between speech and action requires that persons or groups who articulate a moral position should act accordingly. Persons and institutions who draw on theological resources to advocate social justice should embody those practices in their personal and institutional lives. Integrity of principle calls persons and groups articulating a moral position to apply those principles consistently across a variety of issues. Thiemann quotes the Gutmann/Thompson example: "[T]hose who oppose abortion out of respect for fetal life should be equally strong advocates of policies to ensure that

   c. We defend the rights of intermediary organisms under the principle of subsidiarity, including the rights of such organisms created by the Church itself, in collaborating to deal with everything that relates to the common good. (paras. 1212–1214)

The Bishops recognize that they do not have the only voice in society, as they openly accept pluralism. Yet they demand that the church have the power to speak – in its own prophetic terms: no limits on the range of the issues on which it can speak are offered. Indeed the Bishops stress "contact and dialogue" between the church and "the builders of temporal society" (para. 1226). "This dialogue calls for initiatives that will permit encounter and close relationship with all those who are collaborating in the construction of society, so that they may discover their complementarity and convergence" (para. 1228). In a remarkable series of passages, the Bishops claim that the church has things to say to all of the following groups: politicians and people in government, intellectuals, scientists, communications experts, artists, jurists, workers, peasants, economists, military persons, and public functionaries (paras. 1238–1248). The language used in these passages varies from quite theological to "generic." When the Bishops choose to employ non-theological language, it is undoubtedly for reasons of communication. This application is on the church's right to speak to various persons and sectors of society in terms that it chooses. This can be done while upholding the norm of mutual respect.

[45] Amy Gutmann and Dennis Thompson, "Moral Conflict and Political Consensus," in R. Bruce Douglass, Gerald M. Mara, and Henry S. Richardson (eds.), *Liberalism and the Good* (New York and London: Routledge, 1992).

children are properly fed."[46] More controversially, Pope John
Paul II claims an integrity of principle – the "Gospel of Life" –
across Catholic positions against abortion, the death-penalty,
and dehumanizing economic practices.[47] Thus, "Moral integrity asks that citizens seek consistency in their speech, action,
and application of principles."[48]

Importantly, Thiemann emphasizes in his discussion of moral
integrity that there is a need to have moral (and legal) space, in
public life, for *dissent*. Moral integrity sometimes requires vocal,
public rejection of policies or actions that run counter to one's
moral worldview. Thiemann suggests that even in severe
dissent, whether in the publication of critical analyses or in acts
of civil disobedience, participants can still uphold the three
norms of publicity.

Citizens engaged in acts of dissent should seek, so far as possible, to
make the moral reasons for their actions available to a broad democratic public. They should also comport themselves in such a way that
their dissent manifests the moral seriousness of those committed to
the practice of mutual respect . . . To dehumanize one's opponents in
the process of dissent is to undermine the moral integrity of the very
conscience that motivates these actions.[49]

In a genuine, pluralistic democracy it must be appropriate for
citizens and groups to evaluate the basic structure and social
arrangements according to their conception of justice, as long
as they uphold these norms.

Public accessibility, mutual respect, and moral integrity together serve to help to order a public sphere in which moral
discourse, including disagreement, can yield just and compas-
sionate public policies. Thiemann emphasizes that to accept
these three "conditions of publicity" is to realize that "there is
no fundamental incompatibility between public religious arguments and the essential conditions of publicity in a pluralistic
democracy."[50] Citizens in a society with an expanded public
sphere will have cultivated the ability to give weight to those

[46] Thiemann, *Religion in Public Life*, 137, quoting Gutmann and Thompson, "Moral
Conflict and Political Consensus," p. 137.
[47] John Paul II, *The Gospel of Life* [*Evangelium Vitae*] (New York: Random House, 1995).
[48] Thiemann, *Religion in Public Life*, p. 137.
[49] Ibid., p. 139.   [50] Ibid., p. 140.

arguments – religious or otherwise – that uphold these three
norms. Such a public sphere would promote the quality of
moral discourse likely to yield creative solutions to the most
urgent political, social, and economic problems – including
inequality.

FRAMING A CHRISTIAN ETHICAL APPROACH TO INEQUALITY

A Christian ethical approach to inequality draws on "particular" religious resources not shared by all citizens while
seeking to offer perspectives on socioeconomic problems that
concern the population as a whole. Thiemann's norms of
publicity help to clarify how the approach can make a faithful
and fruitful contribution. The theologically informed approach
to disparity in economic life is a constructive perspective
integrally linked to the author's involvements with and formation within particular Christian communities.[51] At the same
time, it is influenced by insights from economics and philosophy
as well as theology. The approach is philosophically informed
and economically informed as well as being theologically
informed.

Yet these various factors should influence the approach in
non-analogous ways. The theological concepts and commitments hold a prior status; in particular, social scientific insights
are employed toward normative ends. As is perhaps best
articulated in the theology of H. Richard Niebuhr, the commitment to God claims central importance, as one's ultimate
loyalty must be directed theocentrically. Other loyalties – to
persons and indeed to intellectual frameworks – should claim
less-than-ultimate status.[52] Still, intellectual resources from a

[51] I am a citizen of the United States seeking to make a constructive contribution to
public discourse in this country and to international development debates. I write as
a Christian raised within the Protestant, Reformed tradition, serving the Presbyterian Church (USA) as an ordained minister. I have also been informed by the Latin
American (largely Catholic) liberationist tradition, through travel and study in Latin
America and through work with Latino/Latina migrant workers in the US.

[52] See chapter 6, below, for a discussion of these ideas in H. Richard Niebuhr's
theology. See also Ronald Thiemann, "Public Religion: Bane or Blessing for

variety of sources are necessary components of any theologically informed approach to issues of public life. In Thiemann's words: "Religious convictions and principles may provide a basic framework within which policy reflection takes place for the believer, but those resources do not determine choices in the public realm . . . The underdeterminate character of religious beliefs provides another reason why people of faith should welcome the conversation and debate that characterizes pluralistic democracy."[53] The perspectives outlined in this project have already benefited from such pluralistic interchange.

One implication is that often the approach is neither wholly similar to nor wholly distinct from "non-theological" positions. Of course, in the wide public sphere theorized by Thiemann and developed herein, it is not as necessary as it is in political liberalism even to determine where an argument is explicitly "theological." The important point for engagement in public discourse is attention to the three conditions of publicity.

Public accessibility

The norm of public accessibility extends to modes of reasoning and language beyond theology. Academic discourse of various kinds can remain inaccessible to a wide public. In a genuinely public sphere, it is incumbent upon people working in theological ethics, philosophy, and social science to state their arguments in as straightforward a way as possible. Thus the economic-empirical analyses in the policy sections of this book are presented in as non-technical a fashion as possible. (In particular, the technical aspects of measures of inequality are relegated to the appendices.) The theological discussions seek to name clearly their appeals to authority and the moral implications of theological doctrines.

There is only a rough analogy between modes of theological and economic reasoning – not only because of the differences in their sources of authority but also because of the nature of the

Democracy?," in Nancy Rosenblum (ed.), *Religion and Law: Obligations of Citizenship, Demands of Faith* (Princeton: Princeton University Press, forthcoming).

[53] Thiemann, *Religion in Public Life*, pp. 169–170.

commitment to the communities in which those modes of reasoning are practiced. Yet on both the theological and economic sides of this loose analogy, the norm of public accessibility suggests that, although "outsiders" do not stand within the communities in which the steps of reasoning are fully comprehensible, all should be able to view those steps by which "insiders" arrive at the conclusions they do.

Mutual respect

The most important point to make vis-à-vis the norm of mutual respect is that a Christian ethical approach is not coercive – either towards those who accept the theological starting points or towards those who do not – in the effort to promote the normative perspective and policy-oriented proposals. Rather, while one approach to inequality is offered, other perspectives are invited. The approach is informed by a commitment to the truthfulness of the theological claims developed in the following chapters. But (following Thiemann) such assertions about truth require neither the coercion of others to accept them nor the denouncing of other perspectives as untrue.[54]

Further, it is not necessary to argue that the theological accounts of moral equality are exclusively tied to the policy-oriented initiatives that are proposed. Indeed, even accepting the specific constructions of Niebuhr's and Gutiérrez's accounts of equality, it would still be quite possible to arrive at different policy perspectives. The claim is a more modest one: that there is consistency between the Christian ethical approach constructed in part two and the contributions to public and policy-oriented discourse described in part three.[55]

Mutual respect calls for openness towards other normative approaches and insights – and more important, it requires respect for the agency of all people making arguments. This position admittedly entails a certain confidence that just and

[54] In fact, following Thiemann, I would offer a theological perspective for renouncing such claims about exclusivity or coercion.

[55] This claim illuminates my discussion of mutual respect of people who differ on one or more of these dimensions of my project. It also addresses the question of moral integrity, since I am attempting to present a morally and logically coherent project.

humane public policies will result from a genuinely *democratic* deliberation characterized by mutual respect. There are potential objections to this confidence in democratic process, of course, but these are problems shared by all people who favor some form of democracy.[56]

Two further points about mutual respect and religious perspectives require consideration. First, different people holding similar theological doctrines can – and often do – arrive at very different public policy (political, social, and/or economic) conclusions.[57] The norm of mutual respect, then, is required not merely among people from distinct religious communities or worldviews, but it is required in relations among co-religionists on matters of public concern. This point relates also to the need for public accessibility (to assess how different people move from particular theological convictions to policy-oriented perspectives) and for moral integrity (to determine if the applications of their convictions correspond to the convictions themselves). But the point here is that those who say they share the "same" faith perspectives may still need to exercise mutual respect when tempers flare over matters social, political, or economic.

The second point is that this proposal for theorizing and constructing a wide public sphere bears similarities to calls by Christian groups on the political right for a moral and religious "renewal" of civil society.[58] The public sphere outlined here grants room for persons and groups from various religious and moral perspectives – Buddhist, Hindu, Muslim, Jewish,

---

56 Stanley Hauerwas would argue, of course, that Christians have no stake in democracy for its own sake: "The church does not exist to provide an ethos for democracy or any other form of social organization, but stands as a political alternative to every nation, witnessing to the kind of social life possible for those that have been formed by the story of Christ" (*A Community of Character*, p. 12). In order to respond adequately to Hauerwas on this point, it would be necessary to develop a normative account of democracy – and the particular ends that it does (or does not) serve. While beyond the scope of this project, I would assert that Christians would be interested in defending forms of democracy that further people's sense of stake in their communities and that help to enlarge their capability. These terms need specification as well. The question is not merely about expanding their "choice" and freedom but what kinds of choices and liberties are expanded.

57 See Thiemann, *Religion in Public Life*, pp. 169–170.

58 For one set of such perspectives, see Dan Coats, "Can Congress Revive Civil Society?" with responses by Gertrude Himmelfarb, Don Eberly, and David Boaz, *Policy Review* 75 (January–February 1996).

Christian, humanist, liberal, or conservative – to engage in public debate. In contrast, some but not all proposals for a "remoralized" civic life advocate a particular, conservative Christian agenda, such as through appeals for America to be a Christian nation. Stated positively, emphasis on the norm of mutual respect seeks to ensure that public discourse is enriched by a wide variety of perspectives.

Moral integrity

Attention to moral integrity, conceptually the most complex of the three norms, can illuminate various aspects of this project. It suggests that those who articulate a strong commitment to realizing moral equality – including this author – would also engage in efforts to promote a more just and humane economic order, and would therefore not promote the kinds of excessive inequalities criticized in the analysis. There is another crucial point here related to the fact that the theological perspectives of this project have *institutional, ecclesiastical contexts*. That is, theological concepts like the "equality before God" and the "preferential option for the poor" are endorsed and espoused by communities of faith, in the United States and beyond, who also should hold themselves to the norm of moral integrity. For example, statements of the Catholic church have emphasized that their church is a powerful economic actor that is called to live up to the principles it espouses. The US Bishops stated in 1986:

All the moral principles that govern the just operation of any economic endeavor apply to the Church and its agencies and institutions; indeed the Church should be exemplary. The Synod of Bishops in 1971 worded this challenge most aptly: "While the Church is bound to give witness to justice, she recognizes that anyone who ventures to speak to people about justice must first be just in their eyes. Hence, we must undertake an examination of the modes of acting and of the possessions and lifestyle found with the Church herself."[59]

---

[59] National Conference of Catholic Bishops, *Economic Justice for All: Pastoral Letter on Catholic Social Teaching and the US Economy* (Washington: United States Catholic Conference, 1986), para. 347, citing the Synod of Bishops, *Justice in the World*, para. 40, in O'Brien and Shannon (eds.), *Catholic Social Thought*.

Consequently, part of the analysis considers precisely the relationship of the witness of persons and groups within Christian churches to wider public discourse and public policies. While this element is not developed in significant detail in this project, attention is given to the ways in which the preferential option for the poor and the call to evangelical poverty and solidarity apply particularly, and especially, to church institutions and their members. (The requirements for the practice of such beliefs are more compelling for Christian communities than for societies as a whole.) The norm of moral integrity suggests that the public arguments will be more effectively communicated if they are attached to communities engaged in exemplary practice.

One further aspect of the norm of moral integrity involves granting the opportunity and room for *dissent*. The theological accounts presented below – both the Reformed and liberationist perspectives – emphasize that theological loyalties are ultimate and, when necessary, call for denunciation of social, political, or economic realities that dehumanize people by denying their worth as equals before God. The socioeconomic analyses of the project reveal significant and in some cases severe inequalities; the normative approach emphasizes that such forms of inequality matter morally. Taken together, these perspectives suggest the need for significant reorientation of priorities in domestic policymaking and in international development contexts. Of course, these claims raise a number of questions to be addressed below; but the important point is that "room for dissent" demanded by the norm of moral integrity enables such critical inquiry into contemporary social conditions and structures.

This project has been framed in order to participate in and contribute to a pluralistic conversation about the "meaning" of equality and inequality in socioeconomic life. The extended consideration of Thiemann's conditions of publicity demonstrates that participating in pluralistic, public discussions about important moral questions and policy issues should not preclude people from drawing upon religiously (or non-religiously) based moral convictions. There are dangers, of course, that Christians who engage in public debate will be ignored, or they might sacrifice their faith-based convictions on the altar of relevance and effectiveness. Yet as will be developed below, there are theologically compelling reasons for understanding inequality and promoting concrete actions to remove those that dehumanize. The goal of forging a Christian ethical approach is not effectiveness any more than it is distinctiveness. The framework outlined here, however, should enable Christians to make contributions to public discourse that are indeed distinctive and effective while maintaining faithfulness to their God.

CHAPTER 6

Equality before God in the thought of
H. Richard Niebuhr

THEOLOGICAL ACCOUNTS OF EQUALITY

It has already been shown that disparate moral frameworks and narratives differ in the construction of moral equality. Notably, they entail distinct responses to the question, "Equality of what?"[1] This point suggests that it is not promising to ask whether contemporary Christian moral accounts *are* or *are not* egalitarian – for equality functions in them all. Rather, the fitting and potentially fruitful inquiry would examine *how particular theologies are egalitarian.*

This chapter and the next one examine the ways in which equality operates within Reformed and liberation theologies, and, specifically, in the thought of two representative, seminal thinkers, H. Richard Niebuhr and Gustavo Gutiérrez. Of course, there are central dimensions of theological accounts that are not present in the philosophical accounts of moral equality discussed in chapter 2. Most clearly, the "equality among persons" is above all else a theological claim about persons' moral status not only in relation to one another, but principally in relation to God. From distinct religious and social positions, both Niebuhr and Gutiérrez would concur with William Temple's assertion: "Apart from faith in God, there is really nothing to be said for the notion of equality."[2] Stated in

---

[1] Amartya Sen, "Equality of What?" and *Inequality Reexamined*. Similarly, in the words of Douglas Rae, "The question is not 'Whether equality', but '*Which* equality?'" (Rae et al., *Equalities*, p. 19). See my discussion of "Equality of what?" in chapter 2.

[2] William Temple, *Christianity and the Social Order* (Harmondsworth, UK: Penguin, 1977 [1942]), p. 37. Quoted in Robert Veatch, *The Foundations of Justice: Why the Retarded and the Rest of Us have Claims to Equality* (New York: Oxford University Press, 1986), p. 67.

more positive terms, their accounts of moral equality become comprehensible in the context of God's relation to humanity.

Within the theologies of Gutiérrez and Niebuhr, the regulative idea of human equality bears *directly* and *dynamically* on political and socioeconomic relations – in individual actions as well as in wider social structures. In Niebuhr's words: "As a pledge the principle of equality is subject to ever new commitment. It must be re-enacted in decision after decision in courts of law, in legislation, in daily administration of common goods, and in national and international political actions."[3] For Gutiérrez, a liberationist notion of equality critically reflects on those social and material conditions that can, at their worst, dehumanize people, all of whom are subjects of God's universal love and will.

The proclamation of a God who loves all human beings in equal fashion must be enfleshed, incarnated, in history – must become history . . . [The gospel's] proclamation to the exploited, the laborers and *campesinos* of our lands, will lead them to perceive that their situation is contrary to the will of God who makes himself known in events of liberation.[4]

Both Niebuhr and Gutiérrez offer theological accounts of equality that are informed by, and address, the cultural, political, and socioeconomic signs of the times. The care with which each considers the social-ethical implications of theology makes attention to their writings potentially fruitful for constructing a theologically informed approach to economic inequalities and well-being. Insights drawn from their respective accounts of the equality before God can be fruitfully engaged within, and can contribute to, public discourse and policy debates related to inequality.

At the same time, neither Niebuhr nor Gutiérrez develops his account of equality with public policy debates about inequality and well-being as a principal context of application. Indeed, Gutiérrez has stated explicitly that the first task of his theology

---

3 H. Richard Niebuhr, *Radical Monotheism and Western Culture* (New York: Harper and Row, 1970), p. 73.
4 Gustavo Gutiérrez, *The Power of the Poor in History* (Maryknoll, NY: Orbis, 1983 [1979]), p. 19.

is to address impoverished persons (who may even see themselves as "nonpersons"), including those in his parish in Lima,
Peru. His theology seeks to help such people discover and
exercise their own agency for personal and social transformation. Policymakers have not sufficiently addressed the
plight of the poor; parish-based projects, base communities,
and local cooperatives are most frequently initiatives undertaken precisely because of the *failure* of political leaders and
officials to enact just policies.

H. Richard Niebuhr's theology is often discounted as
standing one step removed from the daily fray of public debate
and policymaking. The contrast is made between H. Richard
and his brother Reinhold: Reinhold is seen as the engaged
social ethicist and activist, while H. Richard is then read as the
detached Christian thinker. To be sure, Reinhold Niebuhr
wrote more prolifically and in detail about specific social and
policy-related issues, and the sole occasion on which the
brothers debated an issue in print, the title of H. Richard's
essay was "The Grace of Doing Nothing."[5] Yet a fuller reading
of H. Richard's corpus reveals rich resources for confronting
inequality and other aspects of socioeconomic life.[6]

The policy implications of each thinker's account of equality
can be developed in a way that is faithful to their wider
theological aims and approaches. Gutiérrez's interest in the
nonperson is consistent with a conception of public discourse
and policy-oriented debate that emphasizes the agency of all

[5] H. Richard Niebuhr, "The Grace of Doing Nothing," *Christian Century* 49 (3/23/1932).
[6] R. Melvin Keiser, in his *Roots of Relational Ethics: Responsibility in Origin and Maturity in
H. Richard Niebuhr* (Atlanta: Scholars Press, 1996), offers a creative analysis of the
potential of H. Richard Niebuhr's ethics of responsibility to inform a critique of "the
various forms of social domination – sexism, environmental exploitation, the Christian imperialism of anti-Judaism, war, racism . . . and classism" (pp. 127–128).
Keiser's exploration into the liberative and transformative aspects of Niebuhr's
thought for socioeconomic life moves in the same general direction as my project,
though he does not deal in any detail with questions of distributional inequalities. (For
his treatment of Niebuhr's "socioeconomic critique," see his chapter 8.) One
interesting claim by Keiser is that Niebuhr's most serious treatment of social and
economic issues occurred before his "conversion" (around 1929) from Protestant
liberalism to what Keiser calls "relational realism." Keiser seeks to reintegrate
Niebuhr's early economic interest with his later theological framework. My work
shares such a goal; while I do not "periodize" Niebuhr, all of the sources I employ
date after 1940, and most are from the final twelve years of his life (1950–62).

people and that even pays preferential attention to the voices of the marginalized. While liberation theologians have focused on local initiatives, their calls for structural transformation have also served as a call for just public policies – and in many contexts, for more radical response. With respect to H. Richard Niebuhr, this chapter provides a reading of his deliberate, hopeful, theologically informed participation in public life.

CREATED EQUAL BEFORE GOD, THE SOURCE AND CENTER OF VALUE

In the theology and ethics of H. Richard Niebuhr, the idea of an equality of all people is first an assertion about their worth in relation to God. Based on any empirical or "finite" standard of valuing – standards such as social or economic productivity, biological fitness, reasoning ability, and so on – people are readily shown, in fact, to be unequal.[7] Niebuhr's understanding of equality requires the qualifier *before God*; in the divine–human relation people are endowed equally with dignity – and this is not reducible or equivalent to any empirical determinant.

H. Richard Niebuhr's overall approach is "theocentric." God is the sovereign ruler and judge, creator and redeemer of all that exists. In "radical monotheism," which Niebuhr offers as the most faithful and true description of Christianity, all living creatures derive both their *being* and their *value* from God, because God is the very principle of being and the principle of value. God alone is the One beyond the many, the absolute good who relativizes all other goods that are valued by persons and groups. Thus God is the center – of life, of being, of reality, of value – from whom all beings in creation receive their own worth. Stated succinctly, "worth is worth only in relation to God."[8] This is worth in an ultimate sense; as will be developed below, this theocentric framework of valuing people sets the context for and coexists with complex, multiple, and competing values. Within a web of social, economic, and political relationships, people of different abilities and capacities hold different

[7] Niebuhr, *Radical Monotheism*, pp. 74–75.
[8] H. Richard Niebuhr, *Christ and Culture* (New York: Harper & Row, 1951), p. 18.

value in terms of the specific ends or tasks. But these very ends and tasks are relativized in relation to the Absolute who is God.[9]

This theocentric understanding undergirds Niebuhr's account of equality. That equality is outlined in the essay, "Religion and the Democratic Tradition" (1940):

[T]he idea of equality which stems from faith in the creator and judge of all men is . . . perhaps . . . not a doctrine of equality at all, since it does not measure men by men or by some common human standard; it affirms rather that all men have immediate worth to God, the last measure of value, whatever be their worth or lack of worth to each other and to society. It demands of the believers not that they treat all men alike but that they deal with each person as uniquely sacred and ignore all claims to special sanctity. Seeing all men before the final judge, faith discounts all temporal privileges and claims and in this sense treats all men as equal.[10]

Thus at its theocentric root, equality is a statement about the relationship of all people to God their creator; and specifically, it claims that God, from whom all receive life as a gift, values each human person equally. Niebuhr can assert that each human being is created in the "image of God" as unique and sacred but equally valuable to God.[11] While he will proceed to speak of humans as also "equal in sin" (considered below), theologically prior to that understanding is this first sense of equality: humans as equal in origin, created in God's image.

Niebuhr's Reformed theological understanding of equality thus emphasizes the primary, definitive relationship of each human to her or his creator. Yet theocentric equality bears directly, in at least three ways, on human relationships. First, *all* people are dependent on God for their very being; each receives life as a gift, without merit. Thus the scope of the equality before God is *universal*. No one is excluded from God's valuing. No special privilege can allow people to claim equality for

---

[9] Ibid., pp. 237–240.
[10] H. Richard Niebuhr, "The Relation of Christianity and Democracy," in William Stacy Johnson (ed.), *Theology, History, and Culture: Major Unpublished Works of H. Richard Niebuhr* (New Haven, Yale University Press, 1996), p. 155.
[11] See, for instance, "The Idea of Original Sin in American Culture," in Johnson (ed.), *Theology, History, and Culture*, p. 178.

themselves or for any in-group; no form of exclusion can be justified by assertions of differential human worth. The social ethic resulting from this theocentric vision must extend to all.[12]

Second, humans are called to live all of life as a *grateful response* to the One who has given them life. Their life is a gift, and so are the lives of all those with whom they interact. In each moment of life, people respond not just to the human actors they confront, but also to God: "God is acting in all actions upon you. So respond to all actions upon you as to respond to his action."[13] Such responding should be based in the gratitude for life and leads to the *ethic of responsibility*: each person is responsible *to* God but *for* one's neighbors.[14]

Third, and no less important, Niebuhr's theological anthropology is grounded in *relationality*[15] – not merely the central relationship of God to each human but the myriad webs of relationships among people. As Niebuhr describes this relationality in the context of *The Responsible Self*, all actions and

12 For one attempt to employ H. Richard Niebuhr, among other thinkers, to provide an account of justice based on the equality of all persons, see Robert M. Veatch, *Foundations of Justice*. Veatch focuses in particular on the justice-claims of "the retarded" and argues that in order for all people to have "an opportunity for equality of well-being over a lifetime," public policy towards those with handicaps of various sorts deserves public resources that "should, as much as is possible, exactly compensate for the handicap" (pp. 151–152). Veatch's approach draws policy conclusions that move in the same direction as the constructive recommendations of this book – though I would not be able to specify how to "exactly compensate" for any particular handicap. My overall approach differs in at least two significant ways. First, while Veatch wants to claim that "religious" and "secular" bases for equality result in roughly one broad, Western view of equality, I am arguing that theocentric visions of equality make stronger claims about equality and inequality than secular, liberal versions do. See a fuller discussion in chapter 5. Second, my normative vision is more specific than Veatch's in tracing a wide variety of spheres of goods to be considered, and the need to combat inequality in each sphere.

13 H. Richard Niebuhr, *The Responsible Self: An Essay in Christian Moral Philosophy* (San Francisco: Harper & Row, 1963), p. 126.

14 Nicholas Wolterstorff, in his *Until Justice and Peace Embrace* offers another Reformed theological vision in which grateful response to God plays a central part in moving from Christian faith to "world-transformative" actions on behalf of a fuller social justice.

15 Melvin Keiser asserts that he coined this term with respect to H. Richard Niebuhr in a master's thesis at Yale Divinity School: "Relationality in the Theology of H. Richard Niebuhr: A Study in Niebuhr's Understanding of Man and God," 1964. As discussed in note 6 above, Keiser sees the relevance of Niebuhr's ethics for informing careful analyses of socioeconomic questions of justice and oppression. See Keiser, *Roots of Relational Ethics*, pp. v–vi.

decisions are made within a "continuing community of agents," without which the genuine self could not develop or exist. This "fundamentally social character of selfhood," examined most explicitly in Niebuhr's ethical writings, fits within his theocentric vision of the relation of self to God.[16]

In addition to human relations, Niebuhr's theocentric vision extends to human relations with the whole of creation. Niebuhr argues that all beings, not merely humans, are created by God and all beings possess positive value in relation to God, who is their source and creator. Faith that is truly and radically monotheistic does not separate the *being* and *valuing* bestowed by God, and accordingly, all of being is good – that is, each being possesses positive worth.[17] At the same time, Niebuhr does not call into question the traditional assumption of Christian theology (as well as of most modern, Western thought) that humans are valued *more than* other living creatures and creation. This view is evidenced in a passage from *Christ and Culture*:

The value of man, like the value of sparrow and flower, is his value to God; the measure of true joy in value is the joy in heaven. Because worth is worth in relation to God, therefore Jesus finds sacredness in all creation, and not in humanity alone – though his disciples are to take special comfort that they are of more value to God than the also valued birds.[18]

Niebuhr's theological and ethical vision extends to all of creation, promoting "a life of *responsibility* in *universal community*."[19] *Responsibility* derives from the grateful response of humans for the life they receive from God as a gift; *all* human agents created in the image of God hold responsibility within creation;

---

[16] Niebuhr, *Responsible Self*, pp. 65, 71. For the linkages between God–human and human–human relations seen especially through Christ as divine–human mediator, see especially Niebuhr, *Christ and Culture*, pp. 18–19.

[17] Niebuhr, *Radical Monotheism*, pp. 36–37.

[18] Niebuhr, *Christ and Culture*, p. 18. Some implications for the non-human elements of creation result from the *human responsibility* developed in Niebuhr's ethics and in this book. My project focuses on human agency in providing for the material well-being of all people; but this analysis could be extended along H. R. Niebuhrian lines to consider directly the well-being of all of creation. See, for instance, James Gustafson, *A Sense of the Divine: The Natural Environment from a Theocentric Perspective* (Cleveland: Pilgrim Press, 1994). See also Melvin Keiser, *Roots of Relational Ethics*, pp. 135–137.

[19] Niebuhr, *Responsible Self*, p. 89.

and the relations among all people should be marked by a spirit of community,[20] since they share in common with one another the being and value that result from their central relation with God.

EQUALS IN SIN: HUMAN FINITUDE, IDOLATRY, AND SUFFERING

Corruption and finitude

Niebuhr's Reformed vision stresses that in another important way, humans are equals: "Reference to our origin may lead us to say: I am equal to the best among us; reference to our sin may lead us to confess: I am not better than the worst among us."[21] Niebuhr embraces the classic Christian assertion that no person is without sin.[22] This claim suggests an equality related to humility. This dimension of the equality before God "convict[s] men of their sin, humbling the proud and privileged while exalting the lowly."[23]

Equality in sin does not imply, for Niebuhr, that the image of God is destroyed in each person, or that humans are totally, wholly, or intrinsically bad. Humans are essentially good, they have positive value, and sinfulness is only a distortion of that prior and more basic goodness: "Man in the Protestant view is a ruin but he is the ruin of a Coliseum or a Parthenon, not the ruin of a hovel. He is diseased tree, a warped oak, and not a sick tumbleweed."[24] Niebuhr is careful to clarify that the Reformed understanding of sin as "*total* depravity" or "*total* corruption" means two things. First, sin is *universal*: all people remain mired in sin. Humans can do nothing, as participants in a creation that suffers from sinfulness – even though redemption of all

---

[20] Ibid., p. 65. See chapter 8 for a fuller discussion of equality and human relations.

[21] Niebuhr, "Idea of Original Sin," p. 190.

[22] Following a long line of Reformation thinkers, Niebuhr quotes Paul on this theme: "There is none righteous, no not one . . . For all have sinned, and come short of the glory of God" (Romans 3:10, 23; quoted in Niebuhr, "Idea of Original Sin," p. 179).

[23] Niebuhr, "Relation of Christianity and Democracy," p. 155.

[24] Niebuhr, "Idea of Original Sin," pp. 181–182. See also Niebuhr, *Christ and Culture*, p. 194.

being is taking place – to escape the influence of sin in their lives. While they are called to strive in gratitude toward God's righteousness and justice, they must not think more highly of themselves than they do of others. This includes, of course, those who are or seek to be followers of Christ. "Universality of original sin always meant to believers that they must think of themselves as equally corrupt with all other men, non-Christians and overt criminals."[25]

The second aspect of "*total* depravity" is this: all aspects of life are affected (or infected) by sin. It affects the "total person" or the "whole person." "The Protestant affirms that the corruption enters into every action and part of man: reason, conscience, instinct, passion, personal, and social affections."[26]

While neither of these aspects – the *universality* of persons or the *whole* person – destroys the prior sacredness and goodness of each human being, this understanding of "total depravity" does call for vigilant attention to the actions of individuals and groups. H. Richard Niebuhr does not argue, as his brother Reinhold does, that groups tend to be more immoral than individuals in motive and in action.[27] H. Richard emphasizes that the influence of sin is great enough to affect all human endeavors, individual and collective. Contrasting his view with more optimistic anthropologies such as "Jeffersonian and romantic philosophy," he states: "The Protestant philosopher sees that . . . dangers arise from the tendencies of individuals to abuse their powers as well as from such tendencies in the corporations. Hence he restricts and balances all powers, for sin

---

[25] Niebuhr, "Idea of Original Sin," p. 182.

[26] Ibid.

[27] H. Richard Niebuhr explicitly rejects the view of "romantic liberalism" which asserts that group power must be limited by the actions or power of uncorrupted or "natural men" ("Idea of Original Sin," pp. 189–90). For his part, Reinhold Niebuhr's suspicion of group actions, in contrast to individual actions, is captured in the title of his 1932 classic: *Moral Man and Immoral Society: A Study in Ethics and Politics* (New York: Charles Scribner's Sons). Reinhold's *An Interpretation of Christian Ethics* (New York: Harper & Brothers, 1935) offers a fuller vision of his understanding of individual versus group morality. In that work he argues that Jesus' love ethic can be directly relevant only to personal morality, whereas in the wider social sphere, the love ethic may only be approximated by regulative principles such as "equality" and "justice." See also Robin Lovin, *Reinhold Niebuhr and Christian Realism* (Cambridge: Cambridge University Press, 1995), pp. 191–234.

is universal, not particular; total, not confined to one part of life."[28] At the same time, it is important to note here (and to discuss in detail below) that H. Richard Niebuhr emphasizes that both groups and individuals, while infected by sin, can be transformed by God's gracious intervention.

The most logical social ethic deriving from this worldview is not, he argues, a conservative or *status quo* political or social system, but rather a "radically equalitarian" one in which political and social power is (relatively) balanced among various groups and persons. There is a logical and perhaps an historical linkage, he asserts, between this "Protestant" view of human sinfulness and the federal, three-branch system of American government.

If in Protestant logic the doctrine of original sin and human depravity implies the assertion of human equality, it also implies the rejection of any human absolutism, of any absolute authoritarianism . . . If we are such [sinful] men as this, then it is evident to the Protestant that none of us, individually or collectively, ought to be allowed to exercise anything like absolute authority over the rest of us.[29]

Power, ultimately, is from God, and in itself is therefore good.[30] But particularly when concentrated it can be abused by human agents. Equality in sin, affecting all the disparate spheres of human life, results in potentially oppressive situations when excessive power is permitted in any of those spheres. Such an insight, developed in Niebuhr's critique of political systems, is also suggestive for understanding and ordering socioeconomic relations. The social ethic associated with this view of equality in sin would constrain excessive accumulation of economic power as readily as it would limit excessive concentration of political power.

---

[28] Niebuhr, "Idea of Original Sin," p. 188.
[29] Ibid., p. 179.
[30] H. Richard Niebuhr, *Faith on Earth: An Inquiry into the Structure of Human Faith* (New Haven, Yale University Press, 1989), p. 100. For a careful analysis of power and its complex relations to force, authority, and morality, see an earlier work in New Studies in Christian Ethics: James P. Mackay, *Power and Christian Ethics* (Cambridge: Cambridge University Press, 1994).

Idolatry

To have faith in the radically monotheist God is to place one's ultimate *trust* in God and to show complete *loyalty* to God. In this view, when people orient their lives toward God, they can enjoy the integrity of a genuine self. Because all humans are sinful, each fails (though in distinct ways) to demonstrate such a faith in God, placing faith in a variety of "gods." More specifically, people hold as ultimate values what should be commitments informed and indeed constrained by the prior commitment to God. They revere and serve any number of values besides God – such as nation-state, organized religion, pleasure, economic efficiency or consumer goods. "Value-centers" demand commitment in ways that usurp one's absolute commitment to God, and consequently, to an ethical orientation marked by responsibility in a universal community of equals. Humans can experience life as a struggle to integrate involvements in and commitments to a variety of systems offering meaning and fulfillment. Life, rather than being lived as gratitude, is then experienced as conflict.[31]

Niebuhr labels such behavior as "idolatry," a rejection of the radically monotheist motto: "Thou shalt have no other gods before me."[32] The proper relativizing of all finite values occurs when they are placed in the context of God as the center and principle of value. When the monotheist motto is enacted, no other claims are allowed to hold one's absolute loyalty.[33] Based on this account of sin and idolatry, Niebuhr condemns actions that allow finite value-centers to distort the lives of the actors themselves and the lives of others. Such actions based on idolatry lead to oppression and suffering.[34]

---

[31] Niebuhr, *Responsible Self*, pp. 137–141.
[32] Niebuhr, *Radical Monotheism*, p. 37.
[33] See Niebuhr, *Christ and Culture*, p. 28.
[34] Of course, this emphasis in Niebuhr places him in strong continuity with his faith tradition: the rejection of idolatry has served Reformed thinkers in social movements as distinct as the Protestant Reformation, the American Revolution, and resistance to Hitler's National Socialism. See, for instance, Niebuhr, "Idea of Original Sin"; Michael Walzer, *The Revolution of the Saints: A Study of The Origins of Radical Politics* (Cambridge, MA: Harvard University Press, 1965); and the *Barmen Declaration* (1934), in John H. Leith, *Creeds of the Churches: A Reader in Christian Doctrine, from the Bible to the*

Sin and human suffering

For Niebuhr, to have faith (trust and loyalty) in God is to believe that in every action and event of life, God is acting. To remain mired in sin and to hold idols is not to have such faith. It is, instead, to express a "passionate devotion to limited causes"; people stuck in idolatry combat others who also hold their own "restricted loyalties." In the process, they respond to God, the One beyond the many, as an *enemy.* To live in sin and to commit idolatry is to fail to respond in trust and loyalty to God, the worship of whom places all limited goods in context and in harmony.

The consequences of sin and idolatry include human conflicts – including war, political strife, and economic systems of injustice. While Niebuhr leaves much room within his understanding of the sovereignty of God for the mysterious nature and causes of human suffering, he directs most responsibility for it to the hands of human powers, often those with excessive power.[35] Human sin is the root cause of most human suffering.

God's will is never tied to the will of any particular persons or groups; rather, it transcends all human wills. Yet even in the face of unjust human practices and systems, Niebuhr contends, people of faith are called to understand that the will of God is being realized. In "A Christian Interpretation of War," Niebuhr states:

In war the little and the weak peoples, whether we think of racial communities, or of generations, or of economic classes, or of cultural groups, bear the burden of suffering. The maintenance of order in the universe and the internal correction of the justice of groups at war is accomplished, it is apparent, at the cost of individuals and of special people who are not maintained or corrected but slain . . . These facts

---

Present (third edn., Atlanta: John Knox Press, 1982), pp. 518–522. I do not mean to claim that this theme has led Reformed Christians always or even often to condemn situations of oppression and suffering. Rather, I am making an assertion about the potential effectiveness for a Reformed account of idolatry (and equality) for rejecting injustice. The historical examples are meant to highlight some instances when the potential has been at least partially realized.

35 H. Richard Niebuhr, "A Christian Interpretation of War," in Johnson (ed.), *Theology, History, and Culture, passim.*

about war are religiously the most difficult. The faith of the church meets its greatest challenge here; here the faith of every Christian is tested.[36]

Like war, political and economic conflict are seen by Niebuhr as similarly the result of human corruption, self-interest, and conflict, and they often lead to the more overt forms of violence.[37]

Frequently the faithful response to such situations of injustice, according to Niebuhr, is to accept suffering as the will of God, as a requirement of loyalty within the context of "man's misery": "[Such a response] will transcend bitterness by accepting suffering as coming from the hand of the ruling God rather than from the hands of the short-sighted and sinful agents through whom he acts and who, like ourselves, do not know what they are doing."[38] Accepting vicarious suffering as a sign of faithfulness is also consistent with Niebuhr's strong view of God's sovereignty, drawn from his Reformed roots. But Niebuhr proceeds from the above quotation to offer a *crucial caveat*:

It should be evident, but it needs to be made very explicit, that this principle of Christian suffering and obedience is wholly perverted when it is applied to others rather than [to] the self, as when white men recommend it to negroes, when rich men preach it to the poor, or coercionists proclaim it to conscientious objectors. Such a use of the principle is defensive and it perverts it utterly. Under God's rule there are some things men can only say to themselves and this is one of them. The defensive use of the principle of obedience to God in all situations has been the scandal of Christianity at all times and has made it a tool of the powerful. But the fact that the principle can be so abused does not detract from its significance and necessity.[39]

One of the important elements of Niebuhr's account of equality, then, is that while humans are equal in creation and in sin, they suffer the results of human sinfulness *disproportionately*. The oppression resulting from abuses of power in war, politics, and economics is distributed unequally. Niebuhr's theological

---

[36] Niebuhr, "Christian Interpretation of War," p. 166.
[37] Ibid., esp. pp. 163–164 and p. 172.
[38] Niebuhr, "Relation of Christianity and Democracy," p. 147.
[39] Ibid., pp. 147–148.

account not only sheds light on that fact; he goes to great lengths to ensure that his account is not enlisted to further such unequal and unjust treatment. The suffering inflicted by human agents on those who hold a disproportionately small share of social goods is a violation of their sacredness as created equal in God's image.

It bears repeating, at the close of this discussion of Niebuhr's treatment of the "equality in sin," the context in which human sin is understood:

In Protestant thought the principle of man's corruption derives its meaning from its context. It stands among convictions about man's creation in the divine image and about his real redemption from this wickedness and from the inhumanity of man to man. The belief in that liberation as an ongoing process, as a possibility relevant to existence in time as well as eternity, as relevant to political as well as religious life, is for the Protestant even more important than the doctrine of sin.[40]

Sin is about the corruption of that which is good; it requires "liberation as an ongoing process, as a possibility . . . relevant to political as well as religious life." Niebuhr could have added the relevance of this liberation process to *economic* life.

REDEMPTION IN CHRIST, TRANSFORMER OF CULTURE

Niebuhr's thought is theocentric, not Christocentric. Radically monotheistic faith is properly directed to the One beyond the many, the one sovereign, triune God, the God before whom all humans are equals. Christians and the Christian church need always be vigilant against falling into Christo-monism or a "practical monotheism of the Son,"[41] according to which the Christ who mediates between the One and the many is mistaken for that One. Throughout his life Niebuhr was critical of Christians and churches whose theologies implied "the substitution of Christology for theology, of the love of Jesus Christ for

---

[40] Niebuhr, "Idea of Original Sin," p. 191.
[41] H. Richard Niebuhr, "The Doctrine of the Trinity and the Unity of the Church," in Johnson (ed.), *Theology, History, and Culture*, p. 53.

the love of God and of life in the community of Jesus Christ for life in the divine commonwealth."[42]

Yet clearly, Christ plays a central role in Niebuhr's theology and ethics.[43] God's incarnation through Christ is the breaking of the radically monotheistic God into human history, and more generally, into the "realm of being."[44] Christ is thus the transcendent God revealed in history.[45] Christian theologians have emphasized the claim that the transcendent God is also known as the immanent God through the incarnation of Christ. Indeed, these two aspects of theology play a crucial role in Niebuhr's account of equality. God as transcendent stands above all human relations, relativizing and ordering all other value claims. God as immanent illuminates the sacredness of life within the finiteness and relatedness of creation.

Christology is a central site for relating and integrating these themes. As divine and human, Niebuhr asserts, Christ orients humans toward God the Father and mediates God's will to humankind. This dual or two-way role is described at some length in *Christ and Culture*:

To be related in devotion and obedience to Jesus Christ is to be related to the One to whom he undeviatingly points. As Son of God he points away from the many values of man's social life to the One who alone is good; to the One who alone is powerful; from the many times and seasons of history with their hopes and fears to the One who is Lord of all times and is alone to be feared and hoped for; he points away from all that is conditioned to the Unconditioned. He does not direct attention away from this world to another; but from all

---

[42] H. Richard Niebuhr, *The Purpose of the Church and its Ministry: Reflections on the Aims of Theological Education* (New York: Harper & Brothers, 1956), p. 44; quoted in Hans Frei, "The Theology of H. Richard Niebuhr," in Paul Ramsey (ed.), *Faith and Ethics: The Theology of H. Richard Niebuhr* (New York: Harper & Brothers, 1957), p. 97.

[43] In the words of Hans Frei: "Niebuhr's theology is theocentric rather than Christocentric: his theological problem is not in the first instance one of relation to Jesus Christ . . . We are suggesting that in natural religion and Christian faith, Niebuhr's starting point is with God the Father rather than with the Son. And yet the task of Christian theology is to express the conversion of our faith and its *new* understanding of God's power, unity and goodness in the light of God's act in Jesus Christ. Thus Christology is directly involved in Niebuhr's theocentric theology" (Frei, "Theology of H. Richard Niebuhr," pp. 95–96).

[44] Niebuhr, *Responsible Self*, p. 40.

[45] H. Richard Niebuhr, *The Meaning of Revelation* (New York: Macmillan, 1941), esp. chap. 4.

worlds, present and future, material and spiritual, to the One who creates all worlds, who is the Other of all worlds.

Yet this is only half the meaning of Christ, considered morally. The other half has been indicated above by what was said about his love of men in relation to his love of God. Because he is the moral Son of God in his love, hope, faith, obedience, and humility in the presence of God, therefore he is the moral mediator of the Father's will toward men.[46]

These two poles correspond to two dimensions of Christology in Niebuhr's later thought. In his 1962 Earl Lectures, Niebuhr develops these two dimensions: "Christ as paradigm of responsibility" and "Christ as redeemer to responsible being."[47] Christ is paradigmatic in his living because in all that he did, he expressed full trust and perfect fidelity to God the Father. He did not allow any less-than-ultimate or conditioned values to take on ultimate or unconditioned importance. He denounced all idols in his life, a way of life which led to his death. He was, in short, "the responsible man who in all his response to alteractions [*sic*] did what fitted into the divine action."[48]

God's will for all people is, ultimately, their reconciliation to God, with each other, and with all being. Through his life, death, and resurrection Christ brings healing and redemption to all of creation. Reconciliation with God, and consequently with other people and creation, results when every aspect of reality that represents or furthers death can be understood and interpreted within the larger context of life, which ultimately is good. God's action of redemption is made definitively *in Christ*:

For us who are Christians the possibility of making this new interpretation of the total action upon us by the One who embraces and is present in the many is inseparably connected with an action in our past that was the response of trust by a man who was sent into life and sent into death and to whom answer was made in his resurrection from the dead . . .

---

[46] Niebuhr, *Christ and Culture*, p. 28.
[47] Niebuhr, *Responsible Self*, pp. 162–178. While these specific section headings were added by an editor after Niebuhr's death, the two labels are clearly indicative of Niebuhr's own argument.
[48] Niebuhr, *Responsible Self*, p. 164.

Through Jesus Christ, through his life, death, resurrection, and reign in power, we have been led and are being led to *metanoia*, to the reinterpretation of all our interpretations of life and death.[49]

Two important aspects of this Christology need to be considered in more detail in light of this inquiry into the equality before God. First, the process of redemption in Christ extends not merely to all people, but to the breadth of human culture, to all aspects of human doing, making, and relating, as well as to all of creation. That is, regeneration through Christ reaches to every dimension of life in society. In the conversionist social ethic that Niebuhr himself favors, Christ as "the transformer of culture" offers regeneration of every sphere of human life. This includes, of course, socioeconomic relationships.

Second, Niebuhr's account of redemption through the life, death, and resurrection of Christ offers a strong condemnation of human suffering. In Christ God takes on human suffering and makes it God's own. In so doing God reveals that while God's will can be manifested even within and despite such suffering, ultimately suffering is overcome by the power of goodness. In an essay on war, Niebuhr points out that God's definitive answer to the vicarious suffering of the innocent is made in Christ.

[I]t is exactly at this point that the action of God, the Father of Jesus Christ, is most apparent in war, for this is the way of his working which was made evident in the cross of Christ. He gives his best-beloved rather than to allow the work of his creation to dissolve into the anarchy of existence which can recognize no order, to decay internally.[50]

God is a victim of war, one who suffers alongside the innocent (as well as the guilty).

In the spirit of Christian hope, Niebuhr asserts that God, in addition to suffering with the victims, will prevail over all suffering.[51] In Christ God makes it clear that the suffering arising from the sin of human beings – which affects the powerless disproportionately – is also God's suffering. Further,

[49] Ibid., p. 143.
[50] Niebuhr, "Christian Interpretation of War," pp. 166–167.
[51] See William Stacy Johnson, introduction to Johnson (ed.), *Theology, History, and Culture*, especially pp. xxxi–xxxii.

God reveals in Christ that social suffering will ultimately be transformed into social solidarity by removal of the forms of oppression.

This metaphor of God as victim of social suffering can surely be extended beyond the most severe human conflict – war – into other aspects of social, political, and economic life. In all of these spheres, the efforts to end suffering and its human social causes include both divine and human agency. Christ's life, death, and resurrection offer precedent and hope for such cooperative efforts at social transformation.

DIVINE WORK AND HUMAN RESPONSE IN SOCIAL TRANSFORMATION

It should be evident from this examination of Niebuhr's theological account of the equality before God that the primary agent in history is God, not humankind. Those created in the image of God – all humans – are called to respond to their creator in all their actions, including those understood as "economic." But are Niebuhr's theocentrism and strong view of divine agency to be understood as an equality without human agency? Niebuhr answers that question, of course, in the negative; this section explores the complex relationship between divine work and human work in social transformation.

The relationship of divine and human agency begins in the understanding that the sovereign God is always engaging within history as well as beyond history, realizing God's will even through the most immoral and sinful human agents. The maxim, "Whatever is, is good," a motto of radical monotheism borrowed from Augustine, does not imply that "whatever is, is right."[52] For Niebuhr, the good is realized often not with the assistance or contribution of human efforts, but *despite* human intention and action.[53] Within the condition of a creation marred by sin, human motivations such as self-interest, envy,

---

[52] Niebuhr, *Responsible Self*, p. 38. See Johnson, introduction, p. xxiv and Niebuhr, *Christ and Culture*, p. 210.

[53] See, for instance, H. Richard Niebuhr, "Christian Interpretation of War," p. 164 and *passim*.

pride, and faithlessness contradict God's gracious will for all of being. Yet Niebuhr emphasizes that God's will will prevail. In a crucial sense, the most important relation between divine and human agency is this: human action cannot ultimately impede God's action.

This is not all that can be said, however. Humans, like all beings of creation, are called to respond in faith to God, to strive to become God's agents on earth, cooperating with God. In the Niebuhrian view, in order for the reign of God (or the *basileia* of God)[54] to be realized, humans are called to align their wills with God's.

Critics have maintained that such a strongly theocentric theology takes away, or severely impedes, all sense of human agency.[55] In his now classic essay written in response to the

---

54 Following Elisabeth Schüssler Fiorenza (who would not offer the same account as Niebuhr does of divine and human agency), I will employ the original Greek word, *basileia*, to speak of the reign, realm, empire, or kingdom of God. As Schüssler Fiorenza argues, the term *basileia* has polyvalent meanings, including "a royal-monarchical context of meaning that has as its sociopolitical referent the Roman empire." As an *alternative* to the *basileia* of Rome, the *basileia* of God also refers "to a range of ancestral democratic-religious traditions that proclaimed God's kingship and power of salvation. It was also an anti-imperial political symbol that appealed to the oppositional imagination of the Jewish people victimized by the Roman imperial system. The gospel of the *basileia* envisioned an alternative world free of hunger, poverty, and domination" (Schüssler Fiorenza, "A Discipleship of Equals: Ekklesial Democracy and Patriarchy in Biblical Perspective," in Eugene C. Bianchi and Rosemary Radford Ruether [eds.], *A Democratic Catholic Church: The Reconstruction of Roman Catholicism* [New York: Crossroad, 1992], p. 27). Retaining this Greek term is meant to convey the radical alternative to all forms of economic, social, and political domination in order to help provide the dynamic, transformative impetus within my normative approach to socioeconomic life.

55 Even a critic from within the Reformed tradition like Kathryn Tanner asserts that H. Richard Niebuhr's moral realism severely limits human potential to act responsibly in society because too many things must be accepted as "givens." Tanner's normative approach is well laid out in *Politics of God* and "A Theological Case for Human Responsibility in Moral Choice," *The Journal of Religion* 73/4 (October 1993). I would argue that the position developed in this book is also consistent with Kathryn Tanner's feminist Reformed view. Yet contrary to my interpretation and appropriation of Niebuhr, she portrays his approach as entailing a "moral realism" that too willingly accepts the social, economic, and political *status quo*: "[I]n contradistinction to a purported respect for God's prevenient sovereignty, moral realists *restrict* God's active influence over human life, and God's counsels for it." ("Case for Human Responsibility" p. 599). She goes on to claim: "Among the followers of [H. Richard] Niebuhr, God's action and intentions are displayed only in what life forces us to respond to; our own acts of responsible choice in the face of such forces cannot be themselves within the sphere of God's working in the same direct way. At

Manchurian conflict, H. Richard Niebuhr calls for *inactivity* in that specific situation, a response he recommends on the theological basis he calls "The Grace of Doing Nothing." Is he asserting that the proper way to be in relation to the sovereign God is to be passive, to sit on the sidelines as history moves on?[56] Anticipating such a criticism, he suggests that there are various ways of "doing nothing." Some are based in pessimism, self-interest, or moral indignation – all views Niebuhr rejects. In the proper form of inactivity, the most important quality is to have faith that even in the most ambiguous and tragic circumstances, God is acting. Humans must admit, amidst confusion and despair, that the future is beyond their control, but not beyond God's.

The ethic associated with such a faith in the sovereign God is not one of inactivity, but of activity properly contextualized within divine activity.[57] Even within his article on "Doing Nothing," Niebuhr makes this "activist" claim:

most, our own acts may indicate what God is up to in their capacity as restraints on other men and women, in their capacity as forces that befall these others, but not qua responsible choices" (p. 599). Niebuhr is always cautious in equating any human actions directly with God's actions. This is because of his strong view of human sin. But this is not to claim that humans are incapable of acting responsibly in society, and even more important, that human agency cannot be transformed by a sovereign God in order to effect justice. Further, my account emphasizes how H. Richard Niebuhr wanted to distance himself from more conservative positions (like that of "Christ and Culture in Paradox" – a position meant to include his brother Reinhold) in favor of an ethic of (patient, hopeful, deliberate) social transformation. Surely Tanner emphasizes the distinction between her position and Niebuhr's because their positions are so similar.

56 His brother Reinhold makes such a claim in his response, in the following issue of *The Christian Century*, to H. Richard's argument (Reinhold Niebuhr, "Must We Do Nothing?" *Christian Century* 49 [3/30/1932]). More specifically, Reinhold claims that Richard is promoting a "pure love ethic" that paralyzes well-meaning actors while self-interested persons and groups jockey to exercise their power in social relations. As is elaborated in the following paragraphs of my text, Reinhold's criticism misses the force of Richard's argument, which refutes the very view Reinhold attributes to him. See also H. Richard's counter-response to his brother, discussed in the following footnote.

57 In his counter-response to Reinhold's, "Must We Do Nothing?", H. Richard makes this statement: "[T]he issue between us . . . does not lie in the question of activity versus inactivity, to which my too journalistic approach to the problem directed attention; we are speaking after all of two kinds of activity." The debate, according to H. Richard, occurs elsewhere: "For my brother God is outside the historical process, so much so that he charges me with faith in a miracle-working deity which interferes occasionally, sometimes brutally, sometimes redemptively, in this history. But God, I

Like early Christianity and like communism today radical Christianity knows that nothing constructive can be done by interference but that something very constructive can be done in preparation for the future. It also can build cells of those within each nation who, divorcing themselves from the program of nationalism and of capitalism, unite in a higher loyalty which transcends national and class lines of division and prepare for the future. There is no such Christian international today because radical Christianity has not arrived as yet at a program and a philosophy of history, but such little cells are forming. The First Christian international of Rome has had its day; the Second Christian international of Stockholm is likely to go the ways of the Second Socialist international. There is need of and opportunity for a Third Christian international.[58]

The "inactivity of radical Christianity," he writes, "is not the inactivity of a resigned patience, but of a patience that is full of hope, and is based on faith."[59] Such a stance of faithful hope, tempered by patience, involves certain expressions of activity as well as inactivity.

The resultant theocentric ethic is reflected in two dimensions of the equality before God. First, people's "interests" must be seen vis-à-vis the equality before God – by which any special privileges that obstruct the universal scope of God's love are invalid. Second, because of the equality in sin, social agents must realize that the motives of no person or group, including one's own self or one's group, are pure. In the Manchurian conflict these points implied that both US and Japanese interests could (and did) obstruct universal love and community: these national interests did not allow people in other nations to be seen as equals before God. In cases in which self-interest is strong, it may be better to do nothing than to engage actively in conflict.

Sometimes, as in the Manchurian conflict, persons and groups should refrain from action; at other times they should act. But when they act they do so in both faith *and* sin.

believe, is always in history; he is the structure in things, the source of all meaning, the 'I am that I am,' that which is that is" ("A Communication: The Only Way into the Kingdom of God," *Christian Century* 49 [4/6/1932], p. 447). Certainly for H. Richard, God acts in history – indeed, the ethical task involves "fittingly" situating human actions within God's activity.
58 Niebuhr, "Grace of Doing Nothing," p. 379.
59 Ibid., p. 380.

Consequently their efforts are imperfect and will have negative consequences. Niebuhr notes in a 1940 essay:

[S]ince Christians act not only in faith but also in sin they help to enthrone new finite absolutes when they assist in the casting down of old tyrannies. So Protestantism assisted in the development of absolute individualism and of autonomous economic power. Now faith is required to limit by criticism and by law the infinite ambitions of the economic man, to seek in this new realm the recognition of the sacred worth of all beings, to win liberty for those bound in a new slavery.[60]

All people are called to act for positive social transformation within creation in the trust and loyalty that God is the center of value *and* in the humility that all human actions, including one's own, will have negative consequences, some intended and some not intended. (Interestingly, the specific contemporary manifestation of sin he mentions is excessive *economic* ambition.)

Equality before God implies that all humans are called to center their lives on the One beyond the many, before whom they are equal and relate to other people as unique and sacred. In such a view, Christians should not receive special status – in material or soteriological terms – as a result of their worship of and response to God. They are *elected* not for status, but *for service*.[61] Christians are called, collectively and personally, to respond in faith to God. They do so explicitly and reflectively, but most important, they do so in the realization that they are not religiously or morally superior to other people. This humility leads Niebuhr to state that "the church consists of that portion of humanity which, knowing God, knows that man is not God and has made the decision before God that it will not play God but let God be Lord."[62] The church, as a collective of persons who together remember and enact the ongoing narrative of the sovereign, triune God, is therefore striving to know

---

[60] Niebuhr, "Relation of Christianity and Democracy," pp. 157–158. In *Christ and Culture* (p. 212), Niebuhr approvingly attributes such a view to Augustine, for whom "the political order in city and empire is not only confused by wars and oppressions, but the very administration of justice becomes a perverse business in which ignorance seeking to check vice commits new injustice."

[61] Niebuhr, *Radical Monotheism*, pp. 57–58 and "The Church Defines Itself in the World," in Johnson (ed.), *Theology, History, and Culture*, p. 71. See also Tanner, *Politics of God*, pp. 191–192.

[62] Niebuhr, "The Church Defines Itself," p. 72.

the will of God within a sinful creation. At its best, ecclesial life and practice embodies many aspects of the equality before God, including response to God, relationality, and solidarity with victims. In so doing, the church seeks to reflect, and must not therefore be equated with, the *basileia* of God, which will be fully realized only in the reconciliation of the "universal commonwealth" with God.

CONCLUSIONS

Niebuhr's account of the equality before God provides rich resources for ethical deliberation about socioeconomic life. The wide theological vision developed in this chapter, of course, does not "settle" economic matters, but rather informs and deepens discussion – and practice. In Niebuhr's own words:

> Though we start with the bold affirmation of faith that all men have sacred value, because all are related to God, and that they are therefore equal in value, yet we must also consider that all men are in relations to other finite beings, and that in these relations they do not have equal value . . . Priest, Levite, and Samaritan must be considered equal in value as objects of divine valuation; but they are not equal in value to the victim of the robbers, quite apart from anything he thinks about them. In Christ there is neither Jew nor Greek, bond nor free, male nor female; but in relation to other men a multitude of relative value considerations arise.[63]

The affirmation of the equality before God provides the value-framework in which these other "relative values" are not only relevant, but necessary, for ethical evaluation. Niebuhr goes on to say:

> [I]f I consider [my neighbor] in his value-relations to all his neighbors and also in his value-relation to God, then there is room not only for relative justice but for the formation and reformation of relative judgments by reference to the absolute relation. The relation of the Absolute will not come into consideration as an afterthought – as when a priest is sent to accompany a criminal on the way to the gallows – but as a forethought and a cothought that determines how everything is done that is done to him and for him.[64]

[63] Niebuhr, *Christ and Culture*, p. 237.
[64] Ibid., p. 240.

The ultimate value-relation, of humans in equality with one another before God, contextualizes all other value-relations, including those known as political, social, or economic. Humans as equals in creation and as equals in sin can serve as "forethought" and "cothought" in constructing a substantive and meaningful normative approach to the socioeconomic order.

A number of more specific conclusions can be made about the equality before God in Niebuhr's thought. The theological account of moral equality derives from the central assertion that all peoples are created equal before God; God bestows on every person an equal worth that should not be undermined or denied by any structural arrangements or personal relationships. The scope of this moral equality, then, is universal. Further, the very basis in the divine–human relationship contributes the *relational* aspect to H. Richard Niebuhr's account of equality that makes strong claims about responsibility for fellow citizens.

Alongside the awareness of the equal worth of all people in this account, there is also significant focus on the propensity towards evil that all people know and share within creation. Equality before God is also a statement, then, about the limitations that they share in common. Just as important, Niebuhr notes that they do not equally share the *consequences* of sinfulness – like injustice and oppression.

In terms of the question, "Equality of what?" raised in chapter 2, the Niebuhrian account offers no straightforward or specific social space in which equality should operate. Of course, the account defends an equality of human worth or of human dignity, but this claim provides very little additional specification beyond the claim that humans are equals before God. Stated differently, Niebuhr's account offers no precise list of social goods, functionings, or primary goods that must be held equally in order for moral equality to be fully realized and enacted. Rather, Niebuhr's account describes a society or situation in which there exist genuine relationships of "responsibility in universal community," in which God's goodness, love, and order operate. Substantive insights, to be sure, are included in this vision. Specifically, some relative equality – or a limit on excessive inequality – in social and economic power is required, because "absolute" concentrations of power tempt people to act like gods. This claim to relative balancing of economic power plays a significant role in the normative and constructive work of later chapters.

Central to the Niebuhrian account is the *transformative potential* of Christian commitment in general, and the commitment to the equality before God in particular. One task of social ethics, for Niebuhr, is to determine thoughtfully what kinds of human activity can most faithfully and responsibly transform persons and societies towards God's *basileia*. As H. Richard states in reply to his brother Reinhold's critique: "Man's task is not that of building utopias but that of eliminating weeds and tilling the soil so that the kingdom of God can grow."[65] Weeding and tilling are transformative human activities within the greater transformation, toward the *basileia*, of which God is the central, principal agent. Such weeding and tilling require attention to, and the limitation of, certain social and economic inequalities.

Theocentric faith from a Reformed, Niebuhrian perspective calls all people to strive, individually and collectively, toward realizing more fully God's will for humankind and creation. Humans are intended to live life in community with one another, a form of living that is modeled, albeit imperfectly, by the Christian church. Actions in economic life are made knowing that no social system or structure completely or even adequately reflects God's will.[66] "Subject to ever new commitment," equality as a regulative idea moves people to act within their present contexts to defend the distinctiveness and sacredness of each human person.[67] This vision of the equality before God is actualized in diligence, humility, and hope – diligently acting to relativize all value-centers and manifestations of social power that claim ultimate status and which consequently dehumanize people; humbly recognizing that justice is always incomplete in a sinful world; and proceeding in the hope that

[65] Niebuhr, "A Communication."
[66] Niebuhr, "Relation of Christianity and Democracy," p. 158.
[67] Niebuhr, *Radical Monotheism*, p. 73.

God's final work is "a deed not of final destruction but of final recreation. Not of enslavement to futility but of liberation to action, not of death dealing but of life-giving."[68]

The Niebuhrian account of equality is arguably more focused on the dangers of excessive accumulation of power than on the deprivation of power. (Of course, the two are related, as they reflect the opposite ends of a distribution of power.) Niebuhr emphasizes that the realization of moral equality requires the limitation of special privileges of people with power. In contrast, the liberationist account of equality, in the following chapter, will begin with the ways in which equality calls for at least the minimum provisions needed for personhood.

---

[68] H. Richard Niebuhr, "Man's Work and God's," in Johnson (ed.), *Theology, History, and Culture*, p. 214.

CHAPTER 7

Equality before God in the thought of Gustavo Gutiérrez

LIBERATION THEOLOGY AS THEOLOGY

At its root, liberation theology is a method of making sense of people's experiences in the contemporary world in light of a belief in a loving, powerful, gracious being called God. Theology is a "critical reflection on praxis," entailing the evaluation of a reality that includes a God of life and a world of vast disparities of cultural experience and socioeconomic condition.[1] This requires the employment of various tools and resources, but all in the service of the theological task. It also requires the prioritizing of *theodicy*: "God-talk and the suffering of the innocent."[2]

Theology, for Gustavo Gutiérrez, is distinct from the modern, "progressive" theological quest, which most fundamentally engages the question of the existence or non-existence of God in the contemporary world: "How can one proclaim God in a world become adult, a world grown up, a world come of age?" The interlocutor of such modern theology is the "non-believer."[3] In contrast, Gutiérrez states that

the interlocutor of the theology of liberation is the "*nonperson*," the human being who is not considered human by the present social

[1] Gustavo Gutiérrez, *A Theology of Liberation* (Maryknoll, NY: Orbis, 1988 [1973, 1971]), fifteenth anniversary edn., pp. 5–12. All subsequent references to *A Theology of Liberation* are to this 1988 edition.

[2] This phrase comprises the subtitle of Gustavo Gutiérrez's *On Job: God-Talk and the Suffering of the Innocent* (Maryknoll, NY: Orbis, 1987 [1985]).

[3] Gutiérrez, *Power of the Poor*, p. 57. See also Elisabeth Schüssler Fiorenza (ed.), "Introduction: Feminist Liberation Theology as Critical Sophialogy," in *The Power of Naming: A* Concilium *Reader in Feminist Liberation Theology* (Maryknoll, NY: Orbis, 1996), p. xxii.

order – the exploited classes, marginalized ethnic groups, and despised cultures. Our question is how to tell the nonperson, the nonhuman, that God is love, and that this love makes us all brothers and sisters.[4]

In order for a theology to be liberative, it must take into account the situations of these marginalized and oppressed people. Such is the context in which liberationist concepts of inequality and equality operate.

Liberation theology – particularly the Latin American strand – has been portrayed as political ideology, economic ideology, or social theory dressed up in religious vestment.[5] Such criticisms typically accuse liberationist thought of being "Marxist" – with varying degrees of nuance about what aspects (philosophical, historical, political-economic, and/or cultural) of "Marxism" are being appropriated. While liberation theology clearly draws upon "secular" social theories – employing Marxist sources among others – the central task of liberationist thought is in fact *theological*.[6] It is fitting and important to sharpen the theological and moral dimensions of the contri-

---

[4] Gutiérrez, *Power of the Poor*, p. 193.

[5] For an example of the sharpest criticism of liberation theology, see Michael Novak, *Will it Liberate?: Questions about Liberation Theology* (New York: Paulist Press, 1988). The two Vatican "Instructions" also offer severe criticism of the methodological and substantive dimensions of liberation theology – and particularly liberationist claims about the use of Marxism in its discussion of social theory and transformation (Congregation for the Doctrine of the Faith, "Instruction on Certain Aspects of the 'Theology of Liberation'," reprinted in *Origins* 14 [9/13/1984]; Congregation for the Doctrine of the Faith, "Instruction on Christian Freedom and Liberation," reprinted in *Origins* 15 [4/17/1986]). A thoughtful, extended critique is contained in Dennis P. McCann, *Christian Realism and Liberation Theology: Practical Theologies in Creative Conflict* (Maryknoll, NY: Orbis, 1982).

[6] Two important examinations of the relationship between liberation theology and the social sciences are Arthur F. McGovern, *Liberation Theology and Its Critics* (Maryknoll, NY: Orbis, 1989), especially chapters 6–8, and Enrique D. Dussel, "Theology of Liberation and Marxism," in Ignacio Ellacuría, S.J. and Jon Sobrino, S.J. (eds.), *Mysterium Liberationis: Fundamental Concepts in Liberation Theology* (Maryknoll, NY: Orbis, 1993). While Dussel is a liberation theologian and philosopher and McGovern is an amiable critic, the two concur in their assessment that liberation theology is first of all theology, and that the social scientific methods drawn upon do not obscure the central theological task. For an important claim that liberation theology too wholeheartedly rejects one rational, modern "metanarrative" – capitalism – only to embrace too wholeheartedly another rational, modern, but ultimately flawed "metanarrative" – Marxism – see John Milbank, *Theology and Social Theory: Beyond Secular Reason* (Oxford: Blackwell, 1990).

bution that liberationist perspectives can make to particular socioeconomic problems – including inequality.

CREATION, HUMAN SUFFERING, AND THE GOD OF LIFE

In Gutiérrez's liberationist vision, the reflection on equality centers on "who God is" vis-à-vis the social reality that produces nonpersons. Liberation theologians thus do not develop, *a priori*, any notion of equality. Rather, they emphasize the ongoing, active role of the God of life within a socio-historical situation of vast inequalities. Equality-talk should be formulated in response to such signs of the times.

The equality before God, Gutiérrez emphasizes, is first a claim that all humans possess dignity bestowed on them as creatures of a loving God. The liberating God is the creator/creating God who gives life to all of creation – including, of course, people.[7] God is also parent (as "Father") of *all* people, even those whose humanity is denied within the present order. As children of God, people are therefore siblings, brothers and sisters.

Gutiérrez develops these claims about "the equality of all human beings before God" in *On Job*, citing Job 31:13–15:

> If I have ever infringed the rights of slave
> or slave-girl in legal actions against me –
> what shall I do, when God stands up?
> What shall I say when he hold his assize?
> Did he not create them in the womb like me,
> the same God forming us in the womb?[8]

Here as in most cases, Gutiérrez's exposition of equality before God addresses the mistreatment of marginalized persons and groups (e.g., slaves). Within a context of injustice, humans-as-

---

[7] Thus the title of Gutiérrez's most systematic reflection: *The God of Life* (Maryknoll, NY: Orbis, 1991 [1989]).

[8] Gutiérrez, *On Job*, pp. 41–42. In this passage Job is trying to come to terms with his own suffering; Gutiérrez's own discussion of equality also occurs in the context of various forms of suffering. Gutiérrez invokes equality not only to understand, but also to transform, them.

siblings emerges as a crucial aspect of theological anthropology. Social relations are evaluated in light of the rightful fraternity/sorority that should operate among equals.

This theological emphasis illuminates directly the social-relational aspect of equality. People experience their identities not only as children of God who is their loving parent, but also in relation to their sisters and brothers of humanity. Equality in the liberationist framework thus concerns the quality of inter-action, or social cohesion, among persons within (local, national, global) societies. Only within such societies will all people be able to realize their dignity bestowed by God.[9]

In the face of human suffering, Gutiérrez draws upon the book of Job in order to emphasize the *gratuitousness* of God's love expressed in creation. Gutiérrez compares Job's complaints to God to the questions raised up to God by poor people in Latin America. Notwithstanding the human suffering of both Job and the contemporary afflicted, Gutiérrez contends, "Job is invited to sing with Yahweh the wonders of creation – without forget-ting that the source of it all is the free and gratuitous love of God."[10]

Still, to admire God's gratuitous love and to express awe at creation does not enable humans to comprehend God's mystery – humans' ways are not God's ways.[11] For Gutiérrez, the divine mystery includes the paradox that God limits God's own power so that human beings can enjoy their freedom – and that there might consequently be a "communion" between divine and human freedom. If God were to destroy evil and those who perpetrate it, God would at the same time be destroying that human freedom God has promised.[12] The liberating God is a self-limiting God.

Human equality originates in this gratuitous love of God. All people are equally God's children; they each receive their life as a gift of pure love. Within the ongoing historical process, some of those children experience deprivations that hinder their self-

---

[9] This claim is further developed in my discussion of preferential and inclusive solidarity in the next chapter.
[10] Gutiérrez, *Power of the Poor*, p. 75.   [11] Gutiérrez, *God of Life*, p. 116.
[12] Gutiérrez, *Power of the Poor*, pp. 72–81.

consciousness as human beings. While these deprivations cannot be fully explained, they nonetheless must be understood as obstructions to full personhood. In this framework, the central theme of equality in creation is that God's love is intended at the same time for *all* people but *especially* for people who in some important sense(s) are deprived or marginalized:

[The preference for the poor] is a testament of life that is the pure gratuitousness of God's love and that consequently directs itself to the least valued. The basis of the preference is located in the central theme of biblical revelation: the gratuitousness of the love of God. Therefore there is no way to separate preference and universality, because the universality of God's love is also in God's gratuitousness.[13]

God's love is, paradoxically, universal and preferential. Such a tension runs through liberation theology, and it plays a significant role in the normative framework for socioeconomic life developed in this book. The paradox sheds light on the social context of a creation in which people suffer unequally: in order for God to reach out in free and full love to all people, God's care will be fitting to the situation in which they find themselves, socioeconomically, religiously, emotionally, politically, and so on. In Stephen Pope's helpful schema, in order for God's love to be universal, God's care is not equal. Rather, it is extended according to "need."[14]

In response to God's universal and preferential love, people are called into relationships, personal and societal, that enable all human beings to realize their dignity, equally bestowed on each by the God of life. To respond to divine love in this way is to participate with God in the *process of liberation and salvation*. For Gutiérrez (as well as most liberation theologians), creation is an integral component of that ongoing process. While "creation is regarded as the first salvific act and salvation as a new

---

[13] Gustavo Gutiérrez, *Evangelización y Opción por los Pobres* (Buenos Aires: Ediciones Paulinas, 1987), p. 53, my translation.

[14] Stephen J. Pope, "Proper and Improper Partiality and the Preferential Option for the Poor," *Theological Studies* 54/2 (1993), pp. 256–262. Here Pope rightly defends the liberationist claim that God's love for the poor is preferential but not exclusive. See my discussions of "basic needs" and solidarity, in chapters 2 and 8.

creation," both are seen within the narrative of liberation.[15]
Creation serves thus as more than an isolated, originating *event*
in which people are equally created in the image of God.[16]
Rather, creation is a dynamic movement that includes transforming nature and human relations in order "to build a society
that is more just and more worthy of humankind – as Marx
clearly saw."[17] Gutiérrez emphasizes that "history is one," and
God's movement and human response to God are intended to
work in harmony toward a communion of divine and human
love, which would entail full respect for each person's human
dignity.[18] In assisting and accompanying the poor to realize
their dignity, humans become agents in the liberation process
which moves toward the full realization of the equality before
God.

SIN – STRUCTURAL AND PERSONAL – AND EQUALITY

The very emphasis on the struggle for liberation recognizes the
need for liberation *from something*. Human sinfulness obstructs
the divine loving will from being realized on earth. Because
humans abuse the freedom granted by a self-limiting God,
"communion" among humans and between humans and God
is not realized. The *scope* of sin, like the scope of God's love,
extends to all aspects of human life and relationships, affecting
all people and all relations, personal and structural.

Gutiérrez defines sin as "a rejection of friendship with God
and, in consequence, with other human beings."[19] To sin is also

---

[15] Gutiérrez, *Theology of Liberation*, p. 101.
[16] Liberation theologians do employ the language of the *imago Dei*, but it remains less
central to their account than it is, for example, in either Catholic papal social
teaching or the Reformed framework examined above. Its employment in liberation
theology tends to reflect the urgency of social transformation. The Puebla *Final
Document* (in Eagleson and Scharper [eds.], *Puebla and Beyond*) contains this passage:
"[T]he poor merit preferential attention, whatever may be the moral or personal
situation in which they find themselves. Made in the image and likeness of God
(Genesis 1:26–28) to be his children, this image is dimmed and even defiled. That is
why God takes their defense and loves them (Matt 5:45; James 2:5)" (para. 1142; also
quoted in Pope, "Proper and Improper Partiality," p. 259).
[17] Gutiérrez, *Power of the Poor*, p. 32. See also Gutiérrez, *Theology of Liberation*, p. 101.
[18] Gutiérrez, *Theology of Liberation*, pp. xxviii–xl.
[19] Ibid., p. 226, n. 101.

"to create relationships of injustice, to make an option for oppression and against liberation."[20] All human beings, including those described as poor, are sinful – when sin is understood in either of these ways.[21] Gutiérrez defends his position against critics who claim that liberation theology glorifies "the poor" as somehow morally superior to "the non-poor." No one is free from the effects of human sinfulness in any sphere of life. In particular, Gutiérrez emphasizes that all people are in need of continuous personal transformations, requiring constant efforts at reconciliation with God and with other humans.[22]

Sin and response to sin entail *social* dimensions – a claim often associated with liberation theology. Sin can be seen as "social" in at least three related, but distinguishable, respects. First, the "social" aspects of sin disallow any merely "spiritual" interpretation of sin. That is, sin affects social, economic, and political dimensions of life, producing this-worldly situations of injustice and oppression that dehumanize people. Second, sin is "social" in the sense that neither the causes nor the consequences of sin are confinable to personal relationships. The consequences of sinful actions, whether committed by persons or groups, extend beyond the actors most directly involved. Third, groups and institutions – persons acting corporately – commit sins and can put in place *social structures* that are unjust.[23]

---

20 Gutiérrez, *Power of the Poor*, p. 9.
21 Gutiérrez, *Evangelización y Opción*, p. 37.
22 See Gustavo Gutiérrez, *We Drink from Our Own Wells: The Spiritual Journey of A People* (Maryknoll, NY: Orbis, 1984 [1983]), pp. 97–98; Gutiérrez, *Theology of Liberation*, p. xxxviii; see also Pope, "Proper and Improper Partiality," for important distinctions among cognitive, moral, divine partiality. Pope argues that the preferential option for the poor is based not in any cognitive or moral superiority of the poor, but rather as a (paradoxical) result of the universal love of God.
23 On this third point, see Gutiérrez, *Theology of Liberation*, p. 24. The systemic, socioeconomic situations of sin are certainly emphasized in liberation theology and ethics – and some critics of liberation theology fail to give liberationists sufficient credit for acknowledging the personal dimensions of sin. See, for instance, the Vatican's 1984 "Instruction on Certain Aspects of the 'Theology of Liberation'" and the 1986 "Instruction on Christian Freedom and Liberation." In an important footnote, Gutiérrez traces recent Catholic social teaching to acknowledge that social sin and structures of sin are rooted in the personal wills of people who are thus sinning against God and human beings (Gutiérrez, *Theology of Liberation*, p. 226, n. 101).

Situations of structural injustice resulting from social sin create ruptures in social solidarity. As the social analysis of liberation theology has long asserted, systems of injustice create often severe divisions among persons, groups, and classes. In simplistic models of unjust societies, groups of oppressors and oppressed are distinguished according to the former's holding of economic power and the latter's lack thereof. Society is divided along a single axis, most often in Marxist terms of class that implicitly prioritizes material forms of oppression over all others. Some writings of liberation theology have expressed this view.[24] In more complex social models, *overlapping* forms of oppression are shown to operate within societies. Many people experience two or more forms of marginalization – such as racial- and gender-based injustice – and the results are thus "multiplicative" in nature.[25] Each form of oppression is traceable to human sin.

The social disparities and divisions that result from injustice make the realization of genuine moral equality and solidarity impossible. Social, economic, and political ruptures caused by sin affect not merely nonpersons who are "othered" by forms of marginalization and oppression, but they also impact on better-off people who by their participation in personal and social sin do not fully realize "communion" with God or with others. In

---

[24] In recent liberationist literature, theologians reject such a dichotomous view, noting in particular that material forms of oppression are inextricably related to, but distinct from, other oppressions. Yet even earlier accounts, such as Ignacio Ellacuría's focus on the common good and human rights in a "divided society," emphasize various overlapping forms of oppression in societies marked not just by class structure, but by political and military violence ("Human Rights in a Divided Society," in Alfred Hennelly, S.J. and John Langan, S.J. [eds.], *Human Rights in the Americas: The Struggle for Consensus* [Washington: Georgetown University Press, 1982]). Ellacuría's El Salvador, at least through the civil war period, serves as a prime example of multi-dimensional oppression.

[25] The multiplicative nature of oppression is developed in the work of Elisabeth Schüssler Fiorenza, *But She Said: Feminist Practices of Biblical Interpretation* (Boston: Beacon Press, 1992); *Discipleship of Equals: A Feminist Critical Ekklesia-logy of Liberation* (New York: Crossroad, 1993); and Schüssler Fiorenza (ed.), *Power of Naming*. In the last, see especially Ivone Gebara, "Option for the Poor as an Option for Poor Women." See also Gutiérrez, *Power of the Poor*, p. 218, n. 14. The question of multiplicative oppression as it relates to a "cluster" of preferential options is taken up in chapter 8.

Marxist terms, such divisions are a source of alienation for all people in society. Seen in terms of contemporary economic language, social inequalities can entail serious social costs of fear, distrust, and violence.

From the liberationist interpretations of sin and creation, at least four, related implications of the equality before God emerge. First, the human dignity that God has bestowed equally on all people is blocked for everyone by the spiritual and material effects of sin. Because of the social-relational nature of everyone, the denial of the personhood of any limits the personhood of all.[26]

Second, the degree of impact of social sin is *disproportionately* felt by people (or "nonpersons") at the bottom of socioeconomic (and political) distributions. Oppressors and the oppressed each need liberation, but by definition the former group benefits from the latter's lack of social power or agency.[27] The effects of sin are thus not only distinct across socioeconomic distributions, they are also unequal.

Third, all people are sinners, equally unable to effect their own liberation or salvation without God's help. No one group, including "the poor," is morally superior to any other group; as will be discussed below, ethical orientations such as "preferential solidarity" require particular *responses* by persons and collectives to structures of injustice caused by sin.

Finally, severe political, social, or economic deprivation can block the attainment of human relationality intended for all people as children of God and as siblings to one another. A commitment to equality can thus call for praxis to overcome forms of deprivation (either relative or absolute) that dehumanize.

---

[26] The costs of structural injustice borne by well-off people as well as the marginalized will serve as an important element of my argument against excessive inequalities. See the discussion of solidarity in chapter 8.

[27] It bears repeating that oppression is a multi-faceted concept; the same person can be both oppressed and oppressor at the same time in different spheres.

THE POOR CHRIST, INTEGRAL LIBERATION, AND SOLIDARITY

Integral liberation

God's response to human suffering in a world of personal and structural sin is liberation; that liberation is most fully manifest in Jesus Christ. Borrowing from Pope Paul VI's social encyclical, *Populorum Progressio* (1967), Gutiérrez emphasizes the *"integral* liberation" willed by God and enacted in human history by Christ.

Paul VI had emphasized the *"integral* development" of peoples, rejecting mere economic growth of production in favor of "authentic," "complete," or "integral" development that would "promote the good of every man and of the whole man."[28] The key paragraphs from the papal encyclical bear inclusion:

If further development calls for the work of more and more technicians, even more necessary is the deep thought and reflection of wise men in search of a new humanism which will enable modern man to find himself anew by embracing the higher values of love and friendship, of prayer and contemplation. This is what will permit the fullness of authentic development, a development which is for each and all the transition from less human conditions to those which are more human.

Less human conditions: the lack of material necessities for those who are without the minimum essential for life, the moral deficiencies of those who are mutilated by selfishness. Less human conditions: oppressive social structures, whether due to the abuses of ownership or to the abuses of power, to the exploitation of workers or to unjust transactions. Conditions that are more human: the passage from misery toward the possession of necessities, victory over social scourges, the growth of knowledge, the acquisition of culture. Additional conditions that are more human: increased esteem for the dignity of others, the turning toward the spirit of poverty, cooperation for the common good, the will and desire for peace. Conditions that are still more human: the acknowledgment by man of supreme values, and of God their course and their finality. Conditions that, finally and

---

[28] *Populorum Progressio* (1967), para. 14, reprinted in O'Brien and Shannon (eds.), *Catholic Social Thought*.

above all, are more human: faith, a gift of God accepted by the good will of man, and unity in the charity of Christ, who calls us all to share as sons in the life of the living God, the Father of all men.[29]

Gutiérrez and other liberation theologians cite this text with approval because it recognizes the many dimensions of life involved in the process of human liberation. Further, within a complex anthropology, material needs (often unmet because of oppressive social systems) are prioritized as more basic steps – necessary but not sufficient steps – for the awareness of human dignity.[30]

Human sinfulness requires liberative action, from God and from humans, in all spheres of human life. The ministry of Jesus is seen to address these various dimensions of life (spiritual, cultural, political, social, economic); integral liberation is bound up with Christology.

Christ's life, death, resurrection

In liberation theology, God's desire and action for integral liberation are revealed in the unified narrative of Jesus Christ's life, death, and resurrection. This approach is articulated by Ignacio Ellacuría:

> [T]he resurrection points back toward the crucifixion: the Crucified One rises, and rises because he was crucified; since his life was taken away for proclaiming the Reign, he receives a new life as fulfillment of the Reign of God. Thus, the resurrection points back toward the passion, and the passion points towards Jesus' life as proclaimer of the Reign.[31]

Such a unified account rejects Christologies that emphasize Easter at the expense of overlooking the human suffering that Christ experiences in his life and death. Conversely, the kinds of suffering experienced by Jesus are not seen as final, because of

---

[29] *Populorum Progressio*, paras. 20–21.
[30] Gutiérrez, *Theology of Liberation*, pp. 98–105, esp. p. 100. See also *God of Life*, pp. 136–139. Jon Sobrino also stresses the Christological basis of integral liberation. ("Systematic Christology," in Ellacuría and Sobrino [eds.], *Mysterium Liberationis*, p. 458).
[31] Ignacio Ellacuría, S.J., "The Crucified People," in Ellacuría and Sobrino (eds.), *Mysterium Liberationis*, pp. 585–586.

the importance of hope in the resurrection. Christ's life, death, and resurrection together fit centrally into divine/human salvation history. But Christ also points beyond himself toward the realization of God's *basileia*, within history and beyond history.[32]

Further, this unified, or integrated, account of the Christ narrative corresponds to the vision of integral liberation. For just as liberation encompasses the material, social, and religious dimensions of life, so the liberating experience of Christ entails healing injuries and divisions, teaching justice, suffering and dying at the hands of injustice, and proclaiming the victory of life over all death-dealing realities.

The integrated vision of Christ's life, death, and resurrection enables liberationists to stress the relationship between Christ and the contemporary poor as God's agents within that salvation history. There is a commonality of experience and work between the crucified God and "the crucified people" – those who comprise "a vast portion of humankind . . . actually crucified by natural oppressions and especially by historical and personal oppressions."[33] The liberation effected by Christ extends to these people, not merely in the sense that full and equal respect for their dignity is intended by God, but also because they are called to exercise their own agency in personal and social transformations toward justice.

Kenosis

In liberation theology, Jesus Christ is the poor Christ who embodies the divine love and will for all humans to experience integral liberation. He is God become human, but more particularly, he is God become poor. The traditional understanding of *kenosis*, of God emptying God's self for the sake of humankind, is interpreted in this two-fold light – God becoming human and God becoming a *poor* human:

---

[32] Gutiérrez, *God of Life*, chap. 6.
[33] Ellacuría, "Crucified People," p. 580. In his essay *On Job* (p. xvi), Gutiérrez supports Ellacuría's use of this term.

> Let the same mind be in you that was in Christ Jesus,
> Who, though he was in the form of God,
>> did not regard equality with God
>> as something to be exploited,
> But emptied himself,
>> taking the form of a slave,
>> being born in human likeness,
> and being found in human form,
>> he humbled himself
>> and became obedient to the point of death –
>> even death on a cross.   (Philippians 2:5–8, NRSV)

Gutiérrez employs this biblical text to indicate Christ's response to human sinfulness in general as well as to the suffering of the neediest in particular. In his words: "The nub, the nucleus, of the biblical message, we have said, is in the relationship between God and the poor. Jesus Christ is precisely *God become poor*. This was the human life he took – a poor life."[34] Elsewhere Gutiérrez's scope is more universal in emphasis. Christ takes on the "human sinful condition and its consequences not to idealize it," but "rather because of love for and solidarity with others who suffer in it." These words illuminate God's solidarity with *all* humans. They are placed, however, within Gutiérrez's chapter advocating a *preferential* stance alongside people who suffer from material poverty.[35] This dual emphasis reflects the dialectic of universality and preference explored above, and which will figure so prominently in the ethical approach and policy implications developed in subsequent chapters. Christ surrenders equality with God to experience human inequalities from the bottom end of the social distribution, the "underside."

Christ's solidarity

The liberationist emphasis on the identification between Christ and the poor illuminates Christ's solidarity with them in their struggle. Since he has become not just human but a poor human, Christ completely embodies a personal option of solidarity. Christ's *kenosis*, or emptying of self, is the highest moral

---

[34] Gutiérrez, *Power of the Poor*, p. 13.   [35] Gutiérrez, *Theology of Liberation*, p. 172.

example of this type of voluntary, personal commitment to society's most needy people.[36] For Christ such solidarity requires the voluntary loss of "equality with God" in order to take on the human condition, and more particularly, the human condition of poverty.

Gutiérrez draws upon the life-example of Jesus in order to call those who are Christ's followers to engage in "evangelical poverty," the voluntary acceptance of the burdens and condition of poverty, not because material poverty in itself is a good. Denouncing poverty requires the solidarity of the non-poor with the poor (as well as solidarity among the poor). As Gutiérrez states, both the poor and the non-poor must continually "opt for the poor." In personal, voluntary terms, this solidarity is reflected in the lives of those who opt to take on lifestyles of "evangelical poverty."[37]

Yet another clear implication of liberation Christology is that the struggle to gain respect for the full and equal dignity of each person requires actions extending beyond personal solidarity to the rejection of systemic oppression and the promotion of policies favoring integral development. Christ as liberator provides a personal example of healing the sick and feeding the hungry. He also embodies the divine rejection of evil, including social structures caused by sin.

Thus, liberation Christology illuminates a number of aspects of the equality before God. First, Christ voluntarily gives up equality with God in order to take on an equal status with human beings. In Christ, God's equal love is extended universally – as equal love *for all people*. But the enactment of that love

---

[36] Chapter 8 contains a lengthy discussion of the various understandings of *solidarity*. Note here that the understanding of Christ as moral example of personal commitment to the poor, as set forth by Gutiérrez, bears similarity to Pope John Paul II's account of solidarity as a *virtue* in his encyclical *Sollicitudo Rei Socialis* (1987), para. 40 (reprinted in O'Brien and Shannon [eds.], *Catholic Social Thought*) – also discussed below.

[37] See Gutiérrez, *Theology of Liberation*, pp. 162–173 and Gutiérrez, "Option for the Poor," in Ellacuría and Sobrino (eds.), *Mysterium Liberationis*. For an insightful and important distinction between this "evangelical" dimension of the option for the poor and the "general" option for the poor to which all Christians are called, see Stephen J. Pope, "The 'Preferential Option for the Poor': An Ethic for 'Saints and Heroes'?," *Irish Theological Quarterly* 59/3 (1993), discussed in chapter 8.

takes place in the actual contexts in which persons and groups disproportionately experience the consequences of evil. God's preferential solidarity is expressed in Christ when Christ becomes a materially poor human. The integral liberation Christ comes to effect seeks respect for the full and thus equal humanity of all; this requires that moral priority, without exclusivity, be given to providing for the basic necessities of all. All people, including the poor, can be agents at the various levels of overcoming sin and working for liberation. The discussion of Christology and integral liberation emphasizes that the principal agency is divine, not human. Yet these Christological emphases serve as a moral call for Christians to engage in transforming actions in all aspects of life – including the social and economic.

ESCHATOLOGY AND SOCIAL TRANSFORMATION: REALIZING FULL AND EQUAL PERSONHOOD

The eschatological dimensions of liberation have been suggested in the theological and Christological themes already discussed. By more explicit focus on the eschatological themes, the implications for social transformation and public policy can be brought into fuller view.

The various dimensions of the reign of God vis-à-vis human history, as understood in liberation theology, are contained in this negatively stated (and lengthy) paragraph by Ellacuría:

The Reign of God is immune to a whole series of perilous distortions. It is impervious to a dualism of (earthly) Reign and (heavenly) God, such that those who cultivate the world and history would be doing something merely positivistic, while those who devote themselves to God would be doing something transcendent, spiritual, and supernatural. It rejects an identification of the Reign of God with the church, especially with the institutional church, which would imply both an escape from the world into the church, and an impoverishment of the Christian message and mission that would culminate in a worldly church – a secularization of the church by way of a conformation of its institutional aspect to secularistic values of domination and wealth, and by subordinating to it something greater than it by far, the Reign of God. It rejects a manipulation of God, a taking of the name of God in vain in support of injustice, by insisting that that name and reality are properly invoked in the historical signs of justice, fraternity, freedom, a preferential option for the poor, love, mercy, and so on, and that without these it is vain to speak of a salvific presence of God in history.[38]

Ellacuría states well the pitfalls that liberationists have attempted to avoid. It is worth exploring, in more positive fashion, how the reign or *basileia* of God does function in liberation theology.

For Gutiérrez and the liberation theologians, the proper movement of history is toward the full realization of God's *basileia*. God is the primary actor in this movement; all of creation and all of salvation history result from God's gratuitous love. The *basileia* serves as a goal and a vision toward which people strive as God's agents in the effort to overcome all aspects of sin. Full integral liberation will only occur when God's *basileia* is reached.

Gutiérrez is clear that human history cannot contain the whole of God's mysterious, transcendent, divine reality; while rejecting clean distinctions between natural and supernatural orders, he is also clear in denying that the *basileia* will be fully realized *within* human history or as a result of human efforts. That being said, however, the liberationist vision stresses the undeniable, inextricable relationship between the alleviation of human suffering that obstructs full and equal personhood and the realization of God's *basileia*, on earth as well as in heaven.

As Gutiérrez emphasizes, liberation always entails a transcendent element. Liberation does not just require the overcoming of socioeconomic structures of injustice or the transformation of oneself personally; the depth of sin always requires God's gratuitous action, "the unmerited redemptive effort of the Lord." The struggle toward the *basileia*, even if it

---

[38] Ignacio Ellacuría, "Aporte de la Teología de la Liberación a las Religiones Abrahámicas en la Superación del Individualismo y del Positivismo," manuscript of an address to the Congress of Abrahamic Religions held at Córdoba, Spain, in February 1987. Quoted in Jon Sobrino, "Central Position of the Reign of God in Liberation Theology," in Ellacuría and Jon Sobrino (eds.), *Mysterium Liberationis*, p. 355.

were to consist of wholehearted, committed human work, depends ultimately on God's action to eradicate sin.[39]

In this liberationist eschatological view, creation is an element in the process of moving toward God's *basileia*. Human beings attain their personhood as salvation history moves closer to this vision. Actions to overcome dehumanizing deprivations and structures of marginalization in themselves reflect movement towards the new creation in which the "imago dei" is made more evident; a continual re-creation of people takes place when they work for a more just and good society.[40]

Jesus Christ is seen as the initiator of God's *basileia* and as the embodiment or incarnation of God's liberating presence amidst structures resulting from sinfulness. Christ is, in Jon Sobrino's terminology, "the Absolute Mediator of the Reign of God," who both in his "person" and in his "praxis" reflects the coming of God's reign, "the ultimate will of God for this world."[41] In terms of the relationship between the Christ narrative and integral liberation, Christ initiates[42] the work of liberation that will be made complete only in the realization of the *eschaton*. Christ's works of healing and feeding are efforts on behalf of the *basileia*; his teachings describe God's reign; his suffering and death, in liberationist terms, occur at the hands of injustice of the anti-reign; and his resurrection signals hope of

[39] Gutiérrez, *Theology of Liberation*, pp. xxxviii–xxxix.

[40] For instance, Ellacuría puts it this way: "Hence, to connect creation and resurrection is false from a Christian viewpoint, whatever the understanding of the original 'image and likeness,' the historic process of death and resurrection. Every process in history is a creation of the future and not merely a renewal of the past. The fallen human is not restored, but rather the new human is built up . . ." ("Crucified People," p. 585).

[41] In Sobrino's words: "Jesus himself asserts this relationship between the Reign of God and his person. At times his assertion is explicit: 'If it is by the Spirit of God that I expel demons, then the reign of God has overtaken you' (Matt. 12:28 and par.). At other times he posits this relationship in an implicit but real way: in various of the actions of his praxis which can and should be interpreted as signs of the coming of the Reign on behalf of the poor (his miracles, his exorcisms, the welcome he extends to the weak and oppressed); in his struggle with the anti-Reign (controversies, denunciations, exposé of oppressors); or in his celebration of the presence of the Reign (meals)" ("Systematic Christology," p. 441).

[42] Of course, I employ the term "initiates" not in a chronological sense, since God is seen to work in the Hebrew Bible (most paradigmatically for liberation theology, in the Exodus) to effect achievements of human/divine liberation. Jesus is initiator of the reign in liberation theology as the definitive response of God to human suffering.

overcoming all of the forces of death which hinder the arrival of God's *basileia* on earth and beyond it.

Most of these dimensions of the relation of Christology to eschatology are illuminated in an often-quoted text in liberation theology, Matthew 25:31–45. This is the parable of the Great Judgment, in which Jesus praises and rewards those who served "the least of these who are members of my family" (v. 40, NRSV), identifying himself with these very people who suffer from some sort of basic deprivation. Gutiérrez asserts that Jesus, by favoring the "least of these," draws disfavor from those in authority – those at whose hands Jesus dies.[43] Gutiérrez employs this passage, and others, to illuminate the relationship of God's love (in Christ) and the care of neighbor as well as the moral priority of helping those lacking basic necessities. At the same time, he notes that this passage indicates not just God's care for the needy, but also the universal scope of God's love. The Christ who reveals the universality and integral quality of God's love not only suffers with the poor, but invites all people into the drama of social struggle for the *basileia*.

These eschatological themes illuminate important aspects of the relation of the moral-theological understanding of equality and the existence of the kind of socioeconomic inequalities that dehumanize. Because God is a God for whom "the last shall be first," humans are called to struggle in contemporary situations on behalf of the least of these, even though such justice-work involves personal risks. The *basileia* of God would include the full and equal respect for the dignity of each person. In order to proceed from actual realities towards the eschatological goal, a preferential care for those in greatest need is required. The kind of "preference" that is called for, by God and consequently by human actors on personal and policy levels, is that which promotes the full inclusion of all people within society. The call is for preferences that move towards, and not away from, the universality of divine love and, consequently, towards inclusive participation in various dimensions of human society.

---

[43] Gutiérrez, *Theology of Liberation*, pp. 85, 98, 112, 132.

GUTIÉRREZ, INEQUALITY, AND "EQUALITY OF WHAT?"

As a way of drawing together the various insights of Gutiérrez's liberationist account of equality, it will be helpful to return to some of the terminology of equality developed in chapter 2. The liberationist account, most importantly, offers no straight-forward answer to the question, "Equality of what?" It does entail the claim that all people are equally bestowed by God with human dignity – no human should be treated as a nonperson, one without dignity. This is indeed the most central point of the liberationist vision. Yet "equality of dignity" requires further specification in order to address socioeconomic life. The *scope* of equality in liberation theology is, as in most modern philosophical accounts of equality, universal. But the crucial *preferential* component of the liberationist account can be understood by broaching not the question of scope, but rather by considering the *space* of moral and social attention. Like Amartya Sen's call for an equality of basic capability, the liberationist position prioritizes the provision of basic function-ings over the acquisition of more "luxurious" products, in order that all people can experience a sense of stake in their societies.[44] Such an approach is preferential to those lacking basic (often material) goods and services, even while it retains a universal commitment to the equality of all. Indeed, the prefer-ential orientation is intended to create societies in which the social effects of moral equality are more fully enacted.

Like the approach of Michael Walzer, the liberationist account of equality is "complex."[45] The emphasis on integral liberation reflects a commitment to the provision of multiple social goods in multiple *spheres* of life. Partially in response to the 1984 and 1986 Vatican "Instructions," recent liberationist writ-ings have carefully stated the centrality of socioeconomic dimensions without making them lexically prior to, or determi-nistic of, cultural, religious, political, or other dimensions. (Still, most basic needs require provision of one or more socio-

---

[44] The discussion of the relation of basic capability, functionings, and basic social goods is further taken up in chapters 8 and 9.
[45] Walzer, *Spheres of Justice*.

economic goods.) Attention to the whole person encompasses these various spheres of life; integral liberation is in this sense "complex."

Equality before God is a claim about one's moral status; it is not a claim advocating sameness in any moral, cultural, or social sense. The liberationist account rejects oppression, marginalization, and deprivation, but not differences.[46] Particular attributes should help to reflect one's personhood, but too often in actual societies these attributes lead to marginalization or oppression for those who do not hold significant social position, including "the unemployed, the poor, the blind, the crippled, public sinners, Ayacuchan Indians, landless peasants, populations looking for shelter"[47] – or for women who can be "doubly oppressed."[48] Equality as a regulative idea calls for, rather than rejects, the distinctive expression of personhood amidst differences.

ON DRAWING TOGETHER NIEBUHR AND GUTIÉRREZ

Chapters 6 and 7 have traced two theological accounts of the equality before God. While these examinations have covered a wide range of theological issues (creation, sin, redemption, *inter alia*), the accounts have prepared the way for the normative approach to economic disparities and well-being, which is developed in the following chapter. The two distinct theological accounts have been explored in parallel fashion. Thus far, very little explicit comparison has been included. As much as possible, each account has been examined critically on its own terms as a respective coherent whole.[49] At this point, some

---

[46] As discussed in chapter 2, "difference" must not itself be formulated in a way that essentializes certain attributes (for instance, of women or of men) as prior to people's social formation. To avoid this problem, I follow Schüssler Fiorenza's call to speak of differences, in the plural (*Discipleship of Equals*, esp. p. 370).

[47] Gutiérrez, *God of Life*, p. 117.

[48] Gutiérrez, *Power of the Poor*, p. 137.

[49] I do not mean to deny the methodological difficulty of drawing on multiple resources, even from within "the Christian tradition," and even if my intention is not explicit comparison. A number of methodological points are at issue. Perhaps most significant, as I have attempted to do, I must acknowledge that the act of comparison (or of contrast) involves not merely two objects, but also the subject undertaking the

further theological lessons and even common insights can be drawn. The insights drawn in this section will be revisited and expanded in the next chapter.

Theocentric approaches

Gutiérrez and Niebuhr each begin their theological and ethical systems with the claim that God is the central actor within history and in all of reality. Critical deliberation about personal and social living begins with reflection on the relationship of God to creation, and more specifically, on the divine's relation to each human. Both Gutiérrez's understanding of "theology as critical reflection on praxis" and Niebuhr's notion of offering a "theology of the present moment"[50] entail understanding and acting within the current human situation vis-à-vis belief in a transcendent and immanent God.

In both frameworks, the God–human relationship sets a theocentric context for human relations. The will of the God of life is fully realized when humans, in their complex (and multi-dimensional) relationships to one another, acknowledge one another as possessing dignity bestowed by God. This dignity can be realized only within just structures and relations that

enterprise. I thus identified in chapter 5 my own social location, because surely the accounts of equality in Niebuhr and Gutiérrez involve my own constructive concerns and biases. As Lee Yearley has helpfully described, the act of comparison involves employing the "analogical imagination," seeking similarities in differences and differences in similarities. In a methodological discussion of his own work comparing Mencius and Aquinas on their theories of the virtues, Yearley notes that the analogical imagination requires the construction of a terrain on which comparison can be made. To acknowledge this constructive dimension of my project is not to deny that the objects being traced, and compared, are in fact the ideas of Niebuhr and Gutiérrez. See Lee H. Yearley, *Mencius and Aquinas: Theories of Virtue and Conceptions of Courage* (Albany: SUNY Press, 1990), esp. pp. 196–203.

A more explicit (and less methodologically self-conscious) comparison of theological ethics that is relevant to the questions of this study is McCann, *Christian Realism and Liberation Theology.* This work examines relationships between, and compares the respective merits of, liberation theology and the thought of Reinhold Niebuhr.

50 Niebuhr, "Relation of Christianity and Democracy," p. 147: "A Christianity which centers in such faith must always be a religion and a politics of the present moment." See also Niebuhr, "Theology in a Time of Disillusionment," in Johnson (ed.), *Theology, History, and Culture*, p. 115.

recognize the social, interdependent nature of all human beings as children of God.

Niebuhr is more willing than Gutiérrez to acknowledge God's presence in actions and structures that cause human suffering. While Gutiérrez focuses on God's ongoing liberative role within, and beyond, history, Niebuhr's emphasis on God's sovereignty includes the strong view that God is present in the very structures of suffering, acting despite and contrary to those who perpetuate oppression or injustice. Yet Niebuhr alongside Gutiérrez claims that God as God of life is in solidarity with all humans, especially with humans in their various forms of suffering. This solidarity is manifested most clearly in the life and consequent death of Jesus Christ. These theological accounts share the view that equality *before God* is also equality *in creation* and *among humans*; equality and social solidarity are inextricably linked.

Sin

For both Niebuhr and Gutiérrez, sin obstructs humans from playing their part in realizing God's will within creation, which entails God's bestowal of full moral equality on all people. While they certainly acknowledge specific acts of sin, Niebuhr and Gutiérrez each emphasize that sin is a condition in which persons and groups are not able to accord their actions with God's will. The suffering that results from such sin carries intended and unintended consequences that affect all humans, but that impact on some persons disproportionately.

Gutiérrez emphasizes more than Niebuhr God's self-limitation that grants the "room" for humans to act in their own freedom, alienating others (and themselves) as a consequence. Niebuhr's strong view of God's sovereignty leads him to focus on the ways in which God is always acting for good despite human actions. Neither is particularly interested in emphasizing ontological questions about sin's origin or status. They accept, rather, that human sinfulness is a reality that must be overcome, a reality which God is overcoming, sometimes with cooperation from humans, and often without it.

The liberationists are often accused of not taking the sinfulness of all people – what Niebuhr treats as equality in sin – with adequate seriousness. The dichotomy between "oppressor" and "oppressed," while often important for its rhetorical power, does not account for the various and complex ways in which most people, to differing extents, are both oppressor and oppressed. Gutiérrez does not deny this fact, nor the understanding that all, including those oppressed in significant ways, are equal in sin. "The poor are also sinners." The preferential option for the poor, contrary to some of its critics, does not derive from any claims about the "sinlessness" of those who are poor.

At the same time, Gutiérrez is more forthright in emphasizing "class struggle" as a result of and response to human sinfulness. In particular, especially in his earlier works, human sin is often manifested in group form – especially in class conflict described along predominantly Marxist lines. With the constructive critiques of feminist theology and with three decades to develop and nuance his position, Gutiérrez has since offered a fuller vision of oppression and social struggle that incorporates the complex dimensions of human sin and the hope of liberation in Christ.

Both Niebuhr and Gutiérrez account for personal and social sinfulness. While the Reformed tradition can be given less credit than the liberationists for emphasizing structural forms of sin, and while conversely liberationists are criticized for not properly attending to personal sin, the views of Gutiérrez and Niebuhr bear strong similarities. For his part, Gutiérrez defends his position about the social nature of sin by acknowledging that accountability (and culpability) for social structures is held by particular human beings. Niebuhr stresses that the universality of sin affects all persons and groups; he approvingly refers to Augustine's emphasis on the "social sinfulness of mankind."[51] Sin as "social" highlights the ways in which the personal and structural dimensions of sin are interrelated.

The Reformed tradition in which Niebuhr stands offers a

---

[51] Niebuhr, *Christ and Culture*, p. 212.

fuller account of the depth of human sin within every human person and institution, including those fervently struggling for justice. As a consequence, Niebuhr's hopefulness for human-enacted social transformation is more tempered than Gutiér-rez's (although Gutiérrez is more cautious in his expectation than is often acknowledged by his critics). Niebuhr stresses the conviction that any human attempts to actualize justice will lead to further injustices – yet this is no cause for complacency. Niebuhr concurs with Gutiérrez that despite sin and in constant opposition to sin, humans are called to serve as agents of God's will on earth. Inequalities and injustices that obstruct the realization of human dignity are the result of sinful structures and actions; transformation towards God's *basileia* entails over-coming them.

Redemption, Christ, and the church

For both Gutiérrez and Niebuhr, Jesus Christ reflects in a definitive way God's solidarity with humankind and God's will for creation. Those visions differ in emphases. Yet it is important to acknowledge a crucial aspect in which their Christologies are similar. They each offer an *integrated* narrative in which the life, death, and resurrection aspects of Christology play an impor-tant part. More specifically, each denounces visions that (1) stress only Christ's life as a moral example and teacher; (2) understand Christ's crucifixion narrowly as legalistic atone-ment for human sin; or (3) emphasize Christ's victory over death without paying proper heed to the present human condition and its various death-dealing forms. The hope each theologian sees in the Christ narrative is one that takes full account of and addresses the present human condition. Redemption in Christ is universal in scope and ranges over all spheres of life.

To be sure, Gutiérrez's theology emphasizes the "poor Christ" or "the Christ of the poor" in language not present in Niebuhr's theology. Christ expresses and reveals God's soli-darity with humankind in particular by being and living in solidarity with those marginalized within the Roman empire and Palestinian society. There is a relationship, in Ellacuría's words appropriated by Gutiérrez, between the crucified God and the crucified people.

Yet as was suggested in chapter 6, Niebuhr himself employs related language about the crucified God as victim of one severe form of conflict (war), and even in one instance speaks of the working class as the *crucified* class, relating the lower class explicitly to Christ.[52] In human suffering, most pronounced in war, God is present in solidarity with the victims. And the definitive answer to that suffering is in the cross of Christ, by which God takes that suffering onto God's own self.

Within their respective theologies, Gutiérrez and Niebuhr see Christ's relevance and reach within and beyond the Christian church. God's *basileia* is being realized within and beyond history, and churches are one sign and site of that transformation. In fact, both have committed significant energies to understanding the role of the church within human societies and creation as a whole. But for Gutiérrez, another principal site is "the poor," all those who suffer within the present socioeconomic and political order. The option for the poor is made first by God, and should be made by the church, but it is also relevant to Christians in their justice work beyond the walls and ministries of the church. Further (as will be developed below), the option for the poor has implications for all of society, and it can be appropriated and applied in formulating public discourse and policy debate. While Niebuhr is not as explicit about the relation of God's *basileia* and the poor, he is concerned that the community gathered in Christ's name be not confused with the universal commonwealth and he expresses a call for responsible though realistic engagement in social transformation. For Niebuhr and Gutiérrez, God is God

---

[52] Richard R. Niebuhr, in his foreword to Johnson (ed.), *Theology, History, and Culture*, writes the following: "In those early years of the 1930s, I sensed though scarcely comprehended my father's increasing apprehension at what he described as the 'class crucifixion' (not a 'class struggle as Marx believed,' he noted, 'but . . . a class crucifixion as Christ demonstrated') then taking place in our unhappy country and at the growing social and political turmoil he had personally witnessed in Germany as well as at the ominous significance of the Japanese army's occupation of Manchuria" (p. viii).

of all and does work of social transformation beyond all finite institutions, including the church.

Transforming societies

These two accounts of the equality before God share in common the call to transform all dimensions of human life, including the socioeconomic order. God creates and recreates all humans; they are therefore sacred and equals as brothers and sisters in creation, called to live in solidarity with their siblings. Fidelity to the God of life, the God for whom the last shall be first, demands work within finite human structures to realize more fully God's rule "on earth as it is in heaven." Humans have a responsibility to God for their neighbors, to remove or alter structures which make people experience a condition that is less than human and to strive in their own lives to model moral equality in their relationships. H. Richard Niebuhr describes the fitting attitude for social transformation as a "patience that is full of hope based on faith,"[53] while Gutiérrez refers to the "mobilizing and liberating" function of an "active hope."[54] In Niebuhrian language, excessive powers in various spheres of life must be balanced and therefore relativized, for only God – before whom all humans are equal – is absolute. While in practice Gutiérrez would place more emphasis on specific acts of human engagement for justice, Gutiérrez and Niebuhr would concur on the central point of the need to overcome idolatry by treating no persons as lords – or as slaves. The various spheres of life in society should operate in a way that allows all people to be treated as equals before God and amongst each other.

Finally, equality before God provides a transformative impetus in situations of injustice or incomplete justice. Equality is more than a theological dogma; it is a commitment that must be lived out. When deprivations or excessive inequalities

---

[53] H. Richard Niebuhr, "Grace of Doing Nothing," p. 380.
[54] Gutiérrez, *Theology of Liberation*, pp. 123–126. Gutiérrez traces his account of hope in critical conversation with Jürgen Moltmann's *Theology of Hope: On the Ground and the Implications of a Christian Eschatology* (London: SCM Press, 1967 [1965]).

prevent the achievement of solidarity and the actual operation of moral equality, God acts to transform societies towards justice; human beings are called to work together as equals with one another, exercising their own agency as agents of a loving, life-giving God.

CHAPTER 8

Solidarity, selfhood, and social goods

INTRODUCTION

A Christian ethical approach to inequality is built upon the theological commitment to the equality of all people before God. Niebuhr and Gutiérrez provide theological and moral arguments for how excessive inequalities obstruct the conditions that guarantee moral equality. How might the basic contours of a Christian ethical approach draw upon, and be expanded by, insights from political philosophy and social theory?

Amartya Sen's framework of human capability and functionings offers significant resources for sharpening a Christian ethical approach to socioeconomic life, including inequality. Yet Christian ethicists have paid little in-depth, direct attention to Sen's work.[1] And relatively few engagements between Christian ethics and "human development" or "basic needs" have been offered.[2] Theologians and ethicists have long been in conversation with John Rawls's theory of justice – and more recently, his accounts of political liberalism – but these discussions have not focused on questions of inequality.[3] Likewise, the wide-ranging

[1] One explicit discussion of Amartya Sen's work in religious ethics was provided in a panel session: "A Nobel Moment for Ethics and Economics: Amartya Sen's Thought and Religious Ethics," 1999 American Academy of Religion, Religion and the Social Sciences section, November 22, 1999. Panelists included Barbara Hilkert Andolsen, Harlan Beckley, Douglas A. Hicks, David Hollenbach, S.J., and Ellen Ott Marshall.

[2] One treatment of "basic needs" in Christian ethics is Drew Christiansen, S.J., "Basic Needs: Criterion for Development," in Alfred Hennelly, S.J. and John Langan, S.J. (eds.), *Human Rights in the Americas: The Struggle for Consensus* (Washington: Georgetown University Press, 1982).

[3] The most prominent treatment of Rawls's theory of justice in Christian social ethics is

work of Michael Walzer has gained some attention in religious ethics; his writings could be drawn on to expand Christian ethical approaches to disparities in various spheres of life.[4]

This chapter further develops a Christian ethical approach to inequality within a wider context of socioeconomic life. Toward the end of expanding a Christian approach to issues of equality and inequality, three concepts are analyzed in considerable detail: solidarity, selfhood, and social goods. The analysis extends the insights developed by Niebuhr and Gutiérrez – and puts them into conversation with perspectives from political philosophy and approaches to economic development.

SOLIDARITY

Preferential solidarity and inclusive solidarity

The Reformed and the liberationist accounts of equality reflect the universal scope of God's love for human beings within creation. At the same time, most explicitly in liberation theology, God's care is seen as preferential towards those in the greatest need – or variety of needs. A social ethic consistent with these accounts of the equality before God needs to reflect both dimensions of God's love: *universality* and *preference*. A concept that helps to show the tension and the interrelationship between universal inclusiveness and preferential options – and which thus merits close attention – is that of *solidarity*.

Harlan Beckley, "A Christian Affirmation of Justice as Fairness – Part I," *Journal of Religious Ethics* 13 (fall 1985): 210–242; and Beckley, "A Christian Affirmation of Justice as Fairness – Part II," *Journal of Religious Ethics* 14 (fall 1986). A rebuttal to Beckley's argument is Timothy P. Jackson, "To Bedlam and Part Way Back: John Rawls and Christian Justice" *Faith and Philosophy* 4 (1991). An important discussion of "Religion and Rawlsian Liberalism," with essays by Paul J. Weithman, Timothy P. Jackson, David Hollenbach, S.J., and John Langan, S.J., is contained in *Journal of Religious Ethics* 22/1 (fall 1994).

[4] The significance of many aspects of Walzer's writings for religious ethics are considered by Tyler T. Roberts, "Michael Walzer and the Critical Connections"; Elizabeth M. Bounds, "Conflicting Harmonies: Michael Walzer's Vision of Community"; Glen Stassen, "Michael Walzer's Situated Justice"; with Michael Walzer's commentary, "Shared Meaning in a Poly-Ethnic Democratic Setting: A Response," edited by Glen Stassen in "FOCUS: Walzer on Justice, Community, and Social Criticism," in *Journal of Religious Ethics* 22/2 (fall 1994).

From its earliest uses the concept of solidarity has indicated a level of cohesion and social cooperation within a group of people.[5] A perennial issue for the "meaning" of solidarity has been the *scope* of persons included within its purview: does solidarity extend merely to some subgroup who share common interests or attributes within a society, or does it include all members of society (or even all human beings)? Even in nineteenth-century France, J. E. S. Hayward points out in a classic article, solidarity was used disparately, and its employment by different people for distinct ends contributed to the ambiguity of its "meanings." Importantly, the groups that tended to employ the concept in France were those working for *unity within the working classes, especially trade unions and cooperatives.* The term was later adopted by French middle-class politicians as well as by sociologists in order to emphasize the need for *collective cooperation on the part of all persons and groups of society* to solve the complex social problems in a rapidly industrializing age.[6]

These two poles of solidarity – emphasis on the needs of the socially marginalized and the need for society-wide cohesion and cooperation – remain in constructive tension within current usage of solidarity, particularly in Christian social ethics. Drew Christiansen, in his important 1984 article, distinguishes between a number of uses of solidarity, including the "universalistic solidarity of recent magisterial teachings" and the "solidarity with the poor" of liberation theology. While Christiansen insightfully distinguishes between the universal and the preferential dimensions of solidarity, he inaccurately portrays liberation theology as merely "partisan":

For liberation theology, solidarity is a partisan act. It means taking the side of the poor in their liberation from oppression. In this sense solidarity re-enforces the divisions of history. The justification of this, of course, is an eschatology of reversal. By divine favor the poor are

---

[5] Usage of "solidarity" can be traced back as far as Roman times, when it was used in the context of economic cooperation among groups of creditors and among groups of debtors. See J. E. S. Hayward, "Solidarity: The Social History of an Idea in Nineteenth Century France," *International Review of Social History* 4/2 (1959).

[6] Hayward, "Solidarity"; Matthew L. Lamb, "Solidarity," in Judith A. Dwyer (ed.), *New Dictionary of Catholic Social Thought* (Collegeville, MN: Liturgical Press, 1994).

on the right side; by eschatological justice "the lowly are exalted." Liberation solidarity differs from the solidarity of the postconciliar doctrine, therefore, in that it is exclusive. Solidarity does not mean coming together, but going over to the other side.[7]

As chapter 7 asserted, liberation theology is not ultimately exclusive, but inclusive. Gutiérrez's account of equality before God and in society does strive for precisely the "coming together" of inclusiveness. The eschatology in question is not one "of reversal," but rather of working toward God's *basileia* in which the dignity of all people as equals is fully realized.

Yet surely Christiansen is right about liberation theology when it is seen in terms of present-day ethical responses, at personal, collective, and policy levels – responses which indeed call for preferential treatment for marginalized people. In order to realize moral equality, preferential care is required in the space of various, basic social functionings.

Before considering further these two dimensions of solidarity – inclusiveness and preference – some more general points about the concept of solidarity should be raised. While the normative approach constructed herein posits an integral relation between solidarity and equality, solidarity as a concept would not on its own *require* an egalitarian social ethic or structure. Solidarity as a quality of social cohesion and sense of unity is arguably compatible with traditional and/or hierarchical social models. A Christian ethical approach, building on Niebuhr and Gutiérrez, rejects non-egalitarian social structures as incompatible with theocentric understandings of selfhood and the social order. In an important sense, the equality before God is interpreted as theologically and normatively prior to solidarity. The concept, then, is more fully described as "egalitarian solidarity."[8]

José Míguez Bonino suggests six aspects of solidarity that illuminate the development of this concept for socioeconomic

---

[7] Christiansen, "On Relative Equality," p. 671.

[8] I am indebted to Gene Outka for pointing out that solidarity does not logically imply or require an egalitarian society. Hierarchical or caste-based societies can arguably possess a significant degree of social cohesion and sense of interdependence. See also Albert Weale, "Equality, Social Solidarity, and the Welfare State," *Ethics* 100 (April 1990), p. 477.

relations. First, solidarity must be contextual, taking full account of the "peculiar circumstances of the present historical moment." Second, solidarity must be "lived in the conflictive situations created by the struggle of the poor against injustice, exploitation, and alienation" and must therefore avoid "consensus models, which presuppose the existence of a fundamentally just situation." Third, solidarity must be rooted theologically in a dynamic understanding of human nature that draws not merely on creation but on Christological and eschatological themes as well. Fourth, solidarity holds in tension a "committed partiality" and the "universal intention of the solidarity of love." Fifth, this approach must be considered one of "'the greater good' as distinguished from that of 'the lesser evil'." This position contends that love is more ultimate than, and conceptually prior to, sin and social conflict. Finally, Míguez Bonino suggests that eschatology is *both personal and social* and that it is, ultimately, not divisive but inclusive.[9]

Solidarity thus can be seen to refer to a quality of social relations within some population in which all people experience a genuine sense of stake in the ongoing life of that collective. The liberationists helpfully suggest that in order for all people to hold such a stake, preferential attention must be given to those who presently experience forms of deprivation, marginalization and/or oppression. Solidarity can be understood as both a *descriptive* quality of actual societies and as a *normative* orientation, on the part of individuals, collectives, and policymakers toward achieving such a (descriptive) social reality.[10]

---

9 José Míguez Bonino, "Love and Social Transformation in Liberation Theology," in Marc H. Ellis and Otto Maduro (eds.), *The Future of Liberation Theology: Essays in Honor of Gustavo Gutiérrez* (Maryknoll, NY: Orbis, 1989).

10 In his employment of "solidarity" as a moral norm, Pope John Paul II stresses solidarity as a *virtue*. In *Sollicitudo Rei Socialis* (1987; in O'Brien and Shannon [eds.], *Catholic Social Thought*), "solidarity is the correct moral response to the fact of interdependence" (Donal Dorr, "Solidarity and Integral Human Development," in Gregory Baum and Robert Ellsberg [eds.], *The Logic of Solidarity: Commentaries on Pope John Paul II's Encyclical "On Social Concern"* [Maryknoll, NY: Orbis, 1989], p. 148; see also Robert Ellsberg, introduction to *Logic of Solidarity*, p. xi). The moral response springs from the *virtue* of solidarity, which impacts on people in their personal and public relationships; it then should extend to the actions of entire nations in an increasingly "globalized" world. Thus the Pope's account, drawing from Paul VI's and liberationists' critical perspectives on unequal development, suggests solidarity's

With these general understandings of solidarity in mind, it is now possible to explore in more detail both the "inclusive" and "preferential" dimensions of solidarity.

Solidarity, inclusiveness, and the common good

Stephen Pope articulates how partiality can contribute to the more ideal principle of "inclusiveness."

As a general rule it can be said that partiality is justifiable when it contributes to inclusiveness, a value which pertains to our cognitive and affective comprehension, to our recognition of the dignity of every human being, and to our acknowledgement of the comprehensiveness of God's love and of the solicitude for the needy which flows from that love . . . [T]he preferential option appeals to an *expansion* rather than *contraction* of love and wisdom.[11]

Consequently, partiality on the part of human actors and institutions is called for only when it enables, rather than obstructs, marginalized people from participating more widely within their respective communities and societies.

Thus in abstract terms, liberationists do not object to employing language of the "common good," since such language claims to be inclusive. At the same time, liberationists warn against accepting any "false universalism" which does not prioritize the needs of the poor. There are various ways in which to make "universal" claims, including ones about a good held in common – but not all square with a normative vision of egalitarian solidarity.[12]

The liberationist concern about language of the "common good" is carefully articulated by Ignacio Ellacuría in his 1982

relevance for just public policies – in domestic and international arenas. Yet as Dorr argues, the Pope's account of the "partisan" aspect of solidarity is "somewhat bland," since he offers no strong social analysis and less theological emphasis than the liberationists do on the role of the poor in God's liberation (Dorr, "Solidarity," p. 149).

[11] Pope, "Proper and Improper Partiality," p. 265.

[12] Pope (ibid., p. 249, n. 34) quotes Archbishop Oscar Romero on this point. A "false universalism" could treat all people impartially but focus on the wrong "space." For instance, when the "right to private property" is defended as the most fundamental human right, by definition the interests of property holders are disproportionately protected. No attention would be given in an extreme case to those without property.

article, "Human Rights in a Divided Society." Ellacuría notes a number of "commendable" aspects of language of the common good. He argues first that "there is no particular good without the common good," an assertion that rejects actions of privileged people who claim for their own possession goods that should belong to all. Second, he argues that the common good, properly understood, is more than the mere sum of private interests. Against *laissez-faire* political and economic policies, he suggests that some form of "social communitarianism" is required to satisfy the common good. Finally, Ellacuría asserts that "the common good is basically a union of structural conditions" that a society as a whole must provide for its citizens.[13] On each of these points the language of common good serves to promote a society of egalitarian solidarity in which all people could have a genuine sense of stake.

Yet Ellacuría goes on to express deep suspicion regarding the appropriateness of common good language for a divided, violent society, such as the El Salvador in which he was martyred. Within conflictive historical contexts, the common good can be invoked by powerful subgroups of the population in order to further their own interests. Often, that which is claimed to be the common good "is neither good nor common."[14]

In "historicizing" the common good, Ellacuría stresses that it is a goal, a vision, toward which real societies must move. The common good is an eschatological end toward which humans imperfectly strive with their actions and human *teloi*.

Intentions and goals [such as the common good] count for little in history; the truth of what is intended or proposed is the results obtained, the historical actions . . . More concretely, the true picture of a historical process is not found in the actual results which should have been the common good, nor still less is it found in the minorities which appropriate those results for themselves.[15]

Ellacuría goes on to accept a more eschatological interpretation of the common good as a "utopian" goal with clear implications for socioeconomic and political struggles within history.

---

[13] Ellacuría, "Human Rights," pp. 55–56.
[14] Ibid., p. 63.　　[15] Ibid., pp. 62–63.

The common good, therefore, would involve the process which would lead a divided society toward the creation of a true society, where contradictory social interests would not exist. The common good would thus function as a utopia which would recognize the ideological disguise of the common good as currently propounded, as well as the real though concealed denial of the common good. After this, it would become a process with actual stages, leading to a common good which would become a historical reality.[16]

The liberationist perspective, then, holds in tension the eschatological perspective of the common good and the historical forms of oppression that require solidarity-oriented actions in the here and now.[17] A goal like the common good must not be confused with socioeconomic realities within history that require *preferential options* at personal, collective, and public policy levels. The preferential aspects of solidarity now merit fuller examination.

Preferential solidarity and options for the poor

The notion of a "preferential option for the poor" is, of course, a central theological and ethical tenet of liberation theology. Reflecting the emergence of the liberationist movement, the Second General Conference of Latin American Bishops (held in Medellín, Colombia, in 1968) includes a "Document on the Poverty of the Church." This text explicitly recognizes the "wretchedness" of material poverty and calls the church itself to take on "evangelical poverty," in order to foster solidarity with and proximity to the poor.[18] The *Final Document* of the Third General Conference (Puebla, Mexico, in 1979) includes a

16 Ibid., p. 64.
17 Other liberationist perspectives on solidarity include Gustavo Gutiérrez, "Faith as Freedom: Solidarity with the Alienated and Confidence in the Future," in Francis A. Eigo, O.S.A., *Living with Change, Experiences, Faith* (Villanova, PA: Villanova University Press, 1976), especially pp. 33–35; Gutiérrez, *Theology of Liberation*, chapter 13; Jon Sobrino, S.J. and Juan Hernández Pico, S.J., *Theology of Christian Solidarity* (Maryknoll, NY: Orbis, 1985 [1983]); and Ada Maria Isasi-Díaz, "Solidarity: Love of Neighbor in the 1980s," in Susan Brooks Thistlethwaite and Mary Potter Engel (eds.), *Lift Every Voice: Constructing Christian Theologies from the Underside* (San Francisco: Harper & Row, 1990).
18 Latin American Episcopate, "Document on the Poverty of the Church, Documents of Medellin" [1968], in Alfred Hennelly, S.J. (ed.), *Liberation Theology: A Documentary History* (Maryknoll, NY: Orbis, 1990).

chapter bearing the title, "The Preferential Option for the Poor," the first explicit development of this theme.[19] Since Puebla, the preferential option for the poor has played a significant role in liberation theologies in first-world and third-world contexts (including the secondary literature of proponents and critics alike).[20] Official Catholic social teachings of the Vatican and of the US Bishops have also adopted an "inclusive" account of the preferential option.[21]

The simplest articulation of the preferential option expresses attention for "the poor." In this construction, socioeconomic deprivation is prioritized over all other forms of deprivation. As feminist liberation theologians have pointed out, "the poor" as a not-fully-specified category can obscure the particular humanity of those who are deprived, marginalized, or oppressed in a variety of ways.[22] These theorists and activists have

[19] Latin American Episcopate, *Final Document*, in Eagleson and Scharper (eds.), *Puebla and Beyond*, pp. 264–267.

[20] For a detailed tracing of the roots of the preferential option for the poor in Catholic social teaching of the past 100 years, see Donal Dorr, *Option for the Poor: A Hundred Years of Vatican Social Teaching* (Maryknoll, NY: Orbis, 1983). Important, and predominantly positive, analyses of the option for the poor in Latin American liberation theology include Pope, "Preferential Option"; Pope, "Proper and Improper Partiality"; William O'Neill, S.J., "No Amnesty for Sorrow: The Privilege of the Poor in Christian Social Ethics," *Theological Studies* 55 (1994); and Thomas Schubeck, "Ethics and Liberation Theology," *Theological Studies* 56/1 (1995). The two Vatican "Instructions" on liberation theology contain criticisms of "exclusivist" understandings of the preferential option, but they do not deny the importance of preferential care for people in need. Development of the preferential option in feminist theology is considered within this section, below.

[21] For an adoption of the preferential option in papal social encyclicals, see *Sollicitudo Rei Socialis*, para. 42. The pastoral letter of the National Conference of Catholic Bishops of the United States, *Economic Justice for All*, adopts the preferential option for the poor as a moral principle "of the highest priority." My account bears similarity to that of *Economic Justice for All*, but I lay more importance on the eschatological *tension* between preference and inclusiveness, while the US Bishops more clearly state that a common-good framework is *prior* to or more *fundamental* than any preferential options.

[22] A variety of perspectives, particularly on the "option for poor women," are offered in Schüssler Fiorenza (ed.), *The Power of Naming*. See especially the essay by Ivone Gebara, "Option for the Poor as an Option for Poor Women." Interestingly, the Puebla *Final Document* includes a chapter on "The Preferential Option for Young People" (pt. 4/ii, paras. 1166–1205). Leonardo Boff offers a list of just some of the groups that suffer oppression: indigenous peoples, blacks (across the Americas), women, "the handicapped, the old, children, the unemployed, drug addicts, homosexuals, and AIDS victims"; Boff, *Ecology and Liberation: A New Paradigm* (Maryknoll, NY: Orbis, 1995), pp. 131–133. Wolfgang Huber, writing from a German context and

emphasized that some two-thirds of people in a condition of poverty are women and children; women in poverty suffer "doubly" from being marginalized by both class and gender. Liberationists of various approaches have indicated various forms of "classification" that can produce marginalization or oppression: class, gender, race, indigenous or not, sexual orientation, age. The effects of oppression based on these attributes are seen not to be merely additive but "multiplicative." Theologians speak of preferential options for "poor women," "poor indigenous women," and the like. To carry this thinking further, when the preferential option is more fully specified, a whole cluster of preferential *options* is obtained.

These options are most often stated in terms of attributes of people, not according to needs. It would be conceivable to speak of preferences for those in poor health (and thus in need of healthcare), those with poor schooling, those without clothing or shelter, those lacking self-respect or social respect, and so forth. This would express directly that preferential options are to be made according to lack of functioning. Groups like "indigenous women" are included within the cluster of preferential options precisely because those within these groups *disproportionately* suffer deprivations of various (basic and complex) social functionings. Importantly, articulating and enacting preferential options based on these attributes emphasizes the role of *identity* in the attainment or deprivation of social functionings. It is also a way to promote solidarity among people within these marginalized groups. Hence, the emphasis on opting for these groups is not merely a convenient way to understand and address social deprivations; it is also consistent with a normative approach that acknowledges the moral significance of people's identity as socially situated persons who deserve to be treated as equals.[23]

stressing the need to remember the Holocaust, speaks of a "preferential option for the victims" of various social and political systems ("Toward an Ethics of Responsibility," *The Journal of Religion* 73/4 [October 1993], p. 590).

[23] See my section on "Inequalities and differences" in chapter 2 for a discussion of the relation of "redistribution" and "recognition" (in Nancy Fraser's terminology), in which I defend the view that identity and socioeconomic deprivation must be considered in concert.

"Special" and "general" dimensions of opting for the poor

Stephen Pope suggests that the option for the poor in Gutiér-rez's theology can be classified into two aspects – aspects which are not independent of each other but do enable a fruitful distinction. Pope asserts that there are "general" and "special" (or "evangelical") dimensions to the option for the poor. Noting the theocentric roots of the option, including the life-encom-passing example of Christ's solidarity with poor people, Pope considers whether the preferential option is "an ethic for saints and heroes," a moral call that cannot be heeded by most "ordinary" Christians. In particular, are all Christians called to spend their lives accompanying the poor and eschewing material goods? And if they are so called, are they able to live up to this call?

Pope responds that all Christians, while invited to make this "'evangelical' preferential option," *must* enact the more "general" (and less demanding) dimension of the preferential option.

The "general" preferential option entails a commitment to the priority of the poor in both personal and public life; it is especially committed not only to immediate assistance to the poor, but also, and more distinctively, to the empowerment and greater participation of the poor in the life of society (the particular emphasis given to the preferential option by the U.S. Bishops' economic pastoral). The general preferential option is primarily mediated through the ordinary channels provided by one's occupation (either job or career) and family life, and therefore includes socially responsible work and simplicity of lifestyle though it is by no means exhausted by those. It also includes participation in the local parish, voluntary social organizations, the political system, etc. Every Christian must incorporate the preferential option, at least in this general sense.[24]

All Christians are called in their economic life, family life, church life, and political life to act according to the general preferential option. Some critics might argue that Pope is already reducing the demands of the option for the poor: Stephen Pope acknowledges that "[t]he domestication of the

[24] Pope, "Preferential Option," p. 170. The pastoral letter referred to by Pope is *Economic Justice for All* (1986).

preferential option is the obvious danger here."[25] Yet the strong and distinctive nature of the preferential option remains; it makes strong moral demands that challenge people to alter their commitments and activities.

Pope's account of the "general" aspects of the preferential option can be helpful in applying the option to the realm of public policy. Pope himself, in another article, notes that the public policy dimensions of the option for the poor have been little developed in the literature.[26] In order for the preferential option to make a constructive contribution to a pluralistic discourse on poverty, inequality, and well-being, the moral argument must be convincing or compelling to people beyond Christian communities. As developed in chapter 5, people of faith have a rightful and potentially constructive role, along with all other citizens from a variety of (sometimes conflicting) worldviews, to communicate and advocate their understanding of a good and just society. They engage openly, according to "conditions of publicity," to present their views and then to work within legal processes to effect policies and create civic and economic organizations that realize those public visions. In Pope's language, it is the "general" preferential option that is most applicable in such public discussions and policy-oriented debates. It should be added that, based on the norm of "moral integrity," the life-example of some Christians embodying the more demanding "special" aspects of the preferential option would bolster the moral argument for its relevance in public debate.

For pluralistic public discourse, it is necessary to develop more fully the criteria by which preferential options are to be made. The theological criterion of God's universal yet preferential love can be further specified and thus made more accessible within public debate. To this end, it is possible to

---

[25] Pope, "Preferential Option," p. 170.
[26] Pope, "Proper and Improper Partiality," p. 270, n. 89. *Economic Justice for All* considers some important public policy dimensions of the preferential option, though I am arguing that that document does not take as full account of social divisions and systematic forms of marginalization as is called for by the socioeconomic signs of the times. See NCCB, *Economic Justice for All* (paras. 79–94).

draw upon the liberationist claim that God's care is greater for the poor because they have greater *needs*.

At the public policy level, solidarity, the general preferential option, and a cluster of preferential options can contribute to conversations about the formulation of just socioeconomic policies and structures that enable all people to realize their dignity as equals. The constructive tension between preference and inclusiveness can provide moral resources for envisioning just and pragmatic public policies. Constructing social arrangements in which all people hold a genuine sense of stake requires social conditions in which all can secure an adequate level of basic social functionings. A commitment to solidarity requires transformation towards an approximate equality of basic capability.

SELFHOOD

Situating the self – theocentrically, socially, and materially

As both Gutiérrez and H. Richard Niebuhr emphasize, the development of full personhood takes place within a set of interlocking relations. Primary is the relationship between each person and God, a relationship that affirms both the "creatureliness" (as created by God) and the sacred value of each and every human being. Each person's dignity is willed and bestowed by God who is beyond, and active within, finite creation. The centrality of the divine–human relationship implies that life is more than material survival; it is rather life lived with the transcendent God as the source of one's own being and sacred worth. Thus, in Niebuhr's and Gutiérrez's accounts of equality, people are called to know and experience their lives as "theocentrically situated selves."[27]

As developed in the previous two chapters, all of life is properly framed according to this particular relationship; being

---

[27] This phrase is my own creation but it benefits from Seyla Benhabib's helpful notion of "*Situating the Self*," the title of her 1992 book (New York: Routledge). My efforts to situate the self vis-à-vis other people and social goods are further developments of Benhabib's concept.

theocentrically situated orders people's lives as socially and materially situated as well. In the language of the liberationists as well as Paul VI, to be in communion with the divine is the most fully human aspect of well-being. Yet that human dignity is realized within the confines of finite existence in creation. People are situated in two other ways: within webs of human relationships and in the context of the material "goods" of creation. On the one hand, this is a descriptive-empirical claim about how people "are" – as finite beings they require and offer love in relations with others, and they rely on material provisions, from their birth until their death. These are assertions that human interdependence in the context of social goods is a *descriptive* reality of the "human condition," especially the modern condition including globalization, specialization, and differentiation.[28]

"Human interdependence in the context of social goods" also entails a normative claim: while various strands of liberal, modern anthropologies assert that the human being is most fully human when she or he enjoys complete *autonomy*,[29] a theocentric, social-relational framework stresses people's "situated equality" within relations with God, humans, and crea-

---

[28] On this problem of accepting human interdependence as a descriptive reality while normatively calling for solidarity-oriented behavior, see Baum and Ellsberg (eds.), *Logic of Solidarity*, and Pope John Paul II, *Sollicitudo Rei Socialis* (1987).

[29] For the most explicit statement of the Enlightenment stress on autonomy, see Immanuel Kant, "An Answer to the Question: What is Enlightenment?" [1784], in Hans Reiss (ed.), *Kant: Political Writings* (Cambridge: Cambridge University Press, 1991). The reduction of the concern for human dignity to a guarantee of a collection of human rights is a common danger of libertarianism and liberalism. Nozick's *Anarchy, State, and Utopia* is perhaps the most striking example of the former position. Rawls's *Theory of Justice*, taken as a whole, arguably avoids this criticism by his emphasis on two principles of justice. As discussed in chapter 2, while the first principle is concerned with an equal basket of liberties for all citizens, the second principle requires that social, political, and economic inequalities be constrained in order for "primary goods" such as "the social bases of self-respect," wealth, and income to be adequately provided for all citizens of a well-ordered society. (See Rawls's *Political Liberalism* for important refinements of his two principles, as well as a more pragmatic foundation for his theory.) Most often, the liberal reduction of human dignity to human rights occurs not explicitly, but rather because "rights talk" has achieved such predominant currency in modern, liberal discussions about social justice. For a well-stated argument about the dangers of such dependence on human rights language within the US context of discourse, see Mary Ann Glendon, *Rights Talk: The Impoverishment of Political Discourse* (New York: Free Press, 1991).

tion. Like the emphasis on theocentric "situatedness," the stress on social "situatedness" is also an assertion about how life is lived in the most fitting and fulfilling way.

Relationality and egalitarian qualities of social relations

A motley chorus of social theorists share the understanding that human beings are fundamentally "social." Such a social-relational view is well articulated by Seyla Benhabib in her book, *Situating the Self*:

I assume that the subject of reason is a human infant whose body can only be kept alive, whose needs can only be satisfied, and whose self can only develop within the human community into which it is born. The human infant becomes a "self," a being capable of speech and action, only by learning to interact in a human community. The self becomes an individual in that it becomes a "social" being capable of language, interaction and cognition. The identity of the self is constituted by a narrative unity, which integrates what "I" can do, have done and will accomplish with what you expect of "me," interpret my acts and intentions to mean, wish for me in the future, etc.[30]

A socially situated understanding of human selfhood is compatible with both Reformed and liberationist anthropologies in which people are called to relate to other human beings as their siblings who are together striving to do God's work in the world. H. Richard Niebuhr anticipates the emphasis on situatedness with his notion of the "fundamentally social character of selfhood":

To be a self in the presence of other selves is not a derivative experience but primordial. To be able to say that I am I is not an inference from the statement that I think thoughts nor from the statement that I have a law-acknowledging conscience. It is, rather, the acknowledgment of my existence as the counterpart of another self. The exploration of this dimension of self-existence has taken place in many areas of modern man's thinking; many lines of inquiry have converged on the recognition that the self is fundamentally social, in this sense that it is a being which not only knows itself in relation to other selves but exists as self only in that relation.[31]

---

[30] Benhabib, *Situating the Self*, p. 5.   [31] Niebuhr, *Responsible Self*, p. 71.

Personal identity is formed within communities in relation to other selves. In Gutiérrez's framework, personal identity is formed within the societies and communities to which people belong – or do *not* belong. Nonpersons do not have the basic material, cultural, or spiritual prerequisites for knowing that they are human. They are not adequately situated in society, or stated more starkly, they are situated within a sub-human context.

The egalitarian emphasis of these disparate frameworks entails a normative claim about the substantive quality of human relationships. These egalitarian accounts call for full and equal participation within social networks. Socioeconomic structures that make some people "other" through exclusion or marginalization do not promote the realization of selfhood. Patriarchal or "kyriarchal"[32] systems of domination must be rejected because they explicitly or implicitly deny the dignity of particular groups and persons. More generally, hierarchical structures, even when restricted to particular functions or when positions are open to all people, are avoided when more egalitarian ones can be reasonably instituted.

If Marx is correct, then moral claims can never criticize but merely accommodate the socioeconomic "base" of society.[33]

---

[32] The term is coined by Elisabeth Schüssler Fiorenza to denote various forms of master–servant relations. See *But She Said*, p. 117. Schüssler Fiorenza is seeking to develop a vision of an "ekklesia of women" or a "discipleship of equals" in contradistinction to the various forms of oppression that exist in contemporary political, social, and economic forms of "kyriarchy." She employs this framework to reject arguments for "natural" gender differences and to specify the women and men who suffer from distinct forms of oppression. See my discussion of a "cluster of preferential options" earlier in this chapter.

[33] In his "Critique of the Gotha Program" (1875), Marx criticizes the analysis and political platform of the Gotha Congress of the German Social Democratic Party: "Right can never be higher than the economic structure of society and its cultural development conditioned hereby" (pt. 1/3). More specifically, he rejects language of "fair distribution" because it does not address the economic relations on which conceptions of fairness, according to his argument, are dependent. Later in his letter, Marx states that a call for "the elimination of all social and political inequality" is "indefinite," arguing for explicit language about eliminating the "class distinctions" that generate such inequality (pt. 11). Marx's "Critique of the Gotha Program" is reprinted in Robert C. Tucker (ed.), *The Marx-Engels Reader*, second edn. (New York: Norton, 1978 [1972]).

Moral frameworks that consider equality or selfhood in principally or exclusively individualistic terms are open to this Marxist criticism that morality is merely the product of a given socioeconomic system. In contrast, to place normative emphasis on the interdependent, social context of selfhood requires the critical evaluation of the socioeconomic structures in which people live and move and have their being. The scope of the resultant ethic extends beyond merely assuring "fair" exchange, distribution, and contribution *within* the given structures – because the very notion of "fair" is constrained by those structures. Marx (among many others) rightly argues that it entails, in addition, examining whether the socioeconomic arrangements themselves perpetuate exploitation.[34] Elimination of injustice, deprivation, or marginalization thus requires the kind of preferential options discussed above.

Integral selfhood, multiple spheres, and balancing power

The theological emphasis on the "whole" or "total" person (in Niebuhr and in Gutiérrez) and on "integral liberation" (in the latter) suggest that the realization of personhood is related to multiple spheres of life. In the process of liberation, people's "mundane" material needs are held to be important alongside emotional, cultural, and spiritual needs.[35] The discussion of this chapter challenges these very categories: in particular, material goods *are* social goods, and they carry various social meanings that relate to the other spheres, including the spiritual. (A fuller account of the social meaning of goods is offered in the following section.) While selfhood should not be obstructed by distributions of goods in any sphere, the adjective "integral" suggests that selfhood involves *interrelating* these various spheres of life.

Michael Walzer's discussion of the "spheres of justice" helps to illuminate this question of integral selfhood and multiple spheres. Through his sociological-historical examination of

---

[34] I suggest the moral necessity of such analysis within the discussion of the norm of moral integrity and the social room for dissent, in chapter 5.
[35] Gutiérrez, *We Drink from Our Own Wells.*

particular societies, Walzer demonstrates that the "distribution problem" always involves a number of social goods within the various spheres of life. He thus rejects any account of justice or well-being that is based on any one social good – be it money (income or wealth), utility, or political power. Across and within a collection of "relatively autonomous spheres," he asserts, citizens make, share, and compete for goods. Each sphere contains one or more social goods that are distributed according to principles that hold only within that sphere. Walzer favors a notion of "complex equality" according to which the respective holdings of any one social good (like money or political power) are not allowed to "dominate" the distribution of any other social good.[36] For Walzer, "[m]en and women are one another's equals (for all important moral and political purposes) when no one possesses or controls the means of domination." Since this "domination is always mediated by some set of social goods," a just society limits the influence of each social good to its own "proper" sphere.[37] This is partly accomplished through the imposition of what Walzer calls "blocked exchanges," which prohibit the "purchase" of goods like political power or love by potentially dominant goods – particularly money.[38] When such sphere-transcending exchanges are blocked, relatively autonomous distribution can operate within each sphere. As a consequence, domination will be prevented.

Of course, Walzer's vision of "complex equality" requires the successful limitation of domination by social goods like money. He is more interested in this problem of domination than in a problem he calls "monopoly" – by which people hold an excessive amount of any particular social good – because he believes that if domination *across* spheres can be limited, the lingering inequalities *within* spheres will be tolerable.[39] Yet Walzer himself acknowledges that complete autonomy of spheres (which would mean the absence of domination) cannot be achieved. Even within Walzer's "ideal" society embodying

---

[36] Walzer, *Spheres of Justice*, pp. 10–20 and *passim*.   [37] Ibid., p. xiii.
[38] Ibid., pp. 100–103.   [39] Ibid., pp. 10–13.

complex equality, excessive wealth will continue to exercise power, subtly or overtly, in other spheres.[40]

Walzer's account of the complexity, or multiplicity, of social goods within distinguishable spheres is a valuable one, and his argument for limiting the domination of particular goods is compelling. Yet he realizes that even in the best scenario, excessive accumulation of at least a few social goods will need to be addressed. In today's actual society, blocked exchanges have proved remarkably difficult to enact; indeed, increasing numbers of social goods have been "marketized," including perhaps most notably healthcare and the environment.[41] Such signs of the times suggest a trend towards greater, not lesser, domination by the social goods of income and wealth.

Operative in Walzer's account of complex equality is the understanding that most people are talented in at least one sphere of life, and that no one is talented in every sphere. The most gifted money-managers and entrepreneurs are not usually the most able politicians, scholars, friends, or lovers, but almost everyone is talented in one or more such sphere(s). Walzer argues that since in contemporary society money as well as political power do dominate, this wide diversity of talent (and its low correlation across spheres) is not as apparent as it would be under the conditions of complex equality. He acknowledges that autonomous spheres will not allow everyone a chance to excel, but complex equality "will make for a greater sharing of social goods than will any other conceivable arrangement."[42]

Amy Gutmann poses an important question to Walzer about this assertion: "But what happens to those who, even by

---

[40] Ibid., p. 112 and pp. 120–121.

[41] The phenomenon of "marketization" or the spread of "market logic" is not identical to domination of income and/or wealth. "Market logic" entails the notion that in transactions not traditionally seen as purely "economic," such as decisions about marriage and family, or the regulation of pollution, or the administration of criminal justice, the outcome will be made more "efficient" if people's own incentives are allowed to play a role in the allocation of resources. See Becker, *Economic Approach to Human Behavior*, especially p. 5. Often this logic assumes that "costs" and "benefits" can be determined in monetary terms, which *de facto* implies that social goods now have prices expressed in dollar terms. When this is the case, then money as a social good arguably gains in its potential for domination.

[42] Walzer, *Spheres of Justice*, pp. 320–321.

Walzer's pluralistic criteria, fail to contribute anything of value to society?"[43] People who make little contribution to society receive little in return under Walzer's schema. But such an outcome is incompatible with a Niebuhrian or liberationist theocentric claim that persons are entitled to personhood because they are created in the image of God – not on account of any criterion of social or economic productivity.[44] This question will be considered in detail below. The important point here is that the distributions of a number of social goods play a role in the well-being of people; normatively, a Christian ethical account must address both the problems of domination and monopoly in order to guarantee the conditions for moral equality and solidarity.

In actual societies, excessive accumulation of important social goods by a few people is problematic for reasons, in Walzer's terms, of both "domination" and "monopoly." With this critical discussion of Walzer's insightful schema as background, the discussion returns to Reformed and liberationist sources in order to assert that *some level of relative equality of economic power, or at least the limitation of extreme inequalities, is normatively desirable.*

For H. Richard Niebuhr, because power comes from God, it is ultimately good.[45] But the holding of power is properly placed in the theocentric value framework. That is, power accumulated by persons or groups should never enable them or tempt them to claim undue social, political, or economic status, nor should the level of disparity be so great as to degrade the

---

[43] Amy Gutmann, *Liberal Equality* (Cambridge, Cambridge University Press, 1980), p. 113. Gutmann's criticism is directed towards Walzer's earlier works – most notably his essay, "In Defense of Equality" (1973), but the criticism stands against *Spheres of Justice* as well.

[44] Walzer does argue for certain basic provision for all citizens of a society: "No community can allow its members to starve to death when there is food available to feed them; no government can stand passively by at such a time – not if it claims to be a government of or by or for the community" (*Spheres of Justice*, p. 79). The "extent of provision" must be determined within any given society, but in each place the extent must allow for a basic social membership (pp. 78–83). This would seem to indicate a focus on "being a member" as a social *functioning*, though he uses, rather, language of *needs* throughout his chapter on the sphere he calls "security and welfare."

[45] Niebuhr, *Faith on Earth*, p. 100.

humanity of people lacking those goods. Given his strong account of human sin, Niebuhr favors the balancing of powers in the political sphere. As noted in chapter 6, Niebuhr's account suggests an analogous argument for socioeconomic dimensions of life, because economic power, like its political counterpart, can be used to make the "haves" elevate themselves to a higher status than is fitting for humans while forcing the "have-nots" into a dehumanizing social status.

Gutiérrez's framework supports a similar balancing of power in socioeconomic life. Indeed, he argues that in the global market persons and groups have accumulated excessive economic power that allows them to control local and national economies. While most liberationists now eschew monocausal analyses like the early versions of "dependency theory," Gutiérrez and other theologians continue to attribute much socioeconomic oppression to the undue holding of economic power by international and local elites.[46] The liberationist agenda calls not for an eschatological reversal but for full equality in God's *basileia*. In the present moment this calls for movement toward more balanced social, economic, and political power. The import of the distributions of economic goods for a relative balance of overall societal power will now be considered.

THE SOCIAL NATURE OF GOODS

Social goods and situated selves

In addition to being theocentrically situated and situated in human relationships, people are situated within creation by the necessity of socioeconomic goods for their survival and well-

---

[46] See, for instance, Gutiérrez, *Theology of Liberation*, p. xxiv, where Gutiérrez terms the theory of dependence "an inadequate tool" and stresses the need to complexify liberationist social analysis by examinations of domestic conditions of the poor, the various "dynamics" across societies, and transnational problems like foreign debt that displace societies' own power to make independent economic decisions. The analysis of the UNDP and the discussion of contemporary international realities of chapter 3 provide empirical evidence that income and wealth inequalities have significantly increased when the world population is taken as a whole.

being. Material goods are part of a good creation; not only is
there no escape from reliance on material goods, but the *well-
lived* life must be "material" as well as "relational."[47]

Accounts of the "social situatedness" of people typically
place more emphasis on the relational aspects of human interdependence than on human reliance upon material goods. Yet
these two aspects go hand in hand. As Marxist thought has
emphasized perhaps most prominently, social relations are
"mediated" by economic goods within any system of production. No human interaction is non-material; rather, human
relations are constrained by material reality in the same way
that schools of fish are contained by the water of the sea. Marx
goes too far in his claims about the extent to which intellectual,
cultural, and even political factors are *determined* by the capitalist
mode of production. Yet his emphasis on the material dimension of social existence is an important one for understanding
the role that socioeconomic goods can and do play in social
relations.

Most dramatically, Marx's account of "commodity fetishism"
illuminates ways in which economic goods can take on social
meanings that greatly impact on human relationships within
capitalism. For Marx, commodity fetishism occurs when "the
social relation of the producers" (i.e., people) is transformed
into a "social relation among objects." The result is that "the
products of labour become commodities, sensuous things which
are at the same time supra-sensible or social." In this process,
humans are reduced to mere *objects* who are compelled to
contribute labor to a process whose *ends* are commodities, not
the well-being of those people.[48]

This cultural-ideological dimension of the Marxist critique
points to a relationship between material goods and their social
meanings. It is not necessary to accept Marx's mystical account
of how commodities operate, in the extreme case of fetishism

---

[47] There would be room in this analysis for exploring the aesthetic and cultural goods
as well as those more readily described as social or economic. (The terms need not
be mutually exclusive.) Though not the focus of this book, these are other important
kinds of functionings.

[48] Marx, *Capital: A Critique of Political Economy* (New York: Vintage Books/Random
House, 1977 [1867]), I, 1/4, pp. 163–177.

under capitalism, in order to appreciate the fact that material goods convey important, and possibly dehumanizing, social meanings. The quality of human well-being is significantly but not exclusively determined by socioeconomic goods.[49]

In his *Spheres of Justice*, Michael Walzer offers a briefer but more straightforward account of the social nature and significance of goods.[50] In his view, "people conceive and create goods, which they then distribute amongst themselves."[51] Goods are not merely "material"; rather, they are constructed within human relationships and in turn impact on those relationships. Goods are thus both "material" and "socially constructed" – because they are a result of humans mixing their labors with nature's materials.[52] Thus Walzer writes:

All the goods with which distributive justice is concerned are social goods. . . . Goods in the world have shared meanings because conception and creation are social processes . . . John Stuart Mill once complained that "people like in crowds," but I know of no other way to like or to dislike social goods. A solitary person could hardly understand the meaning of the goods or figure out the reasons for taking them as likable or dislikable.[53]

Walzer goes on to emphasize the strong interrelationship between the identity of people and their holdings of social goods:

Men and women take on concrete identities because of the way they conceive and create, and then possess and employ social goods. "The line between what is me and mine," wrote William James, "is hard to draw." Distributions can not be understood as the acts of men and

---

[49] See also Lee Rainwater, *What Money Buys: Inequality and the Social Meaning of Income* (New York: Basic Books, 1974). For a creative interpretation of Marx's notion of commodity fetishism within an anthropological analysis of indigenous peoples' critique of the arrival of Western capitalism, see Michael T. Taussig, *The Devil and Commodity Fetishism in Latin America* (Chapel Hill, NC: University of North Carolina Press, 1980).

[50] Walzer himself accepts that "behind" the notion of commodity fetishism is the "larger truth" that "[c]ommodities are symbols of belonging; status and identity are distributed through the market, sold for cash on the line" (*Spheres of Justice*, p. 106).

[51] Ibid., p. 6.

[52] My language here invokes John Locke's theory asserting the right of private property. Ironically, Walzer develops the social dimension of goods in order to discuss not private holdings of goods, but social distributions.

[53] Walzer, *Spheres of Justice*, pp. 7–8.

women who do not yet have particular goods in their minds or in their hands. In fact, people already stand in a relation to a set of goods; they have a history of transactions, not only with one another but also with the moral and material world in which they live. Without such a history, they wouldn't be men and women in any recognizable sense, and they wouldn't have the first notion of how to go about the business of giving, allocating, and exchanging goods.[54]

As finite, social creatures, humans derive their identity in the context of social relations with other people – relations mediated by social goods. Goods hold particular meanings within human communities: the types and quantities of goods that need to be held are determined within these communities as well. Not all social goods contain tangible, material components, but all socioeconomic goods (including income and wealth, education, and healthcare) are seen, in Walzer's framework and in this Christian ethical approach, as social goods.

On relative holdings of social goods

This account of the self as "situated" suggests that each person's understanding of her or his holdings of socioeconomic goods is a socially constructed understanding. People do not evaluate, or reflect upon, the holdings of their goods in a vacuum, but rather from within their social-relational contexts which this chapter has considered at length. It is not merely a descriptive reality that people understand and evaluate their wider well-being from their socially situated positions; it is also normatively appropriate, a result of their proper understanding of their situatedness within creation. Of course, the question of the values people use to evaluate their situation must also be raised. For instance, they can be completely and narrowly self-interested when they make their comparisons, being motivated by their own well-being to the exclusion of that of all others. The normative, theocentric framework rejects feelings of envy and greed that can result in forms of consumeristic "idolatry." From such a theocentric (or other socially situated) approach, people can incorporate others' well-being into the very conception of their own well-being.[55]

The discussion thus far suggests, importantly, that one's well-being is a function not merely of absolute holding of certain social goods; rather, the situated nature of selfhood implies that relative holdings of important social goods are proper factors in the evaluation of people's well-being. As socially situated, people's place in socioeconomic distributions impacts on their sense of selfhood; if the wider claims of this approach are accepted, then those socioeconomic distributions should be structured so that no one's (absolute or relative) lack of holdings obstructs her or his realization of full personhood.

Social goods, "basic needs," and basic capability

It is now possible to turn to the question of what people "need" in order to realize their full and equal personhood as situated selves. More specifically, it is important to ask what "basic needs" should be met in order for there not to be lingering "need." The issue of "basic needs" relates to discussions of "preferential options" for marginalized people, the multiple "spheres" of life, and the social nature of goods. Any determination of such "basic needs" presupposes some conception of humans and their well-being. The response to the "basic needs" question, then, proceeds from within the context of the theologically informed approach.

The question of "basic needs" is often addressed in economic development, as discussed in chapter 2, by means of a list of

---

[55] The issues of self-interest and well-being here are complex. Amartya Sen ("Rational Fools: A Critique of the Behavioural Foundations of Economic Theory," *Philosophy and Public Affairs* 6 [1977] and "Goals, Commitment, and Identity," *Journal of Law, Economics, and Organization* 1/2 [1985]) demonstrates how self-interest itself is an ambiguous concept that needs further specification in order to be analytically helpful. My main points are that in my normative approach, people's theocentric and social situatedness call them to be interested in the well-being of others as well as in themselves, and that such other-regarding concern can be incorporated into economic modeling, as Sen has helped to show. A further point, briefly discussed in the conclusion, is that those at the higher end of the distribution may have narrow self-interest at stake in lesser inequality, in order to avoid "costs" of crime and violence associated with greater inequality.

material provisions that are arguably essential for human beings to achieve a decent standard of living (however that is defined). The substantive discussions of moral equality and situated self-hood thus far suggest that the kinds of "needs" that are normatively significant are those requirements for people to be able to realize their full and equal personhood. Here the language of Amartya Sen's approach is most helpful: Sen emphasizes that the basic capability of a person is reflected in the set of basic functionings and freedoms that are available to her or him. A Christian ethical approach can employ this conception of "equality of basic capability" as a helpful way to describe the necessary social conditions for moral equality.[56]

At the same time, the normative emphases on the theocen-trically, socially, and materially situated nature of selfhood and on the social nature of goods clarify what is entailed with "basic capability." The basic functionings that comprise capability are each functionings within particular societies; Adam Smith noted that the ability of a person to appear in public without shame, for example, requires that people have the accepted clothing and accessories for that particular society.[57] In other words, as discussed in the previous section, the meaning of goods that reflect functionings are socially determined. The crucial point for this project is that *relative as well as absolute holdings of such social goods play a determining role in a person's capability.* A brief examination of three basic functionings, in the spheres of education, health/longevity, and income, will help to illuminate this point.

Basic functionings that can be described as "being well-educated" and "being in good health" are socially determined.

---

[56] Often these "basic needs" are stated in terms of commodities – particular economic products that must be held in order to escape material deprivation. Yet the "space" of moral and social attention becomes important here – particularly because, as discussed in chapter 2, people vary so significantly in their capacities to "convert" commodities into more intrinsically valuable goods, or into well-being itself. In the Christian ethical approach, capability is more fundamental than holding any commodities, though for socially situated selves, holding commodities is a necessary means of having basic functioning.

[57] Adam Smith, *An Inquiry into the Nature and Causes of the Wealth of Nations* (London: Everyman Edition, Home University Library, 1776), pp. 351–352. For an important discussion of this point, see Sen, "Poor, Relatively Speaking."

Educations differ widely in content and quality across societies and within societies, whatever standard is employed. Within societies, however, certain levels of educational attainment – a high-school diploma, or a college degree, for example – somewhat independent of the content of those years of schooling, convey certain social meanings (and social power). Those social meanings (and empowerment) are relative to the distribution as a whole. In the United States, for example, a high-school diploma is arguably less valuable socially today than it was at the beginning of the postwar period; an associate's degree or baccalaureate degree is needed in many cases to avoid dead-end jobs. (Empirical support for this assertion is provided in chapter 4.) Similarly, "being in good health," while grounded in certain biological realities, is also socially determined. As Norman Daniels points out, similar biological conditions have different social impacts in different societies: dyslexia, as an obvious example, is more inhibiting in a literate society than in a non-literate one.[58] The point is that education-related and health-related basic functionings, while acknowledging the substance of education and the biological factors of health, are always determined relative to the society in which one is located. It follows that a person's well-being is at least partially a function of one's position relative to others in such basic functionings.[59]

[58] Norman Daniels, *Just Health Care* (Cambridge, Cambridge University Press, 1985), pp. 28–35. Clearly, it is normatively desirable both to eliminate illiteracy and to overcome dyslexia in all societies.

[59] This claim is supported by recent research on the impact of socioeconomic inequality on health status and longevity outcomes. Richard G. Wilkinson, presenting extensive empirical evidence, argues that while there is a strong relationship between growth of overall economic production and general improvements in health, at higher levels of development, relative factors (like income inequality within a society) can account for a large part of cross-societal differences in health and longevity. Examining data for the countries of the European Community, Japan, and the United States, Wilkinson concludes: "[B]etween one-half and three-quarters of the differences in average life expectancy from one developed country to another may be attributed solely to differences in income distribution." ("The Epidemiological Transition: From Material Scarcity to Social Disadvantage?," *Daedalus* 123/4 [fall 1994], p. 69). In Wilkinson's view of the social gradient of health, people at the bottom of social and economic distributions suffer from forms of relative deprivation.

It is important to note that Wilkinson is careful not to create a one-way causality running from income to health and longevity. Instead, he further complicates the

The basic functioning of "having adequate income" is arguably one of the most important in contemporary market-based societies. Income carries value which not only can be "exchanged" for consumer goods, but which also can purchase a social and cultural sense of belonging, as well as political influence, *inter alia*. As Lee Rainwater has emphasized, this raises the problem of the relative position of people in the income distribution, not merely for acquiring some absolute minimum basket of commodities, but also for conveying a sense of belonging within their societies. Money from income is a principal resource which people can use to purchase access to "validating activities" within modern, industrial society.[60] But these basic functions of money (to buy basic commodities and to buy basic social belonging) are socially determined and thus relative to particular societies. This point can, of course, be employed to assert the futility of any material growth in a society, since seeking one's well-being by "keeping up with the Joneses" can be a circular enterprise. But it can also be employed to emphasize that distributional concerns matter morally *alongside* aggregate achievements like economic productivity and growth. In this latter view, both distribution and production are morally significant.[61]

Thus the attainment of a set of *basic* functionings by all people is one helpful way to describe the operation of moral equality. Those basic functionings are determined by relative as well as absolute factors. Excessive inequalities in goods reflecting these functionings impair some people from having a sense of adequate participation and basic capability.

analysis, as he states in another article: "Rather than Britain's poor health performance being a reflection of its poor economic performance, it seems that both have common roots in the social division and wastage of human skills and abilities among a substantial proportion of the population" ("Divided We Fall: The Poor Pay the Price of Increased Social Inequality with Their Health," *British Medical Journal* (4/30/1994), pp. 1113–1114). The interrelation of these various factors reinforces the potential benefit of examining inequalities in multiple spheres.

[60] Rainwater, *What Money Buys*, esp. chap. 2.

[61] The relationship of distribution and production – as well as possible moral and economic tradeoffs between them – is considered in the following chapter.

CONCLUSIONS

A view of selves situated vis-à-vis God, human relationships, and social goods is suggestive for various dimensions of a Christian approach to inequality. Since people are equals in sin as well as in creation, the various forms of social, economic, and political power within actual societies must be kept in check. Because people are socially situated, social power is expressed through the relative and absolute holdings of social goods, and thus the balance of social powers is partly realized through limiting the level of disparity of important social goods. Such constraints on inequality can be attained by, and can also help maintain, a just basic structure of society. These contexts of justice will enable people more fully to pursue their own well-being and in turn to make a positive contribution to their communities and societies. Conversely, in actual situations of unequal social power and/or excessively disparate distributions of important social goods, preferential solidarity is required. At the public policy level this calls for special attention to alleviate the relative and absolute deprivations that persons and groups suffer. Attention to the well-being of the most disadvantaged is required for achieving social conditions in which moral equality and genuine solidarity operate.

Clearly the language of capability and functionings helps to clarify and sharpen a Christian ethical approach to inequality. In turn, the constructed Christian account of theocentrically, socially, and materially situated selves helps to specify that functioning well in any society has not only a relational component, but more specifically, a relative or positional one. There is need, as well, to attend to the role of envy in one's sense of position in her or his society – something that is suggested but not pursued in the analysis here.

It bears emphasizing that the Christian ethical approach constructed in this central part of the book has implications for socioeconomic life beyond narrow discussions of inequality. A complete approach to economic life must integrate consideration of distributional issues with economic productivity, technological possibilities, and various other human and material factors. The treatments of solidarity and situated selfhood reveal that Christian ethical approaches to socioeconomic life place fundamental importance on human *identity* and the role of the economy in people's moral formation.[62] Thus while the explicit focus in the book is on empirical inequalities and their moral significance, human beings must not be seen as mere receptacles that are made to hold roughly equal shares of various goods. Rather, shares of any and all goods should contribute to a good and just creation in which human beings experience well-lived lives.

[62] Another book in the series, New Studies in Christian Ethics, makes this point explicitly. A fundamental moral criterion for evaluating any economic system is its impact on human identity. Does the contemporary market economy provide a humanizing or dehumanizing effect on people in their roles as workers or consumers? See Peter H. Sedgwick, *The Market Economy and Christian Ethics* (Cambridge: Cambridge University Press, 1999).

PART THREE

Transforming discourse, persons, and societies

CHAPTER 9

Expanding public discourse on inequality

REFINING THE PUBLIC CONTRIBUTION OF THIS
CHRISTIAN ETHICAL APPROACH

A Christian ethical approach to inequality should provide a framework or tools for understanding the contemporary realities of disparity. Many Christian ethicists (and others) have lamented what they see as morally troubling levels of social and economic division – yet for the most part, they have not provided detailed analyses of what is going on, or how the troubling dimensions of economic life might be addressed. Christian ethics has remained at least one step removed from the empirical and policy-oriented discussions about the levels and trends of inequality. There is no simple way to account for the lack of engagement in the contemporary debate – although reasons would include a widespread view of "keeping faith apart from politics and economics," a lack of understanding of what economic changes are really taking place, and some sort of faith in the "invisible hand" of the "free market" to make things turn out well for everyone. The modest contribution of this book is to bring the moral and economic discussions one step closer together.

What remains to be done is to return to the wide public debates about inequality and to consider the insights that a Christian ethical approach can offer within them. As these final chapters show by example, the kind of engagement ranges from broad (but carefully stated) moral arguments for "why inequality matters" and for "why Christians and other citizens should care and respond," to more specific consideration of policy-oriented discussions about weighing the moral value of inequality alongside other factors in assessing the quality of human well-being and development. The contribution of Christian ethics to inequality is thus itself disparate and multifaceted. Yet there should be a consistency (moral integrity) among all of the initiatives and insights described in this approach.

It should not be surprising that many of the insights of the approach are not wholly distinct from those that have been offered from "non-theological" perspectives. This fact should not be embarrassing to or problematic for Christian social ethics – the goal is not to be distinctive as much as it is to be faithful and truthful.[1] What kind of contribution, then, does the approach make to the wide moral debate? The substantive approach makes at least three types of contribution to public discourse on inequality: it provides a *moral vision and justification* for how inequality matters and why public response is needed; it gives credence to that moral vision by the *moral example* of Christian persons and communities engaged in actions of preferential solidarity; and it provides a *moral call to action* for others (from within and beyond Christian communities) to respond in personal and institutional ways to pressing inequalities.

First, the Christian ethical approach contributes an argument about why certain trends and realities of inequality are morally and socially troubling. The approach does not resolve all of the crucial moral or social dimensions of inequalities, why they matter, or why people should seek to alleviate or constrain them. To contribute to answering all those questions, though, is a central aim.

The *moral vision and justification* for "why inequality matters," in Thiemann's frame discussed at length in chapter 5, has been presented in the spirit of the norm of "public accessibility." In an important sense, drawing from and integrating disparate sources has required an argument that is broadly accessible. The moral arguments are offered in the hope that they will be compelling in public discourse – that is, that they will lead

---

[1] See chapter 5 for a fuller discussion of theological and ethical method.

people to understand and thus to respond to certain inequalities as morally and socially unacceptable. The approach is an answer to this question: "In societies in which serious inequalities exist, what justification(s) would lead people to promote the social conditions of moral equality and social solidarity?" Philosophers like John Rawls have carefully taken up similar questions of justification.[2] The kind of moral justification and vision offered in the present approach is less abstract, and consequently less precise, than Rawls's. Yet drawing on various moral and theological resources to mount a case against certain inequalities, it has been constructed to provide a compelling story for why these inequalities, and responses to constrain them, matter. The discussions of equality, solidarity, and situated selfhood present a moral vision for structuring society in which an equality of basic capability would be established. In a pragmatic sense, the justifications of Rawls and that of other moral theorists, as well as this one, could complement one another in motivating public discussions and policies that move towards lesser inequality.[3]

Second, and related to this question of moral justification is one of *moral exemplification*. As discussed in chapter 5, the theological perspectives that inform this approach have arisen within and have helped to shape the moral vision of Christian

[2] Indeed Rawls's employment of the "original position," with its trappings such as the veil of ignorance and representative persons, is a heuristic tool to allow people precisely to think about justice and equality in a well-ordered society – and about how to transform their societies towards those goals. In Rawls's approach, citizens are invited to think of inequalities not merely in relation to their own interests from their social location, but to take a broader moral scope. I would not dispute that Rawls makes a compelling argument that *once* people have agreed to invoke the reasoning from the original position, then they will agree to his justice as fairness, including the difference principle (see chapter 2). It is the reasons as to *why they would invoke the original position at all* that merit further attention. Posed a slightly different way: representatives in the original position might agree to the difference principle, but why should we? Moral visions such as the one I am articulating address this question.

[3] I do not mean, with this comment, to dismiss the serious differences in approach to inequalities and well-being among these various moral theories. Yet I maintain that in actual public discussions and policy debates about specific issues, some working consensus can be achieved. I have treated some aspects of this question in my "Liberation Theology and Liberal Justice?: The Preferential Option for the Poor and Rawls's Difference Principle," conference paper, American Academy of Religion Annual Meeting, November 1995.

persons and communities. Communities of faith articulate aspects of these theological and ethical perspectives in their weekly (or daily) gatherings. The biblical and theological sources that Niebuhr and Gutiérrez invoke also inform other Christians, not to mention that these two thinkers themselves are widely studied figures. These points are important for two reasons. First, these theological resources have been employed in constructing a normative argument partly in the hope that the approach would be morally compelling to the wide number of Christians for whom Christian theology is central to their own identity. The second point is that all citizens will more likely find a moral vision convincing if it is actually put into practice by particular persons and communities. This is one central insight derived from Thiemann's discussion of the norm of "moral integrity."[4] Thus, the "general" option for the poor will receive a better hearing in public discourse if Christians are engaged in actions that express the "evangelical" as well as the "general" dimensions of the preferential option.[5] In actual practice many churches fall far short of their potential for enacting preferential solidarity in their communal and outreach activities. On the other hand, significant work, both justice-based and charity-based, has been effected by religiously motivated persons and communities in public life; notable figures in this century including Dorothy Day, Martin Luther King, Jr., Archbishop Oscar Romero of San Salvador, Adolfo Pérez Esquivel of Buenos Aires, and Mother Teresa of Calcutta represent myriad nameless persons and groups who have confronted forms of both poverty and inequality. Thus one distinctive aspect of this theologically informed approach to inequality is that it invokes the moral examples of people in practice while inviting others to embrace its vision.

Finally, the theologically informed approach is a *moral call to action*. Alongside the account of why particular inequalities violate the conditions of moral equality and social solidarity, and the narratives of people who are engaged in other-

[4] See chapter 5.
[5] The general and special dimension of the preferential option, as well as a further specification of options in practice, are contained in chapter 8.

regarding efforts of justice and charity, the approach is an argument for why persons and societies as a whole should engage in inequality-reducing actions. This is the transformative impetus emphasized in the work of Niebuhr and even more explicitly in the liberationist account. The reading of the socioeconomic signs of the times, the development of a theological approach, and the "practical mediation" are all aimed at transformative praxis. The call to action has been framed consistent with the norm of "mutual respect," acknowledging the agency of people who hold moral viewpoints that conflict with this one and without engaging in disrespectful attacks on other perspectives. It is the theological and social analyses themselves that are meant to be convincing. The irony, of course, is that extreme inequality itself can readily obstruct people's moral agency.

FOUR "AXES" FOR VALUE-BASED DISCUSSION OF INEQUALITY

It is now possible to describe more substantively some insights that a Christian ethical approach can contribute to the wide public debate. One attribute that marks that debate is a lack of a common approach or language to analyze inequality. That is, discourse about inequality and its relation to justice, well-being, or development is framed in distinct ways by distinct perspectives. When considering the intervention that Christian ethics can make in the debate, it is important to note that none of these descriptions are value-free or uncontroversial. As the discussions of chapters 2, 3, and 4 demonstrate, inequality can be described in relation to various goods, spaces, and people. These accounts differ in their normative emphasis, whether the moral framework is explicit or implicit. The question is not, "Shall discussions of inequality be value-based?" but rather it is vital to ask, "Which values shall matter, and how?"

There is no simple answer to such a question. Yet the Christian ethical approach suggests at least some areas of concern that are called for in any moral or social analysis of inequality. One way to describe these concerns is in terms of four "axes" along which inequality discussions can be focused: multiple spheres of functioning, productivity and/or distribution, scope and differentials, and forms of comparison. The image of "axis" is employed because it captures two important points. First, an axis helps to center or even give order to a number of objects – or perspectives on a problem. Second, axes run along different dimensions of a problem – this image allows us to picture a debate that *expands* in these four directions.

MULTIPLE SPHERES OF FUNCTIONING

This axis emphasizes that public attention and policy-oriented analysis should be directed at various spheres of life – not just at a money-related sphere of income and/or wealth. The normative justification for this claim is located most centrally in the understanding of the sacred worth of the *whole* person, in Niebuhr's account, and in the call to *integral* liberation, in the writings of Gutiérrez. Full and equal personhood is achieved not merely in some spiritual sphere, nor solely in economic, political, or cultural spheres. Rather, all these dimensions of life are integrally related and significant. At the same time, the provision for important, even "basic" socioeconomic needs, such as food, shelter, clothing, health, and education, are necessary but not sufficient conditions for human well-being. In the language of Gutiérrez and liberation theology, such socioeconomic factors provide minimum requirements for personhood. Thus while not overlooking other spheres of life, there is justification for particular attention to socioeconomic goods in discussions of an equality of basic capability.

At the same time, within each sphere of life, the moral force is not placed on any particular commodities in themselves. As Niebuhr's work helps to illuminate, placing excessive value in particular material products of creation can distort one's own proper situatedness. In the extreme, placing too much value in material products can be idolatrous. The goods of creation are to be employed so that people can properly order their lives in relation to God, humans, and all of creation.

It has been suggested throughout that Sen's language of capability and functionings is helpful in clarifying these points. In an important sense, the theologically informed approach contributes one thick moral justification of Sen's position advocating an equality of basic capability. The basic functionings Sen describes, such as "having adequate income," "being in good health," and "being well educated," can be seen as necessary conditions for moral equality and for the attainment of social solidarity. Particular material and social goods contribute to, but must be "converted" into, such forms of basic functioning. In policy-oriented debate, a Christian ethical approach would thus be able to support Sen's proposals for speaking in terms of capability rather than commodities.

In development discourse, the *Human Development Reports* authored by the United Nations Development Programme (UNDP) have embraced much of Sen's language about basic capability and the expansion of people's choices in many spheres of life. As will be further discussed below, the human development index incorporates indicators from three spheres: income, education, and health/longevity. While a Christian ethical approach endorses attending to a host of socioeconomic spheres, it can support the UNDP's efforts to address functionings in these three spheres.[6] Attention to distributional factors, though, is needed in each of these spheres beyond the UNDP's present indicators.

While multiple spheres could be examined, the "sphere-expansion" of public policy analysis is also limited practically by data constraints and conceptual difficulties. For instance, "having access to land" is significant in various societies (though perhaps for different reasons in different societies). Yet practical difficulties exist in determining a person's access to

---

[6] It is also important to note, however, that the normative justification that the UNDP employs for including income – in order to reflect the basic goods and services required to meet a decent living standard – does not note, as explicitly as the present approach does, the ways in which possessing income itself reflects a basic social functioning in contemporary societies. Further, the UNDP's normative explanations for examining health and education do not place as much emphasis on the social dimensions of functionings in these spheres. The discussion in chapter 10 provides further context to these issues.

land: in particular, the relation of land access, gender, and household/family structure raises complex issues of inequality. To varying degrees, societies favor men over women in land-holding; in some cultures, women cannot "own" land at all. Though it may not eliminate access altogether, this severely limits women's access to land. When seeking to apply normative insights into the policy arena, such problems must be taken into account. At the same time, not to focus on land-holding is also problematic because it overlooks the very question of gender inequality in that sphere – a severe manifestation of gender-based marginalization. Efforts to expand policy-related discussions will encounter data constraints and conceptual difficulties in each sphere; yet normative emphasis on multiple spheres should place public priority on overcoming such problems.

PRODUCTIVITY AND/OR DISTRIBUTION

The claim of an expansion along the productivity/distribution axis is that public discourse should attend to questions of distributional inequality as well as aggregate achievement in each sphere of social functioning. This is because relative as well as absolute holdings of social goods factor into personal and societal well-being.

The normative justifications for this claim, supported by Niebuhr's and Gutiérrez's theological accounts of equality, were developed predominantly in chapter 8. People are socially situated: as beings within creation, their relations with other humans are mediated by social goods. No particular functioning, basic or complex, is determined without reference to others in society. Relative deprivation of social goods, when it reaches some level, obstructs people from achieving the related functioning. Of course, this kind of deprivation only matters morally if everyone should attain an adequate level of that functioning. (Thus being well nourished is crucial for treating all as moral equals; being competent at opera singing is not.) Here the discussion returns to the normative question of what basic conditions are required to guarantee the moral equality of all people as well as a general quality of social relations marked by social solidarity.[7]

It is important to emphasize, alongside *distribution*, the importance of *production*, and growth of production, of those goods that contribute to societal and/or personal well-being. Of course, production and growth of production of some so-called "goods" (for instance, tobacco products or pornography) promote inappropriate valuing and/or forms of idolatry.[8] (For such non-goods, concern for their distribution also should take on a different perspective.) For products which rightly are called "goods," the important question is one of balancing (or weighting) of particular distributional and aggregative concerns. When distributional questions are overlooked altogether, the implicit weighting of them is zero. Even this is a form of balancing between distribution and production – an inadequate one.

Production of various goods as well as their distributions should be in service of the normative ends of a society. Such ends can be debated and clarified in public discourse; a Christian ethical approach calls for attention to those distributional *and* aggregative factors in guaranteeing the social conditions for moral equality and social solidarity.

SCOPE AND DIFFERENTIALS

The claim related to expanding public discourse along this axis is as follows: the commitment to the moral equality of all people suggests that an equality of basic capability is a moral goal, and it calls for social transformation towards that situation. Further, any basic-functioning differential among groups' achievement (such as inequality among the races) is morally problematic. It is worth considering the contextual factors related to three "groupings": nationality, race, and gender.

[7] For a fuller discussion relating equality and solidarity, see chapter 8.
[8] Daly and Cobb have helped to shed public light on the fact that measures such as gross national product or gross domestic product include various activities that are arguably not normatively valuable (such as economic processes that produce excessive pollution or other social ills), while many valuable economic activities (such as non-market child-rearing) are not included. See Daly and Cobb, *For the Common Good*.

The moral significance of inequality is based on (descriptive and normative) claims about socially situated selfhood. These claims require an understanding of the contexts in which particular people should "function" well. A person's particular society, or nation, has thus far been considered to be the principal context. The approach could be made much more complex by also incorporating groupings like neighborhood-, gender-, race-, or class-based aggregations as important "reference groups" by which people compare themselves. The analysis could be complicated, in another way, by taking seriously the claims of "global citizenship." Indeed, this approach raises these questions and lays the groundwork for such expansions of discourse. Yet in the present work, and for the sake of parsimony of modeling, the argument has proceeded with the assertion that the principal context, and scope, in which to do analysis of inequalities is the national level.[9] Given such an assumption, in terms of distribution, a prime concern is inequality within nations. This attention to the national level also coincides with the highest level of political authority that can effectively respond to inequality. Significant potential exists for cross-national and global analysis.

Inequality of basic capability within a nation's population should be transformed. Within particular socioeconomic spheres, like income or education, public debate needs to resolve the question of how much inequality is commensurate with approximate equality of basic capability. The Christian ethical framework, drawing here on Walzer and Rainwater, emphasizes the social meanings of income and other goods;[10] the absolute and relative holdings of such goods are integral factors in the determination of basic capability.

Within a given national society, any statistically significant differential across groupings by gender or race, in the achievement of basic functionings, should be eliminated unless a compelling moral justification could account for the differen-

---

[9] An analysis of inequality of global and regional levels and trends is provided in chapter 3. Yet even most of that discussion depends on national data sets.

[10] See the discussions relating to the social nature of goods in chapter 8.

tial.[11] Historical or social analyses considering, for instance, the legacy of slaveholding in the United States or patriarchal household structures can help to *explain* why inequalities exist. But these explanations neither *justify* such inequalities, nor are they inconsistent with transformative efforts to remove them. Rather, inequalities between women and men and among the races are unacceptable signs of the times needing transformation.

Admittedly, gender inequalities in the sphere of income (and wealth) are a complex area for discussion, particularly since gender roles play such a central part. Attention must be given to the empirical realities that more women than men are caregivers of children at home, and that people (disproportionately women) who leave the workforce, even temporarily, forego both present income and future income potential. Victor Fuchs emphasizes the crucial point that as long as more women than men leave the workforce to be caregivers, a phenomenon of "statistical discrimination" against all women (at least against those of child-rearing age) will persist.[12] Yet it is important to analyze these very realities in structural and cultural terms, seeking to uncover the causes that serve to legitimate "essential difference" between men and women and their social roles. The issues here relate to the discussion of inequalities and differences in chapter 2. The burden of moral proof should be placed on those who would justify inequalities of income by appeals to gender roles. The account of basic capability and the commitment to moral equality provide a strong transformative impetus away from the conditions and structures that produce gender-related inequalities in income.[13]

---

[11] Elisabeth Schüssler Fiorenza points out that justifications have long been offered for the unequal treatment – and oppression – of women as well as of other people. My framework for public discourse would require the taking of such arguments seriously as moral arguments, although the conditions of publicity (particularly the norm of mutual respect) offer reasons for rejecting them on substantive grounds. The Christian ethical perspective developed in part two, of course, would oppose (and offer an alternative to) such arguments as being contrary to women's status as moral equals and to the social conditions and structures required by that equality.

[12] Victor R. Fuchs, *Women's Quest for Economic Equality* (Cambridge, MA: Harvard University Press, 1988).

[13] In addition to the work by Fuchs, a number of feminist social scientists have

This treatment of scope and differentials recognizes that the scope of moral equality is universal – and thus the argument for an equality of basic capability is likewise universal. But the determination of the basic functionings that comprise capability are context-dependent, and therefore attention must be paid to the relevant factors of context. An argument to justify significant inequalities in the space of basic functionings would have to be both context-dependent and articulated in moral terms. The presumption remains in favor of equality.

FORMS OF INEQUALITY COMPARISON

The discussion of this fourth and final "axis" is a clarification of the multiple kinds of comparisons that are possible within public discourse on inequality – already expanded along the three axes considered above. This section delineates the various concerns that can be addressed by "comparative" analysis of inequality. Since the very concept of inequality addresses the position of people relative to others, it is in itself already a form of comparison. This primitive type of comparison is reflected in any indicator or measure of inequality. Moving one step beyond this basic fact, *comparative* examinations of those inequality measures can evaluate how the degree of inequality varies across societies, goods, or time periods. Considering each of these forms of comparison in turn will help clarify and enable an expanded public discourse.

Comparisons across societies

This Christian ethical approach has emphasized that the scope of moral equality transcends national (and other) borders. Yet at the same time, the principal context of situatedness, and therefore of one's well-being determination, is one's particular society. Does attention to the national context preclude

addressed the questions related to gender roles and the "time allocation decisions" of women and men between work and family life. Most importantly, see the work of Juliet Schor, *Overworked American*; Arlie Hochschild, *The Second Shift* (New York: Avon Books, 1990) and *The Time Bind: When Work Becomes Home and Home Becomes Work* (New York: Metropolitan Books, 1997); and Sylvia Ann Hewlett, *When the Bough Breaks: The Cost of Neglecting our Children* (New York: Harper Perennial, 1991).

altogether examinations of inequalities across societies – examinations that would seem to be consistent with the universal scope of equality?

As chapter 3 models, international comparisons of inequality can be made in various ways. A truly global perspective on inequality could be undertaken by taking the world population as one whole, and then undertaking inequality analysis for the "society" of all humans. Empirical problems plague such an exercise – for instance, the question of currency exchange and purchasing power come to the fore. More significant, however, are the normative questions related to comparing the well-being of people in very different social contexts – especially if socially situated selfhood is taken with full seriousness. Inequality within a nation is arguably more relevant for one's well-being than is inequality within the global population. Thus, the cultural-social context must be held in tension with the universal scope of moral equality.

Further insight into the relation between social context and universality can be gained by attention to the question, "Inequality of what?" Amartya Sen suggests that while particular basic functionings – such as "having adequate income," "being well educated," or "being in good health" – may be universal, the specific goods required to attain these functionings are context-dependent.[14] Within each society, the attainment of the functioning "having adequate income" is some function of a person's absolute and relative forms of income. The balance among relevant factors varies from one society to another. That the (relative and absolute) components of well-being are context-dependent does not preclude the comparison of well-being across societies.

A distinct type of cross-societal comparative exercise entails seeking to evaluate the level of development for societies as a whole. A narrow form of cross-national comparison examines the per-capita levels of aggregate productivity (of any good) – this is a rough way to gauge the level of holdings of a good for persons in that national population. It is important to note,

---

[14] Amartya Sen, "Poor, Relatively Speaking."

however, that such an exercise pays no attention to the distribution of that good within any nation. One can note, for instance, the differential between per-capita gross national product (GNP) in the United States and the per-capita GNP in Sweden. (This is an international analogue to the kind of "differential" analysis undertaken across race-based and gender-based groupings within the United States, in chapter 4.)

A comparison of the degree of distributional inequality itself can also be made across countries – this exercise would indicate the comparative degree of disparity within particular nations. For instance, the level of income inequality in the United States can be compared with income inequality in Sweden. This second type of comparison pays no direct attention to the level of aggregate production (such as GNP per capita) in the various countries.

Each kind of these comparative exercises – aggregative and distributional – presents potential normative problems for an approach that emphasizes the context-dependence of basic functionings. Yet for purposes of discourse within the international development community, meaningful comparisons can be made about basic social goods related to income, education, and health. General aggregate and distributional indicators can provide important comparative information about basic capability.[15] One such cross-national comparison that includes both aggregative and distributional factors is proposed in the next chapter.

Comparison across goods

Within particular societies, a comparison can be made of distributional inequality of various goods. For instance, it is possible to examine the levels of inequality of income, of education, and of health/longevity within the United States. In order to make such a comparison meaningful, it is necessary to employ a similar summary measure of inequality – such as the

[15] Measures of development like the human development index, as well as other cross-national indicators, provide a precedent for such exercises, though in the following chapter I extend the project from predominantly aggregative indicators to include distributional measures as well.

Gini coefficient – in all three spheres.[16] This exercise reflects a comparison not across societies, but across goods. These two forms of comparison can be combined to explore, for example, the (different) relation of income inequality to education inequality in Brazil and in Guatemala. Such an exercise involves comparisons among people, between two goods, and between two nations.

The important point for comparisons "across goods" is that the level of inequality in any given population differs according to the "currency" in which distribution is considered. Both within and across societies, it matters which goods are taken into account. That income-based data are most readily available should not be allowed to obscure inequalities in various goods – and the various functionings that such goods enable. Normative emphasis on multiple spheres of functioning requires attention to inequalities of multiple social goods.

Comparisons over time

Inequality comparison is made yet more complex when the dimension of time is introduced. Changes in inequality in a good (like income) within some population (like inhabitants of the United States) can be monitored over time to examine the trends in inequality. This type of comparison is particularly important for a framework that prioritizes social transformation *towards* the social conditions of moral equality and social solidarity. By undertaking intertemporal comparison, chapter 4 suggests that trends in income inequality and in some race-based and sex-based inequalities of education and health remain morally troubling. Intertemporal analysis of inequality can be a fundamental method of examining the impacts of specific national (or state or local) policies on distributions.

Finally, introducing intertemporal concerns into public discourse and policy analysis enables a fuller examination of the relationship between inequality and productivity, the second axis discussed above. An account relating inequality and productivity

[16] The construction of the Gini coefficient is discussed in general terms in appendix A, and in relation to income, education, and health, in appendix B.

(in various functionings) requires the examination of their relationship over time. This comparative exercise could further expand public discourse about development and well-being.

CONCLUSIONS

Paula Rayman, an economist and director of the Radcliffe Policy Institute, asserts that "we measure what we value."[17] The moral force of her claim is that people *should* measure what they genuinely value. Her constructive call is to shift economic and policy-oriented analysis to questions that matter morally, and to focus on goods that citizens have reason to value. To that end, public discourse can be expanded along the four axes outlined above. Each of these discussions has raised (sometimes tedious) issues that help to specify public concern about inequality.

Taken together, these discussions serve to clarify the kinds of issues that must be addressed by persons and societies who express significant normative concern about distributional matters. Moving beyond productivity and growth as the central socioeconomic factor in well-being, discourse about inequality must then clarify the spheres of life upon which to focus, the various groupings of people to consider, and the kinds of comparisons to employ. None of these issues are simple or straightforward; but neither can they be overlooked by a normative perspective in which inequalities matter centrally.

It is important to emphasize that the expansion of discourse in this approach is intended, ultimately, to enable a constriction of inequalities – those inequalities that obstruct the social conditions of moral equality and solidarity. Effective policies and personal and civic actions are more likely to be realized if they are shown to address morally unacceptable inequalities *and* if carefully articulated analyses reveal the various dimensions of the problems – and potential solutions. Ultimately there is reason for Christian social ethics to value not only understandings of inequality, but the promotion of justice and well-being for all people.

[17] Paula Rayman, "The New Economic Equation," presentation at the Center for the Study of Values in Public Life, Harvard Divinity School, November 19, 1996.

CHAPTER 10

An application: inequalities and human development

A CONSTRUCTIVE PROPOSAL: THE INEQUALITY-ADJUSTED
HUMAN DEVELOPMENT INDEX[1]

As policy-oriented discussions of inequality become more specific and technical, the insights of Christian social ethics seem less direct. Yet in fields such as international development, it is necessary for policymakers, analysts, and citizens to apply ethical frameworks and insights to very specific problems and issues. Statistical analyses of poverty, water pollution, infant mortality, and the like, as well as rules and regulations for programs to overcome such problems, are framed in a specific way and thus reflect a number of values about what aspects of life are morally significant. Even such technical discussions related to inequality and other economic issues should be consistent with moral frameworks deemed acceptable by the relevant parties.

Insights from the Christian ethical approach developed in the book can be applied to public and policy-oriented discussions. As just one example of how the approach could make a contribution, this chapter provides a constructive proposal for including attention to inequality in the evaluation of genuine, lasting, equitable "human development." The proposal builds on the ongoing project of the United Nations Development Programme (UNDP) and its framework of the current "human development index" (HDI). This index and the UNDP reports that support it have become widely used by governments and

---

[1] This proposal appears in a slightly different form in Hicks, "Inequality-Adjusted Human Development Index." Reprinted with permission of Elsevier Science.

215

non-governmental organizations (NGOs) as they determine economic and social programs.

By expanding that index into an *"inequality-adjusted* human development index" (IAHDI), this chapter demonstrates how attention to particular values can help to shape an important discourse about the meaning of well-being and development. Such an initiative is thus an application of a Christian ethical approach whose normative insights can inform, and build upon, values within contemporary public debates. At the same time, it is important to clarify that any policy-oriented initiative does not capture all important aspects of a moral framework. For instance, achieving positive changes in particular indicators such as adult literacy or infant mortality do not fully account for the moral, social, and economic realities that human beings face in their everyday lives. Yet such data are significant, even morally significant, indicators of personal and societal well-being. If we value moral equality and solidarity, then the evaluation of human development should include attention to socioeconomic inequalities. Devising a way to adjust the HDI for inequality is one way to reflect those values.

THE HDI IN ITS PRESENT FORM

Before offering the constructive proposal, it is first necessary to provide a brief, critical review of the HDI as it is currently conceptualized and measured. As chapter 3 notes, the "human development" approach, articulated in the UNDP's annual *Human Development Reports* 1990–99, seeks to "put people back at the center of development."[2] As a way of indicating the degree of achievement of the goals of this approach, the HDI was devised. A value for the HDI, ranging from 0 to 1, is assigned to each country, with values closer to 1 reflecting greater levels of human development.

As articulated by the UNDP, human development is about the expansion of people's choices; the HDI itself is intended to indicate the level of attainment of some of those choices. The

Human Development Reports have adopted much of Amartya Sen's language about capability and functionings; the common appropriation of Sen's approach makes it unsurprising that this Christian ethical approach could join in and extend the UNDP's normative and policy-oriented discussions. Thus many of the values espoused herein, such as basic functioning in many spheres and removing dehumanizing conditions, are already present in the *Human Development Reports.*

The HDI attempts to encompass the three important spheres of socioeconomic life on which this book has also focused: income, education, and health/longevity. According to the UNDP, income itself is seen instrumentally as a means to acquire basic goods and services, indicating people's access to resources needed for a decent standard of living.[3] The real gross domestic product (GDP) per capita is employed, but as a country's GDP rises, it is discounted at an increasing rate. This discounting is designed to place emphasis on the *basic* income needed to acquire the goods and services required to meet a decent living standard, including things like food, clothing, and shelter.[4]

The education variable is designed to indicate people's choices to acquire knowledge. In its most recent form, it includes adult literacy rates (weighted two-thirds) and the combined enrollment ratios for students at all levels of education (weighted one-third). Together, these variables communicate general information about the educational level of the population of all ages.[5]

The health/longevity variable, life expectancy at birth,

---

[3] As I noted above, my normative approach emphasizes the social meaning(s) of income itself, not merely its instrumental role in acquiring basic goods and services.

[4] Gross *domestic* product is used instead of gross national product in order to avoid problems of exchange rates. The GDP is expressed in purchasing power parity (PPP) dollars in order to obtain rough comparability of access to basic goods and services across societies.

[5] Adult literacy is a "stock" concept, indicating what percentage of adults have acquired some minimal educational functioning (whether acquired from formal schooling or not from schooling). In contrast, school enrollment is technically a "flow" concept, reflecting what proportion of the (school-age) population is currently in school. The *HDR 1995* notes that the indicator of combined enrollment ratios "shows the stock of literacy quite easily for those under age 24" (technical note 3, p. 134). This is only because the literacy rate is such a *basic* educational indicator.

Table 10.1. *Conceptual framework for the HDI*

	Income	Education	Health/Longevity
Indicators of aggregate achievement (as described in text)	Income per capita (adjusted to favor basic income)	Adult literacy rate School enrollment ratios	Life expectancy at at birth

indicates the extent to which inhabitants of a country are able "to live a long and healthy life."[6] To be sure, indicators of longevity do not reveal directly the health quality of those life spans. It is possible to live eighty years in poor health,[7] or to live twenty or fewer years in perfect health before some unexpected death. Life expectancy is, of course, an aggregate measure for a population as a whole; on average, persons living in societies with higher life expectancies do tend to be in better health.

The HDI as it is presently constructed is determined for each country by combining these variables from each of the three dimensions as discussed above. The HDI is calculated by combining, with equal weight, an index for each of the three spheres. The technical aspects of this construction are presented in appendix C. The conceptualization of the HDI is presented in table 10.1.

Distributional problems within the present HDI framework

In its present form, the HDI incorporates little direct information about distributional concerns in any of the three spheres of basic functioning. In the sphere of health/longevity, no attention is paid to how the life expectancy figure varies across particular persons, ethnic/racial groups, rural or urban status, gender, or class/caste. It is, rather, a probability-determined measure based on information drawn from aggregate life

---

[6] *HDR 1995*, p. 11.
[7] Most people who manage to live to eighty years in poor health have benefited from significant medical attention, which is often, though not always, associated with high incomes. I am grateful to Paul Streeten for pointing out that "at low income levels, morbidity and mortality are closely related."

tables, and it is thus not a measure reflecting variation across individuals. For the most significant educational variable, adult literacy, a country's overall rate is given – which conveys only very crude information about how knowledge is distributed across the population.[8] In the sphere of income, the national real GDP per capita measure is employed. Until the *HDR 1999*, this figure was "discounted" for countries whose figure exceeded the gross world product per capita ($5120 in *HDR 1995* and $5,990 in *HDR 1998*).[9] The new methodology discounts GDP for all countries, but at an increasing rate as countries' GDP figure rises.[10] By either the old or the new methodology, there is only an adjustment to a country's per-capita GDP – an aggregate measure. Thus, this discounting illuminates nothing directly about the distribution of income *within* countries. Thus the HDI, while it evaluates conditions in three important dimensions of life, does not adequately address distributional inequality.

One effort to look at issues of "inequality" in the *Human Development Reports* has been to calculate an HDI for various groups and to compare their outcomes.[11] For instance, the *HDR 1995* disaggregates the US data by racial/ethnic groupings, with important results:

[W]ith the HDIs of white, black and hispanic populations separated, whites would rank number 1 in the world (ahead of Canada), blacks would rank number 27 (next to Luxembourg) and hispanics would rank number 32 (next to Uruguay). So, full equality is still a distant prospect in the United States, despite affirmative action policies and market opportunities.[12]

Similar disparities can be shown among groups in various

---

8 Each person is attributed with either a "0" if illiterate or as a "1" if literate.
9 *HDR 1995*, pp. 134–135; *HDR 1998*, p. 107.
10 The formula for discounting GDP was changed in the *HDR 1999* (see "Technical Note," esp. pp. 159–160, which presents and contrasts the old and the new methodology). Note that the proposed IAHDI could be determined by either the old or the new methodology. In the calculation of the IAHDI for the data set of 20 countries (which uses data from the *HDR 1995*), the old methodology is employed. *HDR 1999*, pp. 159–160.
11 This process of data disaggregation is a complex form of the "differential" technique employed in chapter 4 to examine race-based and gender-based inequalities.
12 *HDR 1995*, p. 22.

countries. A similar technique has been used as well to indicate rural-versus-urban disparities.[13]

The *Human Development Reports* have also used disaggregation to explore the disparities between male and female achievements in the three indicators of the HDI. The gender-related development index (GDI) is a calculation made by employing the same social indicators as the HDI but with data disaggregated by gender. The structure for calculating the GDI is particularly interesting because it allows for different weights to be assigned in the "trade-off" between valuing improvements for particular disfavored groups (in this case, women) and valuing improvements for the overall population.[14]

It should be stressed that a measure like the GDI is still aggregative in this sense: no information about the intra-population inequalities *among females* or *among males* is yielded. Hence this type of exercise is "group-based"; it explores the disparities of the respective aggregate measures between (or among) groups. Such an approach has the advantage of illuminating the average disparity between females and males – and thus emphasizing the need for development policies favoring, in this case, females as a group. By definition, of course, it does not address disparities that may be caused by other demographic factors. And, as previously stated, disparities *within* each gender grouping, while significant, are not included. Perhaps the most serious problem with the GDI is that inequalities in the income sphere are implicitly given much more weight than inequalities in either education or in health/longevity, a phenomenon that does not correspond to the UNDP's normative ends. Future refinements should be able to correct this problem.

As a complement to the HDI and GDI, an "IAHDI" attends to inequalities in all three spheres of basic functioning, taking

---

[13] See, for instance, *HDR 1999*, pp. 131–132.

[14] The most significant treatment of the GDI and other gender-related questions of human development is contained in "technical note 1" of the *HDR 1995*. This technical note is based on Sudhir Anand and Amartya Sen, "Gender Inequality in Human Development: Theories and Measurements," Occasional Paper no. 19 (New York: Human Development Report Office, 1995). See also *HDR 1999*, pp. 160–162, which describes an adjustment to the income component of the GDI that is analogous to the *HDR 1999* change in methodology of the HDI.

the population of a society as a whole. Appendix C demonstrates how these three forms of inequality could be weighted in various ways within such an index; the findings reported in the text employ the most straightforward calculation of the IAHDI. The construction of the IAHDI follows the UNDP's lead in reflecting the three spheres of basic functioning. Consonant with the emphasis on values related to equality and constraining inequality, it also incorporates distributional information.

THE IAHDI: EXPANDING THE HDI AND DEVELOPMENT DISCOURSE

Chapter 3 provides the conceptualization and calculation of inequality indices in three spheres of basic functioning: income, education, and health/longevity. It is important to note here that the "social goods" considered in each of the three spheres reflect, as closely as possible, basic functioning in each of these spheres. Specifically, in education, the "good" employed is *years of formal education*. Schooling is both a form of social participation and a form of preparation and access to obtain other important social goods. In terms of health/longevity, the *years of life lived* reflect, as directly as possible, the very basic functioning of people's ability to live long and healthy lives.[15] In the income sphere, the *annual income* of people indicates the "functioning" of having adequate income. (For each of these variables the degree of inequality is estimated by means of the Gini coefficient.) The results from these calculations, for a data set of twenty countries, have been presented in table 3.3 in chapter 3 (page 60): the degree of inequality for the three spheres for each country was found to vary significantly, though Latin American countries, in general, fare poorer than Asian countries in all three kinds of inequality – in income, education, and health/longevity.

---

[15] As discussed in appendix B, I employed mortality statistics for the age-at-death to estimate this functioning. Thus for each society, the "population" of my data set was not the total population, but those people who had died during the 1980s. This is the group for whom "ultimate age attainment" is known, and it can serve as a general indicator for the population as a whole.

In terms of pinpointing specific areas needing public policy attention and social transformation, the information related by the Gini coefficients and by the components of the HDI is more precise than any more complex indicator that combines these indicators. Then why does the UNDP combine its three components (through an equally weighted average) to offer the HDI? The UNDP has consciously – indeed strategically – constructed one simple indicator of "human development" as an explicit alternative (or at least a complement) to income- and growth-centered indicators like GNP per capita.[16]

Thus an important goal of the HDI is to expand public discussion of human development and well-being beyond talk of (income-based) productivity and growth. A Christian ethical approach supports this expansion, while calling for another expansion to attend to inequality as well. The HDI indices for income, education, and health/longevity give an adequate snapshot of human development, but inequalities in each of these spheres can be incorporated for a fuller picture, consistent with the values of human development and capability.

The proposed index, the IAHDI, is constructed as a modification of the HDI. In general terms, the adjustment of the IAHDI involves adding distributional information into each of the three sphere-specific indices of the HDI, then combining these three sphere-specific indices in precisely the way that they are combined to construct the present HDI. This combining of aggregative and distributional data in each sphere – the innovation of the IAHDI – can be described as a process of "discounting" the aggregative data with a variable reflecting the severity of the distributional inequality in that sphere. The IAHDI is calculated by an equally weighted combination of the (now discounted) sphere-specific indices. The framework for

---

[16] In his "Assessing Human Development," Special Contribution to the *HDR 1999* (p. 23), Amartya Sen recounts his discussions with the late Mahbub ul Haq about the goals of constructing and publicizing an HDI. Sen notes that while he has been a central figure in the construction and refinement of the index, the HDI is still a "crude" indicator. The information reflected in the detailed tables of the *Human Development Reports* is far more indicative of the complexities of development than is the HDI itself. But the index serves to promote discourse and action for human development – including attention to the detailed tables – and for this reason it is a valuable exercise.

Table 10.2. *Conceptual framework for the IAHDI*

	Income	Education	Health/Longevity
Indicators of aggregate achievement	Income per capita (adjusted to favor basic income)	Adult literacy rate School enrollment ratios	Life expectancy at birth
Indicators of distributional inequality	Gini coefficient for income	Gini coefficient for education	Gini coefficient for life-span

this process is shown in table 10.2; the technical points of the IAHDI are laid out in appendix C.

The IAHDI thus incorporates distributional patterns and aggregative indicators from all three dimensions of the UNDP framework. Seen in this way, the IAHDI is a refined, scalar index which combines six measures – as can be readily seen in table 10.2.[17] The data requirements for these calculations are not excessively demanding, and they draw largely from census data in specific countries, the most reliable form of socio-economic data. In addition, the IAHDI framework offers significant flexibility in weighting inequalities within the influential UNDP framework for addressing human development and well-being.

What difference does it make, in terms of evaluation of development, to adjust for inequality? The IAHDI as well as the HDI, for the same data set of twenty countries employed in chapter 3, are presented in table 10.3. And in table 10.4, the rankings among these countries by HDI and IAHDI are given. The change in ranks from the HDI to the IAHDI are also indicated, demonstrating the impact on the evaluation of human development and well-being when distributional concerns are introduced.[18]

[17] The aggregate measure for education is itself a composite of adult literacy rate and combined enrollment ratios.

[18] As is well noted in the annual *Human Development Reports*, the correlations of the three respective components with the HDI itself are relatively high: 0.95 for adjusted real GDP per capita, 0.83 for adult literacy rate, and 0.85 for life expectancy at birth. These high correlations have been much discussed in the literature. (See the

Table 10.3. *The HDI and the IAHDI for selected countries*

Country	HDI	IAHDI	Percentage loss
Hong Kong	0.905	0.633	30.1
Costa Rica	0.883	0.561	36.5
Korea (Rep.)	0.882	0.621	29.6
Chile	0.880	0.553	37.2
Venezuela	0.859	0.513	40.3
Panama	0.856	0.499	41.7
Mexico	0.842	0.488	42.1
Colombia	0.836	0.492	41.1
Thailand	0.827	0.539	34.9
Malaysia	0.822	0.519	36.9
Brazil	0.804	0.416	48.3
Peru	0.709	0.393	44.6
Dominican Rep.	0.705	0.375	46.8
Sri Lanka	0.704	0.483	31.4
Philippines	0.677	0.410	39.5
Nicaragua	0.611	0.354	42.1
Guatemala	0.591	0.256	56.6
Honduras	0.578	0.317	45.1
Zimbabwe	0.539	0.316	41.4
Bangladesh	0.364	0.158	56.6

Source: Based on author's calculations and data as described in appendices.

In determining the IAHDI for each country – by the process of discounting the components as described above – the "percentage loss" in HDI ranges from a low of 29.6 for the Republic of Korea to 56.6 for Guatemala and Bangladesh. As a con-

literature review in *HDR 1993*.) The correlations between the inequality measures and the HDI are 0.09 for income inequality, −0.65 for educational inequality, and −0.83 for age-span inequality. For the latter two measures, the correlation runs as expected: lesser inequality in education and longevity corresponds to greater human development. Income inequality has no significant correlation with HDI, and further, the sign is not in the expected direction. Income inequality has almost no relationship to adjusted real GDP per capita – with a value of 0.158. In fact, the correlation between income inequality and non-adjusted GDP per capita is −0.12.

Within the other two dimensions, inequality correlates highly and negatively (as expected) with the relevant indicator. That is, Educ. Gini has a −0.89 correlation to adult literacy (and a −0.69 correlation to educational enrollment). Age Gini has a −0.78 correlation to life expectancy at birth.

Despite such relatively high correlation coefficients, the distributional information is shown to add distinctive information to the UNDP framework, as indicated by the change in rankings presented and discussed in this chapter.

Table 10.4. *Country rankings by HDI and IAHDI*

Country	HDI	IAHDI	Change in ranks
Hong Kong	1	1	0
Costa Rica	2	3	−1
Korea (Rep.)	3	2	1
Chile	4	4	0
Venezuela	5	7	−2
Panama	6	8	−2
Mexico	7	10	−3
Colombia	8	9	−1
Thailand	9	5	4
Malaysia	10	6	4
Brazil	11	12	−1
Peru	12	14	−2
Dominican Rep.	13	15	−2
Sri Lanka	14	11	3
Philippines	15	13	2
Nicaragua	16	16	0
Guatemala	17	19	−2
Honduras	18	17	1
Zimbabwe	19	18	1
Bangladesh	20	20	0

Source: Based on author's calculations and data as described in appendices.

sequence, Guatemala falls by two spots in the rankings, Bangladesh has no further to fall, and the Republic of Korea rises above one of the two countries ahead of it in the HDI rankings. Most Latin American countries, a region known to have the most severe income distribution problem, fall in rank when inequality is factored into the development discussion. That is, if human development and well-being are conceptualized without inequality (by using the HDI in its present form), the Latin American countries do relatively well; that evaluation shifts significantly when inequality is counted in by means of the IAHDI.

The IAHDI, and the Gini coefficients that factor into it, reveal that inequality is significant not just in income, but in education and health as well. Measures of inequality *of income* have been criticized because income-based deprivation is sometimes only temporary; income-inequality measures like the Gini coefficient, reflecting one point in time, thus do not directly address the permanence of the distribution. Educational and health/longevity inequalities, however, are more permanent phenomena whose social and moral import cannot be dismissed with such a criticism.[19]

THE IAHDI AND THE DOMESTIC US CONTEXT

What is the relevance or potential contribution of an index like the IAHDI for discourse and policy-oriented debate within the US domestic context? As illustrated in table 10.2, six kinds of indicators are included in the exercise of constructing the IAHDI – aggregative and distributional measures for income, education, and health/longevity. The innovation of the UNDP has been to expand public discussion beyond the sphere of income; the IAHDI incorporates distributional concern in each of these spheres. In shifting from cross-national discussions of development to the domestic context, it will be helpful to structure the inquiry along these same axes of expansion – considering first the aggregation/distribution question and then the question of multiple spheres.

In a 1994 article, Stephan Klasen addresses the relation of aggregation and distribution in well-being measures for the United States. Klasen constructively considers the proper roles that (income-based) growth and inequality should play in evaluating economic performance in the postwar United States.[20] Invoking various arguments for incorporating distributional concern into well-being measures,[21] Klasen proceeds to offer four related methods to expand well-being measures beyond aggregate indicators (like changes in GNP per capita) to include attention to income inequality. Adjusting growth rates

---

[19] I am indebted to Paul Streeten for noting this important implication of the IAHDI.

[20] Stephan Klasen, "Growth and Well-Being: Introducing Distribution-Weighted Growth Rates to Reevaluate US Post-War Economic Performance," *Review of Income and Wealth* 40/3 (September 1994).

[21] Klasen's three kinds of justification are utilitarianism, the capability approach, and economist Fred Hirsch's account of positional goods and the *Social Limits to Growth*. My own approach draws from, and seeks to integrate, insights from the latter two forms of argument. See Klasen, "Growth and Well-Being," pp. 252–253.

by information provided by the Gini coefficient, two of these methods bear a strong affinity to the construction of the income component of the IAHDI.[22] Empirically, Klasen's findings reveal that when inequality and income-based productivity are factored together, "well-being growth" in the Kennedy–Johnson era far exceeds that in the Reagan era – a result that should not be surprising in light of the inequality discussion of chapter 4.[23] Klasen's framework, then, models an important kind of expansion of public discourse consistent with the values of a Christian ethical approach.

At the same time, Klasen's consideration of productivity and inequality is still confined to the sphere of income. As noted in chapter 4, economists have focused on the sphere of income – particularly when inequality is addressed. Yet on this point, economists Esfandiar Maasoumi and Gerald Nickelsburg note that "[t]here is general agreement among economists that the traditional money-income measures are inadequate and more comprehensive measures of economic status are needed."[24] How would a multiple-sphere expansion look in US domestic discourse? First, examining changes in the HDI for the US

[22] In fact, one of these two "growth indices," which Klasen calls "Gini 1," discounts mean income for each period by a factor of (1 – Gini), the same basic method employed in the IAHDI. See appendix A. Interestingly, Klasen's "Gini 2" is a refinement to "Gini 1" that could also be consistent with my approach. Gini 2 incorporates the same distribution discounting as in Gini 1, but it also includes a further adjustment based on "a function where the utility of a person depends not only on her own income and the overall shape of the income distribution (as in Gini 1), but additionally on the number and the incomes of people ahead of her in the income distribution" (p. 259). Klasen goes on to note that this further refinement may "be particularly suited to Hirsch's analysis" based on positional goods; it is also generally compatible with the socially situated dimensions of my approach. For the sake of parsimony and data availability, the method employed in Gini 1 serves my model.

[23] A. B. Atkinson performs a similar adjustment to national income in the United Kingdom, showing that when distribution is accounted for, UK economic performance in the 1980s is seen as significantly poorer ("Bringing Income Distribution in from the Cold," pp. 302–303).

[24] Maasoumi and Nickelsburg, "Multivariate Measures of Well-Being and an Analysis of Inequality in the Michigan Data," *Journal of Business and Economic Statistics* 6/3 (July 1988), p. 327. This article offers a brief review and helpful bibliography of efforts by economists to expand inequality and well-being analysis beyond "traditional money-income spheres." In their own project, Maasoumi and Nickelsburg propose inequality indicators (based on Theil's entropy-based measures instead of on the Gini coefficient) for net housing equity and schooling.

population as a whole broadens the evaluation of trends of economic well-being. Such an analysis reveals that the HDI for the United States increased from 0.865 in 1960 to 0.942 in 1994. Over that same period, real GDP per capita in the United States rose from $10,707 to $20,500.[25] Since this increase in income was hardly factored into the HDI in its earlier form (since income rises about gross world product had little impact on HDI), most of the rise in HDI can be attributed to improvements in education and health spheres.[26]

As discussed above, the HDI is limited in the domestic context in the same way as in the international discussions: more direct attention to inequality can be given. Chapter 4 discusses the analysis of inequality within the US population in three spheres of basic functioning, and the findings indicated there are: taking the US population as a whole, significant inequalities exist in education and health/longevity as well as in income. As shown in figure 4.3 (page 72), the trends in inequality of basic education and health/longevity are not the same as inequality of income: over the past twenty-five years, the continued steady decrease of overall inequality in the former two spheres contrasts with the rising income inequality figures.

Using the Gini coefficients for the US population presented in chapter 4, an IAHDI for the United States over time could be readily determined. Such a task has not been undertaken, for two reasons. The first was stated above, that until the *Human Development Reports* refined their methodology in 1999, changes in per capita income in wealthy countries were hardly factored into the income component of the HDI framework. Second, and more important, within the US domestic context, information about inequalities of health/longevity and education based on race and gender disaggregation is more precise and

---

[25] *HDR 1997*, table 5, p. 158. The GDP per capita figures are expressed in 1987 US dollars. *HDR 1998* (table 1, pp. 128–130) showed an increase to 0.943 in the HDI for the United States. Note that *HDR 1999* introduced a new adjustment to the income component and thus its figures are not strictly comparable with earlier figures.

[26] A potentially illuminative exercise would be to compare the changes in the HDI for various countries over time vis-à-vis trends in GDP per capita. Table 5 and table 6 of the *HDR 1997*, pp. 158–163, provide the data for such an analysis.

illuminative than the population-wide indicators that are employed in the IAHDI determination. In other words, while the IAHDI is helpful as a general indicator that promotes attention to distributional concerns within the context of international development efforts, it should be complemented in domestic policymaking discussions by more targeted inquiries. Within the US context, such inquiries include various calculations of "differentials" by race and gender groupings – as extensively discussed in chapter 4.

Thus within the US domestic context, the expansion of public discourse can occur along the two axes that comprise the IAHDI – multiple spheres and aggregation-and-distribution. The use of empirical data and indicators is not exactly parallel in international-development and US-domestic contexts, but the proposed forms of expansion share the common normative goal of attending more centrally and carefully to distributional concerns.

CONCLUSIONS

If measures of human development should reflect the relevant values, then a normative emphasis on moral equality should be reflected by attention to distribution within indexes such as the HDI. To incorporate distributional concerns by means of the IAHDI is to promote a "rhetoric of inequality" within discussions of human development. Just as the HDI has managed to shift debate beyond talk of the GNP or GDP, the IAHDI should inject distributional concerns more explicitly into policymaking discussion in the contexts in which the *Human Development Reports* are widely used: UN agencies, NGOs, and national development and social-service agencies. The IAHDI thus helps public discourse about well-being and development to put people at the center of development, but also to care about how those people share in its benefits.

The particularities of the proposed index, while laid out here and in appendix C, comprise a constructive proposal of its own merit. Just as important, the exercise is meant to provide an example of how a policy-oriented proposal can "operationalize" or put into practice the values of a Christian ethical approach. It could be suggested that nothing specific about the IAHDI is "Christian." Yet perhaps the proposal can gain stronger justification among Christians and in the public at large, from arguments like those comprising the Christian ethical approach. The Christian perspective would readily join with other perspectives to put inequality more centrally on the development agenda.

CHAPTER 11

Conclusion: implications for inequality and Christian ethics

What does Christian ethics have to say about inequality? The previous chapters have taken up this question in a variety of ways, engaging with interlocutors theological, philosophical, and social-scientific. Discussions have ranged from empirical analysis of inequality at international and domestic levels, to a reading of equality and inequality in Christian theology, to a policy-oriented proposal for assessing genuine and equitable human development. The "and" in *Inequality and Christian Ethics* proves to be as complex as any of the other words in that title. Particular substantive insights into Christian social ethics and the evaluation of inequality should be valuable in their own right. Yet the most significant innovation or contribution of this book may be its constructive, multifaceted conversation among Christian ethics, political philosophy, and the development literature around the question of inequality.

This concluding chapter does not provide a comprehensive summary of the insights of the book, though some of the arguments and findings are noted. The central task-at-hand, rather, is to name some implications of this project. Like the inquiry itself, these implications relate to a number of dimensions of inequality and to different persons and groups. The approach calls for analysis that is empirical as well as normative and that integrates interdisciplinary perspectives. Action, too, is needed, on the part of Christians, people of other faiths, and those espousing no faith. This action extends to personal, communal, and societal levels. There are implications for understanding inequality as an issue-in-itself and for addressing other social and economic problems. This "conclusion" draws together selected insights of the book while setting an agenda for future analysis and action.

CONSTRUCTING A CHRISTIAN ETHICAL VISION AND EVALUATING ECONOMIC SYSTEMS

The constructive Christian approach to inequality, drawing on the theologies of H. Richard Niebuhr and Gustavo Gutiérrez, suggests that a commitment to equality and social solidarity provides a basic framework for evaluating the moral significance of inequality. The Christian ethical approach developed herein has focused, in language borrowed from Amartya Sen, on inequalities related to functionings and capability. Inequalities that obstruct the conditions for equality and solidarity – and thus the basic sense of stake or participation on the part of all people – should be transformed. Sen's framework calling for an "equality of basic capability" is supported by the approach's emphasis on the social-relational nature of people and on the preferential commitment to those who face absolute or relative deprivation.

A moral examination of the socioeconomic order must reveal and criticize the ways in which present-day social structures do not adequately correspond to the Christian ethical commitment to equality and solidarity. This project opens up space for examination of how particular economic systems – such as those based, to different degrees, on "free" market mechanisms – enable or "generate" specific inequalities.[1] Stated differently, a framework has been provided from which to undertake analysis of specific economic programs and policies in specific times and places. This approach (following Sen on this point) would suggest that any such analysis should address, as directly as possible, distributions of functionings and capability.

This moral-theological vision also entails a call to action. The accounts of equality in Niebuhr and Gutiérrez call people from their present condition to work toward a more good and just society. This is one of the principal contributions that Christian

---

[1] The term "generate" here invokes the title of Lester Thurow's important work on this subject, *Generating Inequality*.

ethical perspectives make in public discourse: theological language and imagery can move people to action. A constructive reading of Thiemann's account of religion in public life has helped to demonstrate how a theologically informed approach can be compelling to citizens from various worldviews and religious and secular communities. This includes, of course, the tremendous unrealized potential of Christians and their (our) churches to effect positive social change. Despite majority status, Christians and churches must neither claim undue social status or privilege in public life nor become separate from public life in private, other-worldly, or sectarian camps. Consistent with the norm of moral integrity, telling the stories of persons and communities engaged in work of charity or justice can increase the impact of the guiding moral-theological vision.[2] In addition, this project can help to inform and motivate people (within and without churches) to engage in outreach and lobbying efforts that would address actual inequalities and their impact on people's lives. At the same time, it should be clear that the task of addressing contemporary inequalities involves more than lobbying government and volunteering in charities; a wide public conversation about the moral, social, economic, and political dimensions of inequality should forge a public will to respond to inequality in a more complete and coordinated way.

EXPANDING DISCOURSE AND PROMOTING WELL-BEING

"Expanding public discourse" has served as a theoretical frame in which to place this project. It has referred to a number of complementary endeavors. First, public discourse can be expanded by adding fuller moral accounts of equality and inequality than contemporary liberalism tends to offer. The

---

[2] David Hollenbach, S.J. suggests that in addition to theological or philosophical accounts of religious language in public life, scholars should engage in empirical studies of actual church-related efforts at public engagement, including religiously motivated activism. Hollenbach, "Politically Active Churches: Some Empirical Prolegomena to a Normative Approach," in Paul J. Weithman (ed.), *Religion and Contemporary Liberalism*, pp. 291–306. See also my discussion of moral examples and moral integrity in the first section of chapter 9.

Christian ethical approach serves as one substantive example and contribution of one perspective. This framework also invites people holding complementary or conflicting viewpoints into a respectful public conversation (guided by the "conditions of publicity" described in chapter 5). In a complementary vein, some analytical tools for the conversation were offered. This latter effort was comprised of four "axes" for centering and expanding public discussions of inequality – including its various technical dimensions. The specific proposal of an inequality-adjusted human development index would put inequality more centrally into public debate about development. While these analytical expansions are consistent with my normative perspective, certainly most of the constructive, policy-oriented insights provided or suggested in chapters 9 and 10 could be supported by people from various moral viewpoints. Rather than being a problem, this is a sign of possibility for common efforts to address distributional problems.

Of course, concern about equality and inequality are already present in public discourse. One predominant way in which the attendant issues are framed is through language of "equality of opportunity." The approach of this book suggests that this language, while promising in theory, can be problematic in practice. At a minimum, it must be further specified. *Outcomes* in one space result from *opportunities* in another space. One must therefore ask, "What is the space in which equality of opportunity should be guaranteed?" From an approach emphasizing an equality of basic capability, social goods in income, education, and health/longevity all provide opportunities to pursue other valuable ends. Language of capability and that of opportunity capture much of this same spirit of "possibility." At the same time, the social nature of goods emphasizes that goods related to basic functionings do more than merely provide opportunities to be or to have something else: holding the goods themselves already represents a valuable form of social participation. Income itself is one important social good, bearing social meanings and providing social possibility. Since relative holdings of income factor into these matters, genuine equality of opportunity would necessitate limiting inequalities of income. In its most common usage, however, language of equality of opportunity is often employed to justify *more* inequality of income, not less.[3] A Christian ethical approach thus contains a concern for opportunity, although the book has tended to employ the associated, and more carefully developed, concept of capability. The commitment to work for an equality of basic capability will require more equality (but not absolute equality) in the sphere of income.

CONSTRAINING INEQUALITIES AND FORGING PRAGMATIC POLICIES

These pages have not provided a generic answer for "how much inequality is too much" in any particular sphere, space, or good. Since capability is comprised of various functionings as well as freedoms, even an absolute equality of capability among persons in a society does not require absolute equality in any single functioning.[4] It has also been noted, though, that when comparing groups (and not individuals), significant inequality in any basic functioning would need to be justified morally – or else alleviated.[5]

The IAHDI is modeled on the assumption that given the inequality levels existing in contemporary societies, more equality is preferred to less in each sphere of basic functioning. Further exploration could consider some "threshold" distributional level, in one or more of the spheres, at which point a society would have achieved a tolerable – that is, morally acceptable – level of inequality.[6] The larger point is that the

---

[3] See the section, "Equality and inequality," in chapter 2 for a discussion of how moral arguments about equality in one space explicitly or implicitly allow for inequalities in other spaces. In his classic work, *Equality and Efficiency: The Big Tradeoff*, Arthur Okun contrasts equality of income and equality of opportunity. (See especially chapter 3.) This usage reflects the standard view that "equality of opportunity" is intended to justify the distribution of income, not to lessen income inequality.

[4] See chapter 2.

[5] See chapter 9.

[6] Consequently, the construction of the IAHDI would need to be refined to evaluate as equivalent all inequality levels below that threshold. See appendix C for a discussion, within the IAHDI framework, of flexible weighting of the indicators of inequality and aggregate achievement.

respective roles of distributional inequalities and aggregate achievements in the assessment of development should be addressed. Without resolving the balance, the approach creates room for public debate to determine how to give weight to these particular concerns. The contribution of this approach is not a precise way to "balance" inequality and achievement, but rather to make sure that inequality gets at least some moral and social attention.[7]

Thus this Christian ethical approach has sought to deepen (but not resolve univocally or unequivocally) a public debate precisely on issues of "how much inequality is too much," and to shift such discussion to an intrinsically important space of functionings and capability. This does not resolve, but rather it begs, the policy-based questions about how to constrain those inequalities that are determined to be morally unacceptable. Programs that target income-based *poverty* can have significant *inequality*-reducing effects in income and, less directly, in other spheres of life. Similarly, programs that target people facing education-based or health-based deprivation have the effect of reducing inequalities. Indeed, reducing severe shortfalls in these spheres – bringing those at the bottom upwards – are arguably the least objectionable form of inequality reduction. Many analysts who acknowledge and illuminate issues of economic inequality thus propose agendas aimed solely at the bottom end of socioeconomic distributions.[8]

---

[7] Stephan Klasen makes a similar point: "Clearly, the case for the alternative measures [that incorporate inequality information] is not based on the certainty of the particular weights attached to distributional concerns but the claim that an incorporation of distributional concerns may approximate changes in welfare better than a total neglect of them" ("Growth and Well-Being," p. 261). While Klasen's examination is confined to the income sphere, his point supports my claim for all three spheres of basic functioning. See also my discussion of equality and efficiency, below.

[8] A few notable examples will reinforce this point. In drawing policy conclusions from a chapter called "Inequality and Economic Rewards," the *ERP 1997* (chap. 5) considers only those policies that raise the income, education, or health prospects of people at the bottom of those distributions. (The distributional effects of a progressive income tax system are noted, but changes to taxation are N O T considered.) In their important 1995 book entitled, *America Unequal*, Danziger and Gottschalk present their constructive proposals in the final chapter, "An Antipoverty Agenda." As they state: "Our primary concern is to improve employment prospects and earnings for those with low skills who want to work . . . We propose an expanded antipoverty initiative that emphasizes assistance to workers. For those who have jobs, we propose expanded

It is important to state in no uncertain terms that such programs targeting the deprivations of people on the margins are crucial elements of societal effort to move toward an equality of basic capability. In fact, talk of a safety net or floor is not precluded by this emphasis on inequality rather than poverty. Yet any net, floor, or threshold should always be determined by taking absolute and *relative* factors into account.

The normative emphasis on preferential care to people in need supports such programs directed towards those at the bottom of socioeconomic distributions. At the same time, in the policy arena, proposals can be couched in as *universal* terms as possible while having the *disproportionate effect* of promoting the well-being of the most disadvantaged. Theda Skocpol's argument for "Targeting within Universalism" has already sparked significant discussion of this issue.[9] The lengthy discussion in chapter 8 on solidarity, universality, and preferential options provides moral resources to extend discussion beyond the pragmatic justifications for universality often presented in these debates.

There are two related points suggested by this approach. First, the very determination of poverty or deprivation depends on the space of the social analysis; if capability and functionings (in spheres including education and health, for instance) are emphasized in policymaking, the type of programs and their targeting will be different than if income alone is emphasized. In terms of the targeting of initiatives within any particular space, the analysis in chapters 4 and 9 has suggested that careful

wage supplements and child care credits. For those who want to work but cannot find regular employment, we advocate transitional public service jobs paying the minimum wage. These proposals follow from our belief that the American public is willing to spend additional government funds to provide opportunities for the able-bodied poor to work their way out of poverty" (pp. 154, 155).

[9] Theda Skocpol, "Targeting within Universalism: Politically Viable Policies to Combat Poverty in the United States," Discussion Paper Series H-90-2, Center for Health and Human Resources Policy, John F. Kennedy School of Government, Harvard University, 1990; Michael Walzer makes a similar point in his *Spheres of Justice*, drawing on examples from Greek city-states and medieval Jewish communities to demonstrate that the redistributive effects of social provision are often more tolerated when they are couched in "general," not "particular," terms. (See especially his chapter 3, "Security and Welfare.") I am grateful to Brent Coffin for discussion of this point.

attention to differentials by race-based and sex-based grouping can be effective in reducing unacceptable inequalities. The respective discussions of these inequalities suggest various ways in which a multiple-sphere approach can illuminate the discussion and targeting of policies. The point is to ask not merely the question, "Inequalities of what?" but also to consider, as specifically as possible, "Inequalities among whom?"

Second, the normative focus on inequality alongside poverty requires attention to the whole distribution of social goods, and not just the bottom end. This is particularly important in the US context, in which the official, income-based poverty rate has fluctuated but remained in roughly the same range over the past three decades, while income inequality has steadily risen. Inequality-based approaches, unlike viewpoints narrowly focused on poverty, understand these trends as morally problematic. Policies addressing the overall distribution of income and wealth, education, and healthcare access and services are required. Such a claim, of course, raises the specter more directly of policies that reduce some people's holdings of social goods in order to reduce inequality.[10] Consideration of such redistributions, within spheres of basic social functioning, should be held within the realm of possibility and debate. At a minimum, discussions of income and inheritance taxes should recognize the recent trends in income (and wealth) inequality. At the same time, in the kinds of measures of well-being suggested by this analysis, a concern for both aggregate production *and* for distributional inequality (in various spheres) is included.[11] This approach requires moral and social balancing, rather than implying that equality is the only social value. Other values, including economic freedom, also figure in discussions about redistributive policies.

[10] In economic language, this raises the possibility of initiatives that are "Pareto-inferior," shifts that could make some people worse off than they were before. For discussions of the Pareto optimality, superiority, and inferiority, see Amartya Sen, *On Ethics and Economics*, chapter 2, and various essays in Sen, *Choice, Welfare, and Measurement* (Cambridge, MA: MIT Press, 1982). For an interesting discussion of these questions vis-à-vis Rawls's discussion of his own normative proposal, "justice as fairness," see *A Theory of Justice*, pp. 66–80.

[11] See chapter 9.

Thus, there is no attempt to solve or resolve the so-called "efficiency–equality" tradeoff – in favor of equality or in any other way. Rather, the equality side needs to be given more careful attention in public discourse and policymaking discussion. It is also worth noting that it is not clear what the complex empirical relations between equality and efficiency are. Questions of economic incentives, savings rates, and the administrative costs of redistribution all figure here.[12] None of these factors are beyond dispute, and the book has not taken them up in detail. These debates notwithstanding, the equality–efficiency tradeoff can be analyzed within various spaces – not just in terms of income.[13] According to the Christian ethical approach (following Sen), the debate would be more fruitfully carried out in the space of functionings and capability than in the space of income alone. That is, it is more important to understand tradeoffs in terms of people's respective capabilities than in terms of their incomes. Further attention can be given to the important claim of recent *Human Development Reports* and their surrounding literature that successful long-term economic growth is strongly linked to egalitarian public policies related to income, education, and healthcare.[14] Surely this literature provides insights for addressing inequalities and productivity growth in the US context as well.

As the resources of Christian ethics are appropriated within more specific policymaking discussions, the necessity to forge "pragmatic" or "implementable" initiatives and programs will come to the fore. According to standard views of *homo oeconomicus*, better-off people would not want to give up their goods even for the benefit of those with less. Two clarifications to this question of "self-interest" can be made here. The first point involves the ambiguities in the term "self-interest" itself. A

---

[12] Arthur Okun's analysis of the "leakages" in efficiency is a very good account of these various factors. See his *Equality and Efficiency*, chapter 4, especially pp. 96–100.

[13] See especially Sen, *Inequality Reexamined*, pp. 136–138.

[14] See especially Speth, "Global Inequality," and Anand and Ravallion, "Human Development in Poor Countries." Further, the *HDR 1999*, with its theme of "globalization with a human face," continues the tradition of seeing the crucial role of economic productivity and growth, but fitting it within the wider framework of human development for all citizens.

person's interests can be focused on one's own well-being as well as on the well-being of others; both of these are interests *of the self*. A person whose own well-being is impacted by the well-being of others exercises what Adam Smith termed "sympathy."[15] Even those who do not experience sympathy can still act in the interests of others – for reasons of moral "commitment."[16] A Christian ethical approach can endorse activities to increase both sympathy and (particular forms of) commitment in all people.

It is important to note, as the second point, that even when self-interest is understood narrowly as exclusively self-regarding, redistributive policies can still be in the "enlightened" interest of economically advantaged people. Specifically, "ruptures in solidarity" can entail serious costs for all persons in a society – but particularly for those who hold the most goods. It is fitting to refer again to the fear and violence present in South Africa, so closely associated with its economic (and other forms of) inequality. As another example, the growth of "gated communities" in the United States, which now include an estimated eight million US citizens, is arguably related to the recent rise in income and wealth inequality.[17] Stated colorfully, the social-relational dimension of well-being raises not just a question of "keeping up with the Joneses"; there may also be a

---

[15] Adam Smith, *The Theory of Moral Sentiments* (Indianapolis: Liberty Press, 1982 [1790]).

[16] This distinction between sympathy and commitment is offered by Amartya Sen in his article, "Rational Fools," especially sections 4 and 8. Sen shows in a later essay that a person's sense of her or his *welfare*, and her or his *goals* that transcend one's own welfare, are distinct from one's actual *choices*. Further, any of these levels – welfare, goals, or choices – can entail either self-regarding or other-regarding preferences. The important point here is that the notion of self-interest fails even to identify these various types of considerations; other-regarding interests can operate at any or all of these levels (Sen, "Goals, Commitment, and Identity"). These issues are taken up in relation to creating social solidarity in Douglas A. Hicks, "Solidarity in Global and National Contexts: Insights from Economic Theory," American Academy of Religion Annual Meeting, November 1997.

[17] Martin Walker, "Behind Bars of Fort Suburbia: Crime Rate Goes Down as Common-Interest Developments Go Up," *Pittsburgh Post-Gazette* (7/13/1997), A9. The quoted source of this estimate in this and other news service articles is Ed Blakely, Dean of the School of Urban Planning and Development at the University of Southern California. I make no attempt to establish causality here; further exploration of this point could shed light on the relationship of inequality to solidarity in the contemporary US context.

phenomenon of "stealing from the Joneses" – or at least the fear thereof. Stated more straightforwardly, self-interest can complement moral commitments in leading people to address excessive inequalities.

Appropriating the resources of a Christian ethical approach in specific policy debates will require contextual and pragmatic consideration. The determination of what inequality levels are "acceptable" may depend not merely on moral visions of equality but also on what is achievable within particular cultural, political, and economic contexts. Programs carefully targeted at people in need may be best couched in terms of universal scope and availability. Arguments about economic freedom, efficiency, and self-interest should be taken seriously as perspectives that deserve clarification, refutation, and/or coalition.

COOPERATING IN HUMILITY AND HOPE

This approach provides a vision of a society marked by the social conditions in which people realize their full and equal personhood in genuine solidarity with one another. Human efforts for a more just and humane society need not be equated with the realization of the *basileia* in order for the approach to have a significant transformative impetus. H. Richard Niebuhr notes the humility and caution with which social efforts should be undertaken; yet he stresses that humans are nonetheless called to act for social transformation.[18] In actual societies, the specifics of the moral goal need not be indisputable in order for transformation in a particular direction to be possible. In practical efforts, people from a variety of worldviews and perspectives may find common ground for actions and policy-making.

At the same time, the normative perspectives of Christian ethics seek to shape people's understanding of themselves, their society, and creation as a whole, not just by analyzing "what is,"

[18] See chapter 6.

but by providing a positive, goal-oriented moral vision of "what could be." The language of "reading the signs of the times" entails a call to understand and to respond to current realities in light of the eschatological vision of God's *basileia*. The liberationist tension between preferential and inclusive solidarity also captures the need to analyze contemporary problems by looking and working towards more just and humane alternatives. As this book has sought to model, careful and constructive engagement with philosophers, economists, and policymakers can lead to new perspectives.

The Christian ethical approach does not permit a simple dichotomy between personal interests and societal arrangements. Articulations of the moral equality of persons, and actions to create social conditions in which all can realize their personhood, go hand in hand. If self-interest is already a socially determined interest, as Marx rightly noted, societies which provide the social conditions of moral equality and solidarity will also tend to form people who exercise both sympathy and commitment for others. The reinforcing circle of personal formation and social structures can be either negative or positive; attention to inequality in public discourse should help to produce the latter result. A central point of expanding public discourse is thus to promote transformative praxis at personal, collective, and public policy levels. These efforts need be neither naïvely optimistic nor flawlessly conceived in order to be personally and socially valuable.

READING THE SIGNS OF THE TIMES . . . AGAIN

This inquiry has been motivated by attention to one particular sign of the times. The methodology, drawing on liberationist understandings of theory and praxis, calls for regularly returning to read the empirical realities of the times with more normatively and analytically focused lenses. Socioeconomic inequality is not the only sign of the times that requires public attention. At the same time, to understand inequality more carefully and completely can shed light on many of the most pressing social and economic problems that define the turn of the century. Problems described as "globalization," "market-ization," "technological revolution," and the "time bind" each entail important distributional dimensions. This project can inform further research into each of these socioeconomic phenomena.

Globalization has opened up both economic systems and human consciousness. A global marketplace has made the flow of capital, technology, and in some cases labor more simple across national borders. The rise in global consciousness has raised the possibility – indeed the inevitability – of compari-sons across national borders. Treatments of inequalities and distributive justice have only begun to address the myriad issues raised by globalization.[19] Public discourse about globali-zation should be expanded beyond talk of aggregate pro-duction and growth to include its various distributional effects.[20] The "axes of expansion" developed in chapter 9 and the normative perspectives of part two provide resources for that undertaking.

"Marketization," like globalization, encompasses a number of aspects. First, marketization concerns thinking about issues not traditionally considered economic – like healthcare pro-vision, the environment, marriage and family, and even religion – as based on "markets" for one or more goods in which people (whose tastes and preferences are seen as static) seek to max-imize their self-interest.[21] The second and related point is that transactions involving such issues can be thought of in terms of money. The Christian ethical approach expresses moral concern about the ways in which marketization shifts analysis not towards the space of functionings and capability, but rather towards a money-related space. And even within the latter, it is not clear that distributional concerns are adequately addressed. The central issue to be examined, then, is whether market-

---

[19] See chapter 9 for a discussion of some of the complex issues involved in international comparisons of inequality.

[20] See the opening paragraphs of chapter 3, and references, for a discussion of the ways in which inequality has been treated in some recent analyses of globalization.

[21] This description follows Gary Becker's account of *The Economic Approach to Human Behavior* (outlined on his p. 5).

ization involves an expansion or a constriction of public moral discourse.[22]

The technological shifts resulting from computer and tele-communications advances raise serious distributional issues – particularly in spheres of knowledge and income, and their interrelation. As discussed in chapter 4, in the United States the skyrocketing "premium" on a college education over the past twenty-five years is a phenomenon closely related to the computer revolution.[23] The structural shift of the US economy in face of globalization, further, is driven by advantages related to technological capacity. Access to the internet will increasingly be a mark of full participation not only in the economy, but in the cultural and social dimensions of citizenship, national and global. In both the US and international contexts, careful exploration of the distributional effects of, and responses to, technological transformation is thus one of the most significant areas for further research that is suggested by this project. The realization of solidarity and capability – and thus equality – will require understanding of and response to technological changes that have led to a so-called "digital divide."

Finally, for contemporary societies like the United States, the "time bind" – a cluster of issues related to balancing and integrating work, family, and community life – has significant distributional components. The most discussed factor is the disproportionate impact of the time bind, over the past three decades, on women. The gender-based differential in converting education and health into income raises calls for further attention to gender roles, moral equality, and the genuine expression of differences. In addition to these gender-related issues, the problems of the time bind are not distributed evenly across race or class. Studies of the time bind tend to examine the lives of middle-class and middle-upper-class families in which one or two members of each household have secured

---

[22] In a related vein, I have developed the claim that seeing human beings increasingly as "customers" or "consumers" can be morally reductive. See Douglas A. Hicks, "The Customer is NOT Always Right," *Sojourners* 28/2 (March–April 1999).

[23] Even George Will acknowledges this point, though he posits a different moral interpretation. See his essay, "Healthy Inequality" and my discussion, in chapter 1.

decent work.[24] William J. Wilson raises a different kind of problem for the segment of the population, disproportionately African American and poor, who live in urban ghettos in which access to the formal labor market has largely "disappeared."[25] In this instance the problem is not as much "overwork" as it is the very limited availability of meaningful and/or adequately paying work. The recent changes in welfare policy raise distinct time allocation questions for people who face the prospect of moving "from welfare to work."[26] These various issues related to the time bind can be more carefully delineated by employing a careful approach to inequality.[27]

Reading socioeconomic inequality as a sign of the times is not only to focus on it for its own sake, but rather to understand its multiple manifestations and the impacts on people's well-being. Focusing on distributional matters will help to show what is at stake in these other pressing socioeconomic issues.

Questions of why and how inequality matters morally cannot be answered in abstract or simple terms. This book has shown how a socioeconomic analysis of inequality can be consistent with – indeed, guided by – a normative approach centrally informed by Christian ethical and theological perspectives. This interdisciplinary endeavor has examined "what is going on,"[28] normatively and empirically, in questions related to inequality.

---

[24] Paula Rayman, for instance, notes that Arlie Hochschild's research in her influential book, *The Time Bind*, is based on a study of 100 mid-level managers of a Fortune 500 company (Paula Rayman, "The Costs of Doing Business as Usual: Reflections on Work, Family, and Community," presentation at the Religion, Values, and the Economy Forum, Center for the Study of Values in Public Life, Harvard Divinity School, February 3, 1998).

[25] William J. Wilson, *When Work Disappears: The World of the New Urban Poor* (New York: Alfred A. Knopf, 1996).

[26] Kathryn Edin and Laura Lein, *Making Ends Meet: How Single Mothers Survive Welfare and Low-Wage Work* (New York: Russell Sage, 1997); Christopher Jencks, "The Hidden Paradox of Welfare Reform," *American Prospect* 32 (May–June 1997).

[27] A recent essay in the *New York Times* notes precisely this distributional dimension of debates about whether "Americans" are working more or less in the formal labor market. This question requires the disaggregating of the population to look at the work and leisure patterns of various groups of people. Hence the lens of inequality can provide insight into the "time bind" debate. See Janny Scott, "Working Hard, More or Less," *New York Times* (7/10/1999), A15, A17.

[28] H. Richard Niebuhr, *Responsible Self*, p. 60.

Yet the analysis of what is going on should also help and lead us to determine what kind of activity to undertake in response to current disparities. To that end, this book has offered new theoretical and policy-oriented perspectives on evaluating and combating excessive inequalities. It bears repeating that this approach is merely one contribution to, and call for, a pluralistic public discourse, for the response to inequality, like inequality itself, relates to the whole population. The leadership challenge is not merely to understand inequalities, but also to transform conditions that marginalize or dehumanize human beings. More deliberate talk of equality, capability, and solidarity should move us in that direction.

Appendix A: The Gini coefficient, inequality, and value-claims

The Gini coefficient is a summary measure of inequality that has been widely employed by economists, other social scientists, and policymakers. Among the various ways to estimate inequality, the Gini coefficient is relatively straightforward to calculate. Its value can fall anywhere from 0 to 1, with values close to 0 indicating little inequality and values nearer to 1 reflecting higher levels of inequality. This appendix discusses some of the analytical and normative questions associated with its use.

The Gini coefficient is most easily conceptualized geometrically, as in figure A.1. In this figure, the proportion of the population is plotted against the population's cumulative holdings of a particular good. Along the x-axis, the cumulative proportion of the population is plotted, from left to right. The population is ordered according to their share of the given good: People with the smallest share are closest to the origin, while those with the greatest share are located to the far right. The cumulative proportion of that population's holdings of the good are represented along the y-axis.

The resulting curve is called the Lorenz curve. At each point of the Lorenz curve, the share of the good held by some proportion of the population is indicated. For instance, the "bottom" 40 percent, or 0.40, of the population might hold 20 percent, or 0.20, of a country's annual income. A completely egalitarian distribution (with thus each person holding the same amount of good x) would be reflected by a 45-degree line, since any given proportion of the population would have that same proportion of the good-in-question. (That is, 20 percent of the

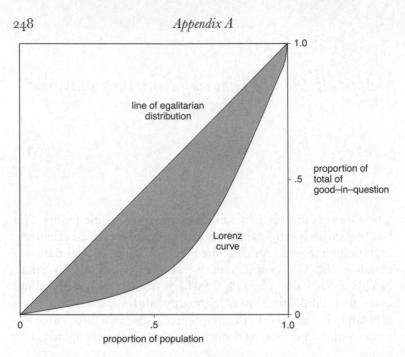

Figure A.1　The Lorenz curve

population would hold a fifth of the total of good x, 40 percent would hold two-fifths of the total of good x, and so on.) For all distributions, the points (0,0) and (1,1) are included on the Lorenz curve, since at the proportion "0" of the population, none of the good is held. At the other end, the "1" on the x-axis represents the entire population who, by design, hold the totality of the good-in-question. This is "1" on the y-axis as well. All (non-egalitarian) distributions will be curves below and to the right of the 45-degree line. The further the curve is from the egalitarian-distribution line, the greater is the inequality.

The Gini coefficient is equal to twice the area between the egalitarian-distribution line and the Lorenz curve (the area shaded in figure A.1).[1] Various other (equivalent) definitions of

[1] The relationship of the Lorenz curve and the Gini coefficient are carefully explored in Sudhir Anand, *Inequality and Poverty in Malaysia: Measurement and Decomposition* (Oxford: Oxford University Press, 1983), appendices B "The Gini coefficient" and D "Lorenz Dominance and Inequality"; and in S. R. Osmani, *Economic Inequality and Group*

the Gini coefficient have also been offered.[2] As noted, the Gini coefficient ranges from 0 to 1, with 0 reflecting complete equality and 1 reflecting that one person holds all of the good, and other persons hold none of it. Hence the greater the Gini, the greater the inequality.

What values, implicit or explicit, does a measure like the Gini coefficient depend upon or assume? Inequality determinations can be distinguished between *descriptive* (or positive) and *normative* exercises.[3] By this classification, the Gini coefficient is a *descriptive* measure; it does not *explicitly* depend upon some normative view of social welfare. Yet from one definition of the Gini coefficient it can be demonstrated that "the Gini coefficient *implies* a welfare function which is just a weighted sum of different people's income levels with the weights being determined by the rank-order position of the persons in the ranking by income level."[4] This point leads A. B. Atkinson to emphasize that "[m]easures such as the Gini coefficient are not purely 'statistical' and they embody implicit judgments about the weight to be attached to the inequality at different points on the income scale."[5] Hence the Gini coefficient does include some

---

Welfare: A Theory of Comparison with Application to Bangladesh (Oxford: Clarendon Press, 1982), appendix 2 "The algebra of the Lorenz curve." A simpler exploration is given in A. B. Atkinson, *The Economics of Inequality*, second edn. (Oxford: Clarendon Press, 1983), chapter 1. See also Amartya Sen, *On Economic Inequality* (1997 expanded edition with a substantial annexe by James E. Foster and Amartya Sen), pp. 29–34.

[2] Anand, *Inequality and Poverty*, offers six equivalent definitions of the Gini coefficient. I employ his definition #1 to estimate Gini coefficients for distributions of income, longevity, and education, below.

[3] That is, one can distinguish between: "positive measures which make no explicit use of any concept of social welfare, and normative measures which are based on an explicit formulation of social welfare and the loss incurred from unequal distribution" (Sen, *On Economic Inequality*, p. 24). Sen applies this distinction to a host of inequality measures. For another careful analysis of inequality measures and social welfare, see Osmani, *Economic Inequality and Group Welfare*, chapter 3.

[4] Sen, *On Economic Inequality*, pp. 30–32 (emphasis added). This formula is:

$$G = 1 + (1/n) - (2/n^2\mu) [y_1 + 2y_2 + \ldots + ny_n] \text{ for } y_1 > = y_2 > = \ldots > = y_n,$$

and where μ = the mean of $(y_1, y_2, \ldots, y_n)$.

For a further discussion, see Sen, *On Economic Inequality*, chapter 2 and Osmani, *Inequality and Poverty*, pp. 314–316.

[5] Atkinson, *Economics of Inequality*, p. 56. For an "intuitive" discussion based on the geometry of the Lorenz curve, see Amartya Sen, "Poverty: An Ordinal Approach to Measurement," *Econometrica* 44 (1976), especially section 6.

implicit weighting, which gives greater emphasis to people with lower holdings of the good-in-question.

Thus it is not possible to say that a lower Gini coefficient unambiguously implies lower inequality. As Atkinson proved in his classic 1970 article, one country A's income inequality can be said to be *unambiguously* less than another country B's *only if* A's Lorenz curve (a curve such as in figure A.1) lies inside B's curve at all points between x = 0 and x = 1. This is a situation of "Lorenz dominance."[6] In other cases, such as when the Lorenz curves *cross* at one or more points, the determination of inequality depends on normative assumptions about how to give weight to the various parts of the distribution.

Thus the Gini coefficient's operation is not purely descriptive, but rather it contains implicit normative assumptions about weighting different members (or classes) of the ranked population. Of course, *any* measure of inequality reflects some set of value-claims and assumptions. The particular assumptions behind the Gini coefficient are not objectionable, but it does mean that when country A's Gini coefficient is greater than country B's, it can be said to have greater inequality according to the weighting scale implicitly contained in the Gini's construction.[7]

The Gini index also satisfies the "Pigou-Dalton criterion," which demands that any transfer from a poorer (or less educated, etc.) person to a richer (or more educated) person, *ceteris paribus*, increases the inequality measure. Yet the Gini coefficient fails to satisfy "the principle of regressive sensitivity to transfer," which would place more weight on transfers to those at the bottom of the distribution. Rather, it is most sensitive to transfers in the middle of the distribution.[8]

---

6 Atkinson, "On the Measurement of Inequality."

7 This is why Amartya Sen, in his "Public Action and the Quality of Life in Developing Countries" (*Oxford Bulletin of Economics and Statistics* 43/1 [1981]), ranks developing countries only partially – according to Lorenz dominance. He concludes that in many cases, the Lorenz curves for income distribution of differing countries cross, leaving only a partial ordering of countries by this measure. He argues that this is the only "non-controversial" way to rank countries for inequality. This implies that the use of the Gini coefficient in this project does not lead to an "objective" ranking of countries' inequalities.

8 These properties of the Gini coefficient were first established by A. B. Atkinson in his

Further, the Gini coefficient is "mean independent"; if every person in one country suddenly doubled her or his endowment of the good in question, the Gini coefficient would stay exactly the same. It is thus a relative measure only.[9] Thus consideration of aggregate or overall holdings of social goods requires attention to other kinds of socioeconomic indicators (GDP per capita, educational attainment, etc.).[10]

While the Gini coefficient is most often employed to analyze distributions *of income*, it can be employed for looking at distributions of other goods as well. A Gini coefficient can be calculated for any good for which we know the amount that is held by each person (or household) within a given society. Appendix B discusses the construction of Gini coefficients for goods in the spheres of education and health/longevity as well as income for an international data set and for a US-based data set.

article, "On the Measurement of Inequality." See also Osmani, *Economic Inequality and Group Welfare*, pp. 38–41 and Sen, *On Economic Inequality* and "Poverty: An Ordinal Approach."

9 Sen, *On Economic Inequality*, pp. 36, 69.
10 Chapter 9 presents an analytical framework for balancing distributional (or relative) concerns with aggregative ones. The IAHDI index proposed in chapter 10 makes use of this framework.

Appendix B: Constructing Gini coefficients in income, education, and health/longevity

This appendix discusses the technical and data-related issues of the actual construction and calculation of Gini coefficients in the spheres of income, education, and health/longevity for the international and US-based comparisons presented in chapters 3 and 4.

Chapter 3 explains that through the construction of the indicators "educational attainment" and "life-span attainment" (and with sufficient data), a Gini coefficient was calculated for goods in each of the dimensions of education and health/longevity. These measures may not be as "intuitive" as is the case for income, because it requires thinking of the total stock of education (in total years of schooling) or of the total stock of life span (in the total number of years lived by persons in a population). Each person in the population holds some share of education and longevity of life. In each of these important dimensions of well-being, there are inequalities that are revealed by a Gini coefficient.

For the cross-national comparison (see table 3.3), the requisite data for all three dimensions were available for an intersection of twenty developing countries. The Gini measures were calculated for these countries in particular, in order that the same countries could be compared in all three dimensions.[1] The data

---

[1] The estimates for educational attainment used by Ahuja and Filmer (see below) appeared to be most reliable and fitting. In order to maintain a reasonably limited time frame among all of the variables in the IAHDI, other inequality data (and human development figures from the UNDP) are drawn from the mid–late 1980s and the early 1990s.

sets, and the calculations, for each of the three dimensions are now considered in turn.

The income distribution data were obtained from the *World Development Report (WDR) 1995*.[2] The data were already given in terms of income shares by quintile. Income share of the top 10 percent was also indicated. From this data, five points of the Lorenz curve, in addition to (0,0) and (1,1) could be derived straightforwardly.[3] The Gini coefficient was determined geometrically from these seven data points.[4]

In terms of educational attainment, *years of schooling* was used as a proxy indicator because it enabled a Gini coefficient to be calculated in an analogous way to *dollars of income*. Yet here the data set was not as neatly packaged for the calculation. The data were taken from the *WDR 1995* Background Paper by Ahuja and Filmer which estimates educational attainment for developing countries.[5] The data were classed by "no educa-

[2] These figures are found in the World Bank, *World Development Report 1995* (New York: Oxford University Press, 1995), table 30 – Income Distribution and PPP estimates of GNP, pp. 220–221.

[3] To be sure, there are reliability and comparability problems with the *WDR* data set. First, for some countries, the data are for consumption and for other countries the data are for income. Income tends to be more unequal than consumption, since the wealthy can more readily use their income for non-consumptive purposes – for example, savings. But there is a precedent for using income and consumption data in comparative exercises. For example, Sudhir Anand and Martin Ravallion ("Human Development in Poor Countries," p. 141) use both household consumption and income data for looking at the distribution of consumption. Further, some countries' distributional data are based on households, and others' are based on individuals; household data obscure intra-household distributions. The data, mostly received from household surveys, are the most recent available for each country, varying from 1979 to 1993. With all these caveats, this is the best income distribution set available. See *WDR 1995* technical notes to tables, pp. 242–244, for further discussion of this data set.

[4] The Gini coefficient was determined by the following definition: For i = 0 to n, let F_i be the cumulative proportion of the population, and let Φ_i be the cumulative proportion of the total quantity of the relevant good. (Thus, the points along the Lorenz curve are (F_i, Φ_i).) Then

$$G = 1 - \sum_{i=0}^{n-1}(F_{i+1} - F_i) * \Phi_{i+1} + \Phi_i)$$

This result can be seen geometrically in Anand, *Inequality and Poverty*, p. 312. The same formula is used to calculate Gini coefficients in educational and life-span attainment.

[5] The Ahuja and Filmer data set appeared to be the best available for the purposes of this project. (Ahuja and Filmer, "Educational Attainment in Developing Countries.") The data set begins with the Barro and Lee estimates of educational attainment,

tion," "some primary education," "completed primary education," "some secondary education," "completed secondary education," and "some higher education."[6]

In the dimension of longevity, data were obtained from mortality statistics listed in the *UN Demographic Yearbook 1992 – Special Topic: Fertility and Mortality Statistics.*[7] Age-at-death statistics were included for males and females for all available years from 1983 to 1991.[8] Since the data were already grouped by age-class, the midpoint number of years was assigned as the life-span attainment for each person in that age-class. This is a reasonable assumption. The areas of possible problem are for the age-class "less than one year," for which a life-span attainment of 0.5 was assigned, and "85 and above," for which a life span of 87 was assigned.[9] With these age classes, it was a

whose data was obtained principally from country-specific census data (R. Barro and J.-W. Lee, "International Comparison of Educational Attainment," *Journal of Monetary Economics* 32 [1993]). Ahuja and Filmer then employ a "flow" analysis based on dropout and enrollment rates to arrive at estimates into the future and to expand Barro and Lee's data set to all those from age six to sixty who had completed their education. The data set employed in my calculations is Ahuja and Filmer's estimated set for 1985.

6 Following the precedent of Ahuja and Filmer, the quantity of schooling-years assigned to each of these classes is, respectively, 0, 3, 6, 9, 12, and 15. There are some comparability problems with this assumption. According to the standards for measuring educational enrollments across countries, the quantity of primary and secondary schooling is not constant. The actual standards are given in table 3 of the *UNESCO '95 Statistical Yearbook* (Lanham, MD and Paris: UNESCO, 1995). Because Ahuja and Filmer utilized the assignment of values discussed above in arriving at their estimates – assuming a six-year span for primary, and a six-year span for secondary education – I have needed to maintain their assumption. Further, even without comparability problems, the educational attainment numbers assigned for each class are imprecise. These caveats must all be noted before making the Gini calculation, which is straightforward once these classes of educational-attainment have been created.

7 United Nations, *UN Demographic Yearbook 1992 – Special Topic: Fertility and Mortality Statistics* (New York, 1992), table 22 – Deaths by age, sex, and rural/urban residence 1983–91.

8 The number of years for which these data were available varied from 1 to 9 years. All available data were used in the case of each country, in order to lessen, where the data were available, the effects of distributional variation across years. In actuality, this variation was slight, and thus countries were not excluded even if data for only one year were available. Other possible problems with this data set are given in the technical notes to table 22, UN, *Fertility and Mortality Statistics*, pp. 86–89.

9 In all likelihood, the actual mean age-attainment of the former class was less than a half-year, due to a high incidence of deaths at or near birth. The actual mean age-attainment of the latter class could have been somewhat higher, but there is no way to know the precise mean. These assumptions were the best that could be conceived.

straightforward exercise to calculate the Gini coefficient for life-span attainment.

Results from these calculations are given in table 3.3, above.

For the examination of inequality trends within the US postwar context, income data are readily available from the US Census Bureau, including the Gini coefficient for families in the United States from 1947 to 1997.[10] The body and notes of chapter 4 discuss the problems of employing *either* family- or household-based data. For periods when data for both are available, the trends for households and families move together. Family-based data are most readily available for the entire postwar period.[11]

Data for educational attainment in the United States are also accessible from the Census Bureau. The Census Bureau changed its methodology of reporting educational attainment in 1992. Prior to that, the Bureau had reported education in years of school completed. In 1992, the Population Surveys began to ask the highest *level* of education attained (e.g., high-school diploma, baccalaureate degree, etc.). Figures such as "median years of education" were no longer employed. For the purposes of the calculation of a Gini coefficient, data were employed according to the earlier Census Bureau categories – that is, in total years of schooling completed. The data set included all people in the United States of ages 25 and over. Educational attainment data were classed by Census Bureau categories of years of schooling completed (0 to 4, 5 to 8, 9 to 11, 12, 13 to 15, and 16 or more).[12] The midpoint value of each class was assigned to all people in each class. For the category "16 or more years," the value of 17 was assigned. That the highest class of attainment is grouped together in this way indicates that

---

10 These data are taken from the US Census Bureau, Historical Income Tables – Families, table F-4, <http://www.census.gov/hhes/income/histinc/fo4/html>. As noted in figure 4.1, the Census Bureau changed its methodology for measuring income after the 1992 figures.

11 See Weinberg, "US Income Inequality," esp. figure 1.

12 The data for years of schooling completed were taken from the US Census Bureau, table A-1, "Years of School Completed by People 25 Years Old and Over, by Age and Sex: Selected Years 1940 to 1996," <http://www.census.gov/population/socdemo/education/tablea-01.txt>. Notes about the change in methodology in 1992 are given at the end of this table.

the measure does not capture well the changes in post-baccalaureate educational attainment. The focus is, rather, on more basic levels of educational attainment.

The Gini coefficient for life-span inequality was calculated using data from various issues of *Vital Statistics of the United States – Mortality Statistics* (1947–92), published by the US Department of Health and Human Services.[13] The available data were classed by ages at death (under 1 year, 1, 2, 3, 4, 5–9, 10–14, . . ., 95–99, and 100 and over). Following the same procedure as in the cross-national calculations, the midpoint value was attributed to all people in each class, including the value of 0.5 year to all those who died before age 1. For all those in the "100 and over" group, the value of 102 years was employed.

The results from these inequality determinations for the US population are given in figures 4.1, 4.2, and 4.3.

---

[13] The most recent issue available is US Department of Health and Human Services, *Vital Statistics of the United States 1992*: vol. II – *Mortality*, table 8.5, p. 176.

Appendix C: The construction of the HDI and the IAHDI

This appendix addresses some theoretical and technical issues of the human development index and the inequality adjustment to the HDI that is proposed in chapter 10.

THE HDI, AS DESIGNED BY THE UNDP

The UNDP's HDI is comprised of three sphere-specific indices, in the spheres of income, education, and health/longevity. The index X_i for each sphere i (i = 1 for income, i = 2 for education, i = 3 for health/longevity) for a given country is determined by the following formula:

$$X_i = \frac{\text{actual } x_i \text{ value } - \text{ minimum } x_i \text{ value}}{\text{maximum } x_i \text{ value } - \text{ minimum } x_i \text{ value}}$$

The assigned maximum value of x_i is the greatest value that a country would be expected to have in that dimension. The minimum value of x_i is the minimum that a country could achieve. In the case of education, the maximum obtainable value is 100 and the minimum is 0 (reflecting a weighted average of literacy rates and educational enrollment, which are each expressed as percentages); in longevity the maximum life expectancy has been set at 85 and the minimum at 25; and in income the maximum real income per capita has been set at PPP$40,000 and the minimum is set at PPP$100.[1]

---

[1] One recent discussion of computing the human development index is contained in the "Technical Note" of the *HDR 1999* (pp. 159–160). See also Sudhir Anand and Amartya Sen, "The Human Development Index: Methodology and Measurement," Occasional Paper no. 12 (New York: Human Development Report Office, 1994), and

Hence the value of X_i for each country in each dimension must fall between 0 and 1 (inclusive). The value reflects the proportion achieved *in the aggregate* for each country, with values closer to 1 reflecting higher achievement levels. Conversely, the proportionate deficiency or shortfall of a country in a particular dimension is equivalent to $(1 - X_i)$.[2] The maximum potential for each country has been standardized, as has the minimum potential, and consequently achievement has been normalized on the 0–1 scale.[3]

The HDI itself is the average of X_1, X_2, and X_3 (the indices for income, education, and longevity). This can be thought of as a weighted average where each index is weighted equally. That is,

$$ \text{HDI} = \frac{\alpha X_1 + \beta X_2 + \gamma X_3}{\alpha + \beta + \gamma}, \text{ where } \alpha, \beta, \gamma = 1 $$

Since each X_i must be a value between 0 and 1 (inclusive), and HDI is a weighted average, HDI also must fall within the same range. The assignment of α, β, and γ is certainly arbitrary, though there is some empirical support, based on principal component analysis, for an equal weighting.[4] Certainly other values could be for α, β, and γ if one's normative purposes called for it.

Anand and Sen, "The Income Component in the HDI – Alternative Formulations," Background Paper (New York: Human Development Report Office, 1999). Chapter 10, above, notes how the income component of the HDI requires a process of "discounting" and how this process was altered beginning with *HDR 1999*.

[2] In earlier editions of the *HDR*, the HDI was calculated with deprivation as a more fundamental concept than achievement. Some people – see for instance, T. N. Srinivasan, "Human Development: A New Paradigm or Reinvention of the Wheel?" *American Economic Review* 84/2 (1994) – continue to discuss the HDI as measuring deprivation, which is no longer the case. The *HDR 1997* introduced a "Human Poverty Index," which does focus on deprivation; its determination is distinct from the HDI. See "Technical Note," *HDR 1999*, p. 163.

[3] To be sure, problems of comparability still remain to the extent that "literacy" does not mean the same thing in one country as in another, or to the extent that the expression of income in PPP dollars does not reflect equivalent access to similar baskets of basic commodities. To such difficulties as these must be added the plethora of data-reliability problems, noted below. Perhaps most serious are the issues of comparisons across contexts, as discussed in the main text of chapter 9.

[4] See *HDR 1993* "Technical Note 2," pp. 109–110.

THE IAHDI, AS PROPOSED IN CHAPTER 10

Recall that each index of the HDI is calculated by the formula

$$X_i = \frac{\text{actual } x_i \text{ value } - \text{ minimum } x_i \text{ value}}{\text{maximum } x_i \text{ value } - \text{ minimum } x_i \text{ value}}$$

The denominator reflects the total span of possible achievement in a given dimension – the distance between the minimum potential value and the maximum; the numerator measures the proportion of that span which has been achieved. In computing the IAHDI, the proportion achieved (the numerator) is adjusted downward, or discounted, by a figure reflecting the inequalities for that dimension. One straightforward way to accomplish this is to multiply the numerator by $(1 - G_i)$, where G_i is the Gini coefficient for each dimension i (i = 1,2,3), a technique for which there is significant precedent.[5]

However, if this calculation were made in each dimension, the index X_i from each dimension would be reduced, on average, by a different factor, since the mean of the respective Gini coefficient of each dimension (i.e., income, education, longevity) is not the same. Further, and just as important, it would not be necessary to adjust each dimension's indicator by an equal proportion (on average). For various normative reasons one could emphasize inequality in particular dimensions and consequently weight some Gini coefficients more than others. In order to enable such a choice of weighting, flexibility can be built into the dimensional indices, called Inequality-adjusted X_i, or IAX_i, for i = 1,2,3:

$$IAX_i = \frac{(\text{actual } x_i \text{ value } - \text{ min. } x_i \text{ value}) * \lambda(1 - G_i)}{\text{maximum } x_i \text{ value } - \text{ minimum } x_i \text{ value}},$$

which is equivalent to

$$IAX_i = X_i * \lambda_i(1 - G_i)$$

[5] See Sen, "Real National Income," *Review of Economic Studies* 43 (February 1976), on the technique and social welfare implications of discounting mean regional incomes by (1–G); see Klasen, "Growth and Well-Being," as discussed in chapter 10, above; and see the *HDR 1993* for an "income-distribution-adjusted HDI." For that calculation, however, only the actual x_1 value, and not the entire numerator, is multiplied by (1–G). See *HDR 1993*, p. 101.

For each dimension i, λ_i is the weight given to inequality-adjustment factor.[6]

Thus, each dimensional index of the HDI is adjusted for inequality by a factor of $\lambda_i * (1 - G_i)$. This weighting, of course, does not change the fact that the dimensional indices comprising the HDI can be weighted differently than their present α, β, $\gamma = 1$. Thus the IAHDI is calculated in an analogous fashion to the HDI:

$$IAHDI = \frac{\alpha IAX_1 + \beta IAX_2 + \gamma IAX_3}{\alpha + \beta + \gamma}$$

While the weights could be adjusted, the IAHDI as reported in chapter 10 was calculated according to a simple weighting system of α, β, γ, λ_1, λ_2, $\lambda_3 = 1$.

---

[6] Presumably, for all i, $(1/(1-G_i)) > \lambda_i > 0$.

Bibliography

Aaron, Henry. *Politics and the Professors: The Great Society in Perspective.*
Washington: The Brookings Institution, 1978.
Ahuja, V., and D. Filmer. "Educational Attainment in Developing
Countries: New Estimates and Projections Disaggregated by
Gender." Background Paper for the *World Development Report 1995.*
Washington: The World Bank, 1995.
Anand, Sudhir. *Inequality and Poverty in Malaysia: Measurement and Decomposi-
tion.* Oxford: Oxford University Press for the World Bank, 1983.
Anand, Sudhir, and Martin Ravallion. "Human Development in Poor
Countries: On the Role of Private Incomes and Public Services."
Journal of Economic Perspectives 7/1 (1993): 133–150.
Anand, Sudhir, and Amartya Sen. "The Human Development Index:
Methodology and Measurement." Occasional Paper no. 12. New
York: Human Development Report Office, 1994.
"Gender Inequality in Human Development: Theories and
Measurement." Occasional Paper no. 19. New York: Human
Development Report Office, 1995.
"The Income Component in the HDI – Alternative Formulations."
Background Paper. New York: Human Development Report
Office, 1999.
Anderson, Elizabeth S. "What is the Point of Equality?" *Ethics* 109
(January 1999): 287–337.
Atkinson, A. B. "On the Measurement of Inequality." *Journal of
Economic Theory* 2 (1970): 244–263.
The Economics of Inequality. Second edition. Oxford: Clarendon Press,
1983.
"Bringing Income Distribution in from the Cold," *The Economic
Journal* 107 (March 1997): 297–321.
Atkinson, A. B., Lee Rainwater, and Timothy Smeeding. *The Income
Distribution in OECD Countries: Evidence from the Luxembourg Income
Study.* OECD Social Policy Studies no. 18. Paris: OECD, 1995.

Augustine of Hippo. *The City of God*. In *The Basic Writings of Saint Augustine* edited by Whitney J. Oates. New York: Random House, 1948.

Barber, Banjamin. *Jihad Versus McWorld*. New York: Times Books, 1995.

Barro, R., and J.-W. Lee. "International Comparison of Educational Attainment." *Journal of Monetary Economics* 32 (1993): 363–394.

Baum, Gregory, and Robert Ellsberg, editors. *The Logic of Solidarity: Commentaries on Pope John Paul II's Encyclical "On Social Concern."* Maryknoll, NY: Orbis, 1989.

Becker, Gary. *The Economic Approach to Human Behavior*. Chicago: University of Chicago Press, 1978.

Beckley, Harlan. "A Christian Affirmation of Justice as Fairness – Part I." *Journal of Religious Ethics* 13 (fall 1985): 210–242.
"A Christian Affirmation of Justice as Fairness – Part II." *Journal of Religious Ethics* 14 (fall 1986): 229–246.

Benhabib, Seyla. *Situating the Self: Gender, Community, and Postmodernism in Contemporary Ethics*. New York: Routledge, 1992.

Benn, Stanley. "Equality, Moral and Social." In *The Encyclopedia of Philosophy*. Vol. III, edited by Paul Edwards, 38–42. New York and London: Macmillan and Free Press, 1967.

Bird, Brian. *Rebel Before His Time: A Study of John Ball and the English Peasants' Revolt of 1381*. Worthing, England: Churchman Publishing, 1987.

Blinder, Alan. "The Level and Distribution of Economic Well-Being." In *The American Economy in Transition*, edited by Martin Feldstein, 415–499. Chicago: University of Chicago Press, 1980.

Boff, Clodovis. "Epistemology and Method in the Theology of Liberation." In *Mysterium Liberationis: Fundamental Concepts of Liberation Theology*, edited by Ignacio Ellacuría, S.J. and Jon Sobrino, S.J, 57–83. Maryknoll, NY: Orbis, 1993.

Boff, Leonardo. *Ecology and Liberation: A New Paradigm*. Translated by John Cumming. Maryknoll, NY: Orbis, 1995 [1993].

Bounds, Elizabeth M. "Conflicting Harmonies: Michael Walzer's Vision of Community." *Journal of Religious Ethics* 22/2 (fall 1994): 355–374.

Bread for the World Institute. *Hunger in a Global Economy: Hunger 1998 (Eighth Annual Report on the State of World Hunger)*. Silver Spring, MD: BFWI, 1998.

Callaghy, Thomas M. "Globalization and Marginalization: Debt and the International Underclass." *Current History: A Journal of Contemporary World Affairs* 96/613 (November 1997): 392–396.

Christiansen, S.J., Drew. "Basic Needs: Criterion for Development."

In *Human Rights in the Americas: The Struggle for Consensus*, edited by Alfred Hennelly, S.J. and John Langan, S.J., 245–288. Washington: Georgetown University Press, 1982.

"On Relative Equality: Catholic Egalitarianism after Vatican II." *Theological Studies* 45 (1984): 651–675.

Coats, Dan, with responses by Gertrude Himmelfarb, Don Eberly, and David Boaz. "Can Congress Revive Civil Society?" *Policy Review* 75 (January–February 1996), 24–33.

Coffin, Brent B. "A View from Below: Justice and the American Welfare Reform Debate." Unpublished Th.D. dissertation, Harvard Divinity School, 1997.

Congregation for the Doctrine of the Faith. "Instruction on Certain Aspects of the 'Theology of Liberation'." *Origins* 14 (9/13/1984): 194–204.

"Instruction on Christian Freedom and Liberation." *Origins* 15 (4/17/1986): 714–727.

Crossette, Barbara. "U.N. Survey Finds World Rich–Poor Gap Widening." *New York Times* (7/15/1996), A3.

"In Days, India, Chasing China, Will Have a Billion People," *New York Times* (8/5/1999), A10.

Daly, Herman, and John B. Cobb, Jr. *For the Common Good: Redirecting the Economy Toward Community, the Environment, and a Sustainable Future*. Boston: Beacon Press, 1989.

Daniels, Norman. *Just Health Care*. Cambridge: Cambridge University Press, 1985.

Danziger, Sheldon, and Peter Gottschalk. *America Unequal*. New York: Russell Sage/ Harvard University Press, 1995.

Danziger, Sheldon, and Peter Gottschalk, editors. *Uneven Tides: Rising Inequality in America*. New York: Russell Sage, 1993.

Danziger, Sheldon, and Robert Haveman. "An Economic Concept of Solidarity: Its Application to Poverty and Income Distribution Policy in the United States." Research Series no. 37, International Institute for Labour Studies. Geneva: IILS, 1978.

Danziger, Sheldon, and Eugene Smolensky. "Income Inequality: Problems of Measurement and Interpretation." In *American Society, Inc.*, edited by Maurice Zeitlin, 110–117. Chicago: Rand McNally, 1977.

Dasgupta, Partha. *An Inquiry into Well-Being and Destitution*. Oxford: Clarendon Press, 1993.

Deininger, Klaus, and Lyn Squire. "A New Data Set Measuring Income Inequality." *The World Bank Economic Review* 10/3 (1996): 565–591.

"New Ways of Looking at Old Issues: Inequality and Growth."

Journal of Development Economics 57/2 (December 1998): 259–287.

Dorr, Donal. *Option for the Poor: A Hundred Years of Vatican Social Teaching.* Maryknoll, NY: Orbis, 1983.

———. "Solidarity and Integral Human Development." In *The Logic of Solidarity: Commentaries on Pope John Paul II's Encyclical "On Social Concern,"* edited by Gregory Baum and Robert Ellsberg, 143–154. Maryknoll, NY: Orbis, 1989.

Drèze, Jean, and Amartya Sen. *India: Social Development and Economic Opportunity.* Oxford: Clarendon Press, 1995.

Dussel, Enrique D. "Theology of Liberation and Marxism." Translated by Robert R. Barr. In *Mysterium Liberationis: Fundamental Concepts in Liberation Theology,* edited by Ignacio Ellacuría, S.J. and Jon Sobrino, S.J., 85–102. Maryknoll, NY: Orbis, 1993.

Dworkin, Ronald. "What is Equality? Part II: Equality of Resources." *Philosophy and Public Affairs* 10 (1981): 283–345.

Eagleson, John, and Philip Scharper, editors. *Puebla and Beyond.* Maryknoll, NY: Orbis, 1979.

Easterlin, Richard. "Does Economic Growth Improve the Human Lot? Some Empirical Evidence." In *Nations and Households in Economic Growth,* edited by P. A. David and M. W. Reder, 89–125. New York: Academic Press, 1973.

Edin, Kathryn, and Laura Lein. *Making Ends Meet: How Single Mothers Survive Welfare and Low-Wage Work.* New York: Russell Sage, 1997.

Ellacuría, S.J., Ignacio. "Human Rights in a Divided Society." Translated by Alfred Hennelly, S.J. In *Human Rights in the Americas: The Struggle for Consensus,* edited by Alfred Hennelly, S.J. and John Langan, S.J. Washington: Georgetown University Press, 1982.

———. "Aporte de la Teología de la Liberación a las Religiones Abrahámicas en la Superación del Individualismo y del Positivismo." Congress of Abrahamic Religions. Córdoba, Spain, February, 1987.

———. "The Crucified People." Translated by Phillip Berryman and Robert R. Barr. In *Mysterium Liberationis: Fundamental Concepts in Liberation Theology,* edited by Ignacio Ellacuría, S.J. and Jon Sobrino, S.J., 580–603. Maryknoll, NY: Orbis, 1993.

Ellacuría, S.J., Ignacio, and Jon Sobrino, S.J., editors. *Mysterium Liberationis: Fundamental Concepts in Liberation Theology.* Maryknoll, NY: Orbis, 1993.

Ellis, Marc H., and Otto Maduro, editors. *The Future of Liberation Theology: Essays in Honor of Gustavo Gutiérrez.* Maryknoll, NY: Orbis, 1987.

Ellsberg, Robert. Introduction to *The Logic of Solidarity: Commentaries on*

Pope John Paul II's Encyclical "On Social Concern," edited by Gregory Baum and Robert Ellsberg, vii-xv. Maryknoll, NY: Orbis, 1989.

Feinberg, Joel. *Social Philosophy.* Englewood Cliffs, NJ: Prentice-Hall, 1973.

Fergusson, David. *Community, Liberalism and Christian Ethics.* Cambridge: Cambridge University Press, 1998.

Frank, Robert. *Choosing the Right Pond: Human Behavior and the Quest for Status.* New York: Oxford University Press, 1985.

Frank, Robert, and Philip J. Cook. *The Winner-Take-All-Society.* New York: Free Press, 1995.

Fraser, Nancy. *Justice Interruptus: Critical Reflections on the "Postsocialist" Condition.* New York: Routledge, 1997.

Freeman, Richard B. "Unequal Incomes: The Worrisome Distribution of the Fruits of American Growth." *Harvard Magazine* 100/3 (January–February 1998), 62–64.

Freeman, Richard B., with responses by Ernesto Cortes, Jr., Heidi Hartmann, James Heckman, Paul Krugman, Michael Piore, Frances Fox Piven, and James Tobin, "The New Inequality." *Boston Review* 21/6 (December 1996–January 1997), 3–18.

Frei, Hans. "The Theology of H. Richard Niebuhr." In *Faith and Ethics: The Theology of H. Richard Niebuhr,* edited by Paul Ramsey, 65–116. New York: Harper & Brothers, 1957.

Fuchs, Victor R. *Women's Quest for Economic Equality.* Cambridge, MA: Harvard University Press, 1988.

Galbraith, John Kenneth. *The Affluent Society.* New York: Mentor Books/ Houghton Mifflin, 1958.

Gebara, Ivone. "Option for the Poor as an Option for Poor Women." In *The Power of Naming: A* Concilium *Reader in Feminist Liberation Theology,* edited by Elisabeth Schüssler Fiorenza, 142–149. Maryknoll, NY: Orbis, 1996.

Glendon, Mary Ann. *Rights Talk: The Impoverishment of Political Discourse.* New York: Free Press, 1991.

Glyn, Andrew, with responses by William Greider, Geoffrey Garrett, Rachel McCulloch, Thomas Palley, and Dani Rodrick. "Egalitarianism in a Global Economy." *Boston Review* 22/6 (December 1997–January 1998), 4–17.

Goldberg, Carey. "Hispanic Households Struggle as Poorest of the Poor in U.S." *New York Times* (1/30/1997), A1, A16.

Gottschalk, Peter, and Timothy M. Smeeding. "Cross-National Comparisons of Earnings and Income Inequality." *Journal of Economic Literature* 35/2 (1997): 633–687.

Gramlich, Edward M., Richard Kasten, and Frank Sammartino. "Growing Inequality in the 1980s: The Role of Federal Taxes and Cash Transfers." In *Uneven Tides: Rising Inequality in America*, edited by Sheldon Danziger and Peter Gottschalk, 225–249. New York: Russell Sage, 1993.

Gustafson, James. *A Sense of the Divine: The Natural Environment from a Theocentric Perspective*. Cleveland: Pilgrim Press, 1994.

Gutiérrez, Gustavo. "Faith as Freedom: Solidarity with the Alienated and Confidence in the Future." In *Living with Change, Experiences, Faith*, edited by Francis A. Eigo, O.S.A., 15–54. Villanova, PA: Villanova University Press, 1976.

——— *The Power of the Poor in History.* Translated by Robert R. Barr. Maryknoll, NY: Orbis, 1983 [1979].

——— *We Drink from Our Own Wells: The Spiritual Journey of a People.* Translated by Matthew J. O'Connell. Maryknoll, NY: Orbis, 1984 [1983].

——— *Evangelización y Opción por los Pobres.* Buenos Aires: Ediciones Paulinas, 1987.

——— *On Job: God-Talk and the Suffering of the Innocent.* Translated by Matthew J. O'Connell. Maryknoll, NY: Orbis, 1987 [1985].

——— *A Theology of Liberation.* Fifteenth anniversary edition. Translated by Robert R. Barr. Maryknoll, NY: Orbis, 1988 [1973, 1971].

——— *The God of Life.* Translated by Matthew J. O'Connell. Maryknoll, NY: Orbis, 1991 [1989].

——— *Las Casas: In Search of the Poor of Jesus Christ.* Translated by Robert R. Barr. Maryknoll, NY: Orbis, 1993 [1992].

——— "Option for the Poor." Translated by Robert R. Barr. In *Mysterium Liberationis: Fundamental Concepts in Liberation Theology*, edited by Ignacio Ellacuría, S.J. and Jon Sobrino, S.J., 235–250. Maryknoll, NY: Orbis, 1993.

Gutmann, Amy. *Liberal Equality.* Cambridge: Cambridge University Press, 1980.

Gutmann, Amy, and Dennis Thompson. "Moral Conflict and Political Consensus." In *Liberalism and the Good*, edited by R. Bruce Douglass, Gerald M. Mara, and Henry S. Richardson, 125–147. New York and London: Routledge, 1992.

Hafner, Katie. "Common Ground Elusive as Technology Have-Nots Meet Haves." *New York Times* (7/8/1999), E8.

Haq, Mahbub ul. Foreword to *First Things First: Meeting Basic Human Needs in the Developing Countries*, by Paul Streeten et al., vii–x. Oxford: Oxford University Press for the World Bank, 1981.

Hauerwas, Stanley. *A Community of Character: Toward a Constructive Christian Social Ethic.* Notre Dame, IN: University of Notre Dame Press, 1981.

Hayward, J. E. S. "Solidarity: The Social History of An Idea in

Nineteenth Century France." *International Review of Social History* 4/2 (1959): 261–284.

The Peaceable Kingdom: A Primer in Christian Ethics. Notre Dame, IN: University of Notre Dame Press, 1983.

Dispatches from the Front: Theological Engagements with the Secular. Durham, NC: Duke University Press, 1994.

Hennelly, S.J., Alfred, editor. *Liberation Theology: A Documentary History.* Maryknoll, NY: Orbis, 1990.

Hennelly, S.J., Alfred, and John Langan, S.J., editors. *Human Rights in the Americas: The Struggle for Consensus.* Washington: Georgetown University Press, 1982.

Heredia, Blanca. "Prosper or Perish?: Development in the Age of Global Capital." *Current History: A Journal of Contemporary World Affairs* 96/613 (November 1997): 383–388.

Hewlett, Sylvia Ann. *When the Bough Breaks: The Cost of Neglecting our Children.* New York: Harper Perennial, 1991.

Hicks, Douglas A. "Liberation Theology and Liberal Justice?: The Preferential Option for the Poor and Rawls's Difference Principle." American Academy of Religion Annual Meeting. Philadelphia, November 1995.

"The Inequality-Adjusted Human Development Index: A Constructive Proposal." *World Development* 25/8 (August 1997): 1283–1298, 4A (section 5: Editorial & Opinion).

"Solidarity in Global and National Contexts: Insights from Economic Theory." American Academy of Religion Annual Meeting, San Francisco, November 1997.

"A Human Face for Economics." *Journal of Commerce* (10/27/1998).

"The Customer is NOT Always Right." *Sojourners* 28/2 (March–April 1999), 24–27.

Hirsch, Fred. *Social Limits to Growth.* Cambridge, MA: Harvard University Press, 1976.

Hochschild, Arlie. *The Second Shift.* New York: Avon Books, 1990.

The Time Bind: When Work Becomes Home and Home Becomes Work. New York: Metropolitan Books, 1997.

Hollenbach, S.J., David. "Public Reason/Private Religion?: A Response to Paul Weithman." *Journal of Religious Ethics* 22/1 (spring 1994): 39–46.

"Politically Active Churches: Some Empirical Prolegomena to a Normative Approach." In *Religion and Contemporary Liberalism*, edited by Paul J. Weithman, 291–306. Notre Dame, IN: University of Notre Dame Press, 1996.

Holmes, Steven A. "Income Disparity Between Poorest and Richest Rises." *New York Times* (6/20/1996), A1, A18.

268 *Bibliography*

"New Reports Say Minorities Benefit in Fiscal Recovery." *New York Times* (9/30/1997), A1, A26.

Huber, Wolfgang. "Toward an Ethics of Responsibility." *The Journal of Religion* 73/4 (October 1993): 573–591.

International Labour Organisation. *Employment, Growth and Basic Needs: A One-World Problem.* Geneva: ILO, 1976.

Isasi-Diaz, Ada Maria. "Solidarity: Love of Neighbor in the 1980s." In *Lift Every Voice: Constructing Christian Theologies from the Underside,* edited by Susan Brooks Thistlethwaite and Mary Potter Engel, 31–40. San Francisco: Harper & Row, 1990.

Jackson, Timothy P. "To Bedlam and Part Way Back: John Rawls and Christian Justice." *Faith and Philosophy* 4 (1991): 423–447.

Jencks, Christopher. "The Hidden Paradox of Welfare Reform." *American Prospect* 32 (May–June 1997), 33–40.

John XXIII. *Pacem in Terris: Peace on Earth.* In *Catholic Social Thought: The Documentary Heritage,* edited by David J. O'Brien and Thomas A. Shannon, 131–162. Maryknoll, NY: Orbis, 1992 [1987].

John Paul II. *Sollicitudo Rei Socialis: On Social Concern.* In *Catholic Social Thought: The Documentary Heritage,* edited by David J. O'Brien and Thomas A. Shannon, 395–436. Maryknoll, NY: Orbis, 1992 [1987].

The Gospel of Life [*Evangelium Vitae*]. New York: Random House, 1995.

Johnson, William Stacy. Introduction to *Theology, History, and Culture: Major Unpublished Writings of H. Richard Niebuhr,* edited by William Stacy Johnson, xi–xxxvii. New Haven: Yale University Press, 1996.

Kanbur, Ravi, and Nora Lustig. "Why is Inequality Back on the Agenda?" Paper prepared for the Annual Bank Conference on Development Economics, World Bank, Washington, DC, April 28–30, 1999 (version: April 21, 1999).

Kant, Immanuel. "An Answer to the Question: What is Enlightenment?" Translated by H. B. Nisbet. In *Kant: Political Writings,* edited by Hans Reiss, 54–60. Cambridge Texts in the History of Political Thought. Cambridge: Cambridge University Press, 1991 [1784].

Keiser, R. Melvin. "Relationality in the Theology of H. Richard Niebuhr: A Study in Niebuhr's Understanding of Man and God." Unpublished S.T.M. thesis, Yale Divinity School, 1964.

Roots of Relational Ethics: Responsibility in Origin and Maturity in H. Richard Niebuhr. Atlanta: Scholars Press, 1996.

Klasen, Stephan. "Growth and Well-Being: Introducing Distribution-Weighted Growth Rates to Reevaluate U.S. Post-War Economic

Performance." *Review of Income and Wealth* 40/3 (September 1994), 251–272.

Knowles, Stephen. "The Evolution of Basic Needs and Human Development." *Rivista Internazionale di Scienze Economiche e Commerciali* 40 (1993): 513–542.

Kristol, Irving. "Inequality Without Class Conflict." *Wall Street Journal* (12/18/1997), A22.

Lakoff, Sanford. *Equality in Political Philosophy.* Cambridge, MA: Harvard University Press, 1964.

Lamb, Matthew L. "Solidarity." In *New Dictionary of Catholic Social Thought*, edited by Judith A. Dwyer, 908–912. Collegeville, MN: Liturgical Press, 1994.

Lardner, James. "Deadly Disparities: Americans' Widening Gap in Incomes May Be Narrowing Our Lifespans." *Washington Post* (8/16/1998), C1, C4.

Latin American Episcopate. *Final Document.* In *Puebla and Beyond*, edited by John Eagleson and Philip Scharper, and translated by John Drury, 123–285. Maryknoll, NY: Orbis, 1979.

"Document on the Poverty of the Church, Documents of Medellin." In *Liberation Theology: A Documentary History*, edited by Alfred Hennelly, 114–119. Maryknoll, NY: Orbis, 1990 [1968].

Lebacqz, Karen. *Justice in an Unjust World: Foundations for a Christian Approach to Justice.* Minneapolis: Augsburg, 1987.

Leith, John H. *Creeds of the Churches: A Reader in Christian Doctrine, from the Bible to the Present.* Third edition. Atlanta: John Knox Press, 1982.

Lewin, Tamar. "Women Losing Ground to Men in Widening Income Difference." *New York Times* (9/15/1997), A1, A12.

"American Colleges Begin to Ask, Where Have All the Men Gone?" *New York Times* (12/6/1998).

Lovin, Robin. "Equality and Covenant Theology." *Journal of Law and Religion* 2/2 (1984): 241–262.

Reinhold Niebuhr and Christian Realism. Cambridge: Cambridge University Press, 1995.

Maasoumi, Esfandiar, and Gerald Nickelsburg, "Multivariate Measures of Well-Being and an Analysis of Inequality in the Michigan Data." *Journal of Business and Economic Statistics* 6/3 (July 1988): 327–334.

Mackay, James P. *Power and Christian Ethics.* Cambridge: Cambridge University Press, 1994.

Marglin, Stephen. "Towards the Decolonization of the Mind." In *Dominating Knowledge: Development, Culture, and Resistance*, edited by Frédérique Apffel Marglin and Stephen Marglin, 1–28. Oxford: Clarendon Press, 1990.

Marshall, Alfred. *Principles of Economics.* Eighth edition. London: Macmillan, 1920.

Marx, Karl. "Critique of the Gotha Program." In *The Marx-Engels Reader,* edited by Robert C. Tucker. Second edition. New York: Norton, 1978 [1972, 1875].

—— *Capital: A Critique of Political Economy.* Edited by Ernest Mandel and translated by Ben Fowkes. New York: Vintage Books (Random House), 1977 [1867].

Mathematical Society of Japan. *Encyclopedic Dictionary of Mathematics.* Vol. 1. Second edition. Edited by Kiyosi Itô. Cambridge, MA: MIT Press, 1968 [1960].

McCann, Dennis P. *Christian Realism and Liberation Theology: Practical Theologies in Creative Conflict.* Maryknoll, NY: Orbis, 1982.

McGovern, Arthur F. *Liberation Theology and Its Critics.* Maryknoll, NY: Orbis, 1989.

Míguez Bonino, José. "Love and Social Transformation in Liberation Theology." In *The Future of Liberation Theology: Essays in Honor of Gustavo Gutiérrez,* edited by Marc H. Ellis and Otto Maduro, 121–128. Maryknoll, NY: Orbis, 1989.

Milbank, John. *Theology and Social Theory: Beyond Secular Reason.* Oxford: Blackwell, 1990.

Miller, David, and Michael Walzer, editors. *Pluralism, Justice, and Equality.* Oxford: Oxford University Press, 1995.

Mitchell, Joshua. "The Equality of All Under the One in Luther and Rousseau: Thoughts on Christianity and Political Theory." *The Journal of Religion* 72 (1992): 351–365.

Moltmann, Jurgen. *Theology of Hope: On the Ground and the Implications of a Christian Eschatology.* Translated by James W. Leitch. London: SCM Press, 1967 [1965].

Morris, M. D. *Measuring the Condition of the World's Poor: The Physical Quality of Life Index.* London: Frank Cass, 1979.

Murray, Alan. "Income Inequality Grows Amid Recovery." *Wall Street Journal* (7/1/1996), A1.

National Center for Education Statistics. *The Condition of Education 1997.* Prepared by Thomas M. Smith, Beth Aronstamm Young, Yupin Bae, Susan P. Choy, and Nabeel Alsalam. NCES 97–388. US Department of Education, Office of Educational Research and Improvement. Washington: NCES, 1997.

National Conference of Catholic Bishops. *Economic Justice For All: Pastoral Letter on Catholic Social Teaching and the US Economy.* Washington: United States Catholic Conference, 1986.

Niebuhr, H. Richard. "The Grace of Doing Nothing." *Christian Century* 49 (3/23/1932): 378–380.

"A Communication: The Only Way into the Kingdom of God."
Christian Century 49 (4/6/1932): 447.

The Meaning of Revelation. New York: Macmillan, 1941.

Christ and Culture. New York: Harper & Row, 1951.

The Purpose of the Church and its Ministry: Reflections on the Aims of Theological Education. New York: Harper & Brothers, 1956.

The Responsible Self: An Essay in Christian Moral Philosophy. San Francisco: Harper & Row, 1963.

Radical Monotheism and Western Culture. New York: Harper & Row, 1970.

Faith on Earth: An Inquiry Into the Structure of Human Faith. Edited by Richard R. Niebuhr. New Haven: Yale University Press, 1989.

Theology, History, and Culture: Major Unpublished Writings of H. Richard Niebuhr, edited by William Stacy Johnson. New Haven: Yale University Press, 1996.

"A Christian Interpretation of War." In *Theology, History, and Culture: Major Unpublished Writings of H. Richard Niebuhr,* edited by William Stacy Johnson, 159–173. New Haven: Yale University Press, 1996.

"The Church Defines Itself in the World." In *Theology, History, and Culture: Major Unpublished Writings of H. Richard Niebuhr,* edited by William Stacy Johnson, 63–73. New Haven: Yale University Press, 1996.

"The Doctrine of the Trinity and the Unity of the Church." In *Theology, History, and Culture: Major Unpublished Writings of H. Richard Niebuhr,* edited by William Stacy Johnson, 50–62. New Haven: Yale University Press, 1996.

"The Idea of Original Sin in American Culture." In *Theology, History, and Culture: Major Unpublished Writings of H. Richard Niebuhr,* edited by William Stacy Johnson, 174–191. New Haven: Yale University Press, 1996.

"Man's Work and God's." In *Theology, History, and Culture: Major Unpublished Writings of H. Richard Niebuhr,* edited by William Stacy Johnson, 208–214. New Haven: Yale University Press, 1996.

"The Relation of Christianity and Democracy." In *Theology, History, and Culture: Major Unpublished Writings of H. Richard Niebuhr,* edited by William Stacy Johnson, 143–158. New Haven: Yale University Press, 1996.

"Theology in a Time of Disillusionment." In *Theology, History, and Culture: Major Unpublished Writings of H. Richard Niebuhr,* edited by William Stacy Johnson, 102–116. New Haven: Yale University Press, 1996.

Niebuhr, Reinhold. *Moral Man and Immoral Society: A Study in Ethics and Politics.* New York: Charles Scribner's Sons, 1932.

An Interpretation of Christian Ethics. New York: Harper & Brothers, 1935.

"Must We Do Nothing?" *Christian Century* 49 (3/30/1932): 415–417.

Niebuhr, Richard R. Foreword to *Theology, History, and Culture: Major Unpublished Writings of H. Richard Niebuhr,* edited by William Stacy Johnson, vii–x. New Haven: Yale University Press, 1996.

Novak, Michael. *Will it Liberate?: Questions about Liberation Theology.* New York: Paulist Press, 1988.

Nozick, Robert. *Anarchy, State, and Utopia.* Oxford: Blackwell, 1974.

Nussbaum, Martha. "Nature, Function, and Capability." *Oxford Studies in Ancient Philosophy* Supplementary Volume (1988).

"Non-Relative Virtues: An Aristotelian Approach." In *The Quality of Life,* edited by Martha Nussbaum and Amartya Sen, 242–269. Oxford: Clarendon Press, 1993.

Poetic Justice: The Literary Imagination in Public Life. Boston: Beacon Press, 1995.

Nussbaum, Martha, and Amartya Sen. *The Quality of Life.* Oxford: Clarendon Press, 1993.

Nussbaum, Martha, with respondents. *For Love of Country: Debating the Limits of Patriotism.* Boston: Beacon Press, 1996.

Oates, Whitney, J., editor. *The Basic Writings of Saint Augustine.* New York: Random House, 1948.

O'Brien, David J., and Thomas A. Shannon, editors. *Catholic Social Thought: The Documentary Heritage.* Maryknoll, NY: Orbis, 1992.

Okin, Susan Moller. "The Complex Inequalities of Gender." In *Pluralism, Justice, and Equality,* edited by David Miller and Michael Walzer, 120–143. Oxford: Oxford University Press, 1995.

Okun, Arthur M. *Equality and Efficiency: The Big Tradeoff.* Washington: The Brookings Institution, 1975.

O'Neill, S.J., William. "No Amnesty for Sorrow: The Privilege of the Poor in Christian Social Ethics." *Theological Studies* 55 (1994): 638–656.

Osmani, S. R. *Economic Inequality and Group Welfare: A Theory of Comparison with Application to Bangladesh.* Oxford: Clarendon Press, 1982.

Passell, Peter. "Rich Nation, Poor Nation: Is Anyone Even Looking for a Cure?" *New York Times* (8/13/1998), D2.

Paul VI. *Populorum Progressio: On the Development of Peoples.* In *Catholic Social Thought: The Documentary Heritage,* edited by David J. O'Brien and Thomas A. Shannon, 240–262. Maryknoll, NY: Orbis, 1992 [1967].

Pope, Stephen J. "The 'Preferential Option for the Poor': An Ethic for

'Saints and Heroes'?" *Irish Theological Quarterly* 59/3 (1993): 161–176.

"Proper and Improper Partiality and the Preferential Option for the Poor." *Theological Studies* 54/2 (1993): 242–271.

Rae, Douglas, et al. *Equalities.* Cambridge, MA: Harvard University Press, 1989 [1981].

Rainwater, Lee. *What Money Buys: Inequality and the Social Meaning of Income.* New York: Basic Books, 1974.

Rawls, John. *A Theory of Justice.* Cambridge, MA: Harvard University Press, 1971.

Political Liberalism. New York: Columbia University Press, 1993.

"Principles of Justice." Mimeographed, Harvard University, 1994.

"The Idea of Public Reason Revisited." *University of Chicago Law Review* 64 (1997): 765–807.

Roberts, Tyler T. "Michael Walzer and the Critical Connections." *Journal of Religious Ethics* 22/2 (fall 1994): 333–353.

Roper, Lyndal. *The Holy Household: Women and Morals in Reformation Augsburg.* Oxford and New York: Oxford University Press, 1991.

Sandel, Michael. *Liberalism and the Limits of Justice.* Cambridge: Cambridge University Press, 1982.

Democracy's Discontent: America in Search of a Public Philosophy. Cambridge, MA: Belknap Press/Harvard University Press, 1996.

Sanger, David E. "Big Racial Disparity Persists Among Users of the Internet." *New York Times* (7/9/1999), A12

Schor, Juliet. *The Overworked American: The Unexpected Decline of Leisure.* New York: Basic Books, 1992.

Schubeck, Thomas L. "Ethics and Liberation Theology." *Theological Studies* 56/1 (March 1995): 107–122.

Schüssler Fiorenza, Elisabeth. *In Memory of Her: A Feminist Theological Reconstruction of Christian Origins.* New York: Crossroad, 1983.

But She Said: Feminist Practices of Biblical Interpretation. Boston: Beacon Press, 1992.

"A Discipleship of Equals: Ekklesial Democracy and Patriarchy in Biblical Perspective." In *A Democratic Catholic Church: The Reconstruction of Roman Catholicism,* edited by Eugene C. Bianchi and Rosemary Radford Ruether, 17–33. New York: Crossroad, 1992.

Discipleship of Equals: A Feminist Critical Ekklesia-logy of Liberation. New York: Crossroad, 1993.

"Introduction: Feminist Liberation Theology as Critical Sophialogy." In *The Power of Naming: A* Concilium *Reader in Feminist Liberation Theology,* edited by Elisabeth Schüssler Fiorenza, xiii–xxxix. Maryknoll, NY: Orbis, 1996.

Schüssler Fiorenza, Elisabeth, editor. *The Power of Naming: A* Concilium

Reader in Feminist Liberation Theology. Maryknoll, NY: Orbis, 1996.

Scott, Janny. "Working Hard, More or Less." *New York Times* (7/10/99), A15, A17.

Scott, Joan. "Deconstructing Equality-Versus-Difference." *Feminist Studies* 14 (1988): 33–50.

Second Vatican Council. *Gaudium et Spes: Pastoral Constitution on the Church in the Modern World*. In *Catholic Social Thought: The Documentary Heritage*, edited by David O'Brien and Thomas A. Shannon, 166–237. Maryknoll, NY: Orbis, 1992 [1965].

Sedgwick, Peter H. *The Market Economy and Christian Ethics*. Cambridge: Cambridge University Press,1999.

Sen, Amartya. *On Economic Inequality*. Oxford: Clarendon Press, 1973.
"Real National Income." *Review of Economic Studies* 43 (February 1976): 19–39. Reprinted in Sen, *Choice, Welfare, and Development*. Cambridge, MA: MIT Press, 1982.
"Poverty: An Ordinal Approach to Measurement." *Econometrica* 44 (1976): 219–231.
"Rational Fools: A Critique of the Behavioural Foundations of Economic Theory." *Philosophy and Public Affairs* 6 (1977): 317–344. Reprinted in Sen, *Choice, Welfare, and Development*. Cambridge, MA: MIT Press, 1982.
"Description as Choice." *Oxford Economic Papers* 32 (1980): 353–369. Reprinted in Sen, *Choice, Welfare, and Development*. Cambridge, MA: MIT Press, 1982.
"Equality of What?" In *The Tanner Lectures on Human Values*, edited by Sterling M. McMurrin, vol. 1, 195–220. Salt Lake City: University of Utah Press and Cambridge University Press, 1980. Reprinted in Sen, *Choice, Welfare, and Development*. Cambridge, MA: MIT Press, 1982.
"Public Action and the Quality of Life in Developing Countries." *Oxford Bulletin of Economics and Statistics* 43/1 (1981): 287–319.
Choice, Welfare, and Measurement. Cambridge, MA: MIT Press, 1982.
"Development: Which Way Now?" *Economic Journal* 93 (December 1983): 742–762. Reprinted in Sen, *Resources, Values, and Development*. Cambridge, MA: Harvard University Press, 1984.
"Economics and the Family." *Asian Development Review* 1 (1983): 14–26. Reprinted in Sen, *Resources, Values, and Development*. Cambridge, MA: Harvard University Press, 1984.
"Poor, Relatively Speaking." *Oxford Economic Papers* 35 (1983): 153–169. Reprinted in Sen, *Resources, Values, and Development*. Cambridge, MA: Harvard University Press, 1984.
Commodities and Capabilities. Amsterdam: North-Holland, 1985.

"Goals, Commitment, and Identity." *Journal of Law, Economics, and Organization* 1/2 (1985): 341–355.

On Ethics and Economics. Oxford: Blackwell, 1987.

The Standard of Living (1985 Tanner Lectures at Cambridge, with contributions by Keith Hart, Ravi Kanbur, John Muellbauer, and Bernard Williams, edited by G. Hawthorn). Cambridge: Cambridge University Press, 1987.

"The Concept of Development." In *The Handbook of Development Economics*, edited by H. Chenery and T. N. Srinivasan, 9–26. Oxford: Elsevier Science Publishers, 1988.

"More Than 100 Million Women are Missing." *New York Review of Books* 37/20 (12/20/1990), 61–66. Revised version of "Women's Survival as a Development Problem," *Bulletin of the American Academy of Arts and Sciences* 43 (November 1989).

"Gender and Cooperative Conflicts." In *Persistent Inequalities*, edited by Irene Tinker, 123–149. New York: Oxford University Press, 1990.

"Justice: Means vs. Freedoms." *Philosophy and Public Affairs* 19 (1990): 111–123.

Inequality Reexamined. Cambridge, MA: Harvard University Press/ Russell Sage, 1992.

"The Economics of Life and Death." *Scientific American* 268/5 (May 1993), 40–47.

"Capability and Well-Being." In *The Quality of Life*, edited by Martha Nussbaum and Amartya Sen, 30–53. Oxford: Clarendon Press, 1993.

On Economic Inequality. Expanded edition with a substantial annexe by James E. Foster and Amartya Sen. London: Oxford: Clarendon Press, 1997.

"Assessing Human Development: Special Contribution." In *Human Development Report 1999*, 23. New York: Oxford University Press, 1999.

Skocpol, Theda. "Targeting Within Universalism: Politically Viable Policies to Combat Poverty in the United States." Discussion Paper Series H-90-2, Center for Health and Human Resources Policy, John F. Kennedy School of Government, Harvard University, 1990.

Smith, Adam. *An Inquiry into the Nature and Causes of the Wealth of Nations.* London: Everyman Edition, Home University Library, 1776.

The Theory of Moral Sentiments. Edited by D. D. Raphael and A. L Macfie. Indianapolis: Liberty Press, 1982 [1790].

Sobrino, S.J., Jon. "Central Position of the Reign of God in Liberation Theology." In *Mysterium Liberationis: Fundamental Concepts in Libera-*

tion Theology, edited by Ignacio Ellacuría, S.J. and Jon Sobrino, S.J., 350–388. Maryknoll, NY: Orbis, 1993.

"Systematic Christology." In *Mysterium Liberationis: Fundamental Concepts in Liberation Theology*, edited by Ignacio Ellacuría, S.J. and Jon Sobrino, S.J., 440–461. Maryknoll, NY: Orbis, 1993.

Sobrino, Jon, and Juan Hernández Pico. *Theology of Christian Solidarity*. Translated by Phillip Berryman. Maryknoll, NY: Orbis, 1985 [1983].

Speth, James Gustave. "Global Inequality: 358 Billionaires vs. 2.3 Billion People." *New Perspectives Quarterly* (fall 1996), 32–33.

Srinivasan, T. N. "Human Development: A New Paradigm or Reinvention of the Wheel?" *American Economic Review* 84/2 (1994), 238–243.

Stassen, Glen. "Michael Walzer's Situated Justice." *Journal of Religious Ethics* 22/2 (fall 1994): 375–399.

Stevenson, Richard W. "Black–White Economic Gap is Narrowing, White House Says." *New York Times* (2/10/1998), A16.

"Black–White Income Inequalities." *New York Times* (2/17/1998).

Stolberg, Sheryl Gay. "Racial Divide Found in Maternal Mortality," *New York Times* (6/18/1999), A18.

Streeten, Paul. "The Distinctive Features of a Basic Needs Approach to Development." *International Development Review* (1977). Reprinted in *Development* 40 (1997): 49–56.

"Human Development: Means and Ends." *American Economic Review* 84/2 (1994): 232–237.

Streeten, Paul, Shahid Javed Burki, Mahbub ul Haq, Norman Hicks, and Frances Stewart. *First Things First: Meeting Basic Human Needs in the Developing Countries*. Oxford: Oxford University Press for the World Bank, 1981.

Synod of Bishops. *Justice in the World*. In *Catholic Social Thought: The Documentary Heritage*, edited by David J. O'Brien and Thomas A. Shannon, 288–300. Maryknoll, NY: Orbis, 1992 [1987].

Tanner, Kathryn. *The Politics of God: Christian Theologies and Social Justice*. Minneapolis: Fortress Press, 1992.

"A Theological Case for Human Responsibility in Moral Choice." *The Journal of Religion* 73/4 (October 1993): 592–612.

Taussig, Michael T. *The Devil and Commodity Fetishism in Latin America*. Chapel Hill, NC: University of North Carolina Press, 1980.

Temple, William. *Christianity and the Social Order*. Harmondsworth, UK: Penguin, 1977 [1942].

Thiemann, Ronald F. *Revelation and Theology: The Gospel as Narrated Promise*. Notre Dame, IN: Univ. of Notre Dame, 1985.

Religion in Public Life: A Dilemma for Democracy. Washington: George-town University Press, 1996.

"Public Religion: Bane or Blessing for Democracy?" In *Religion and Law: Obligations of Citizenship, Demands of Faith,* edited by Nancy Rosenblum. Princeton: Princeton University Press, forthcoming.

Thurow, Lester. "The Income Distribution as a Pure Public Good." *Quarterly Journal of Economics* 85/2 (May 1971): 327–336.

Generating Inequality: Mechanisms of Distribution in the US Economy. New York: Basic Books, 1975.

The Future of Capitalism. New York: W. Murrow, 1996.

"The Boom that Wasn't," *New York Times* (1/18/1999).

Tocqueville, Alexis de. *Democracy in America.* New York: Harper Perennial, 1969 [1840].

Todorov, Tzvetan. *The Conquest of America: The Question of the Other.* Translated by Richard Howard. New York: Harper Perennial, 1984 [1982].

Uchitelle, Louis. "Strike Points to Inequality in 2–Tier Job Market." *New York Times* (8/8/1997), A22.

"More Work, Less Pay Make Jack Look Better Off." *New York Times* (10/5/1997), WK4.

"The Have-Nots, at Least, Have Shelter in a Storm." *New York Times* (9/20/1998), BU4.

UNESCO. *UNESCO '95 Statistical Yearbook.* Lanham, MD and Paris: UNESCO, 1995.

United Nations. *UN Demographic Yearbook 1992 – Special Topic: Fertility and Mortality Statistics.* New York: United Nations, 1992.

United Nations Department for Economic and Social Information and Policy Analysis – Statistical Division. *Trends in International Disiribution of Gross World Product.* National Accounts Statistics *Special Issue* series x, no. 18. New York: United Nations, 1993.

United Nations Development Programme. *Human Development Report 1990.* New York: Oxford University Press, 1990.

Human Development Report 1991. New York: Oxford University Press, 1991.

Human Development Report 1992. New York: Oxford University Press, 1992.

Human Development Report 1993. New York: Oxford University Press, 1993.

Human Development Report 1994. New York: Oxford University Press, 1994.

Human Development Report 1995. New York: Oxford University Press, 1995.

Human Development Report 1996. New York: Oxford University Press, 1996.

Human Development Report 1997. New York: Oxford University Press, 1997.

Human Development Report 1998. New York: Oxford University Press, 1998.

Human Development Report 1999. New York: Oxford University Press, 1999.

US Census Bureau. "Educational Attainment in the United States: March 1995." *Current Population Report*, P20–489. Detailed tables for P20–489: PPL-48. Washington: US Census Bureau, 1995.

US Council of Economic Advisors. *Economic Report of the President 1992.* Washington: US Government Printing Office, 1992.

Economic Report of the President 1995. Washington: US Government Printing Office, 1995.

Economic Report of the President 1997. Washington: US Government Printing Office, 1997.

Economic Report of the President 1998. Washington: US Government Printing Office, 1998.

Economic Report of the President 1999. Washington: US Government Printing Office, 1999.

US Department of Health and Human Services, Centers for Disease Control and Prevention/National Center for Health Statistics. *Monthly Vital Statistics Report* vol. 45, no. 2, supplement 2 (6/12/1997).

US Department of Health and Human Services. *Vital Statistics of the United States 1992.* Hyattsville, MD: US Department of Health and Human Services, 1996.

Veatch, Robert. *The Foundations of Justice: Why the Retarded and the Rest of Us Have Claims to Equality.* New York: Oxford University Press, 1986.

Verba, Sydney, Steven Kelman, Gary R. Orren, Ichiro Miyake, Joji Watanuki, Ikuo Kabashima, and G. Donald Ferree, Jr. *Elites and the Idea of Equality: A Comparison of Japan, Sweden, and the United States.* Cambridge, MA: Harvard University Press, 1987.

Verba, Sydney, and Gary R. Orren. *Equality in America: The View from the Top.* Cambridge, MA: Harvard University Press, 1985.

Verba, Sydney, Kay Lehman Scholzman, and Henry E. Brady. *Voice and Equality: Civic Voluntarism in American Politics.* Cambridge, MA: Harvard University Press, 1995.

Walker, Martin. "Behind Bars of Fort Suburbia: Crime Rate Goes Down as Common-Interest Developments Go Up." *Pittsburgh Post-Gazette* (7/13/1997), A9.

Walzer, Michael, *The Revolution of the Saints: A Study in the Origins of Radical Politics.* Cambridge, MA: Harvard University Press, 1965.

"In Defense of Equality." *Dissent* 20/4 (fall 1973), 399–408.

Spheres of Justice: A Defense of Pluralism and Equality. New York: Basic Books, 1983.

"Shared Meaning in a Poly-Ethnic Democratic Setting: A Response." *Journal of Religious Ethics* 22/2 (fall 1994): 401–405.

"Response." In *Pluralism, Justice, and Equality,* edited by David Miller and Michael Walzer, 281–297. Oxford: Oxford University Press, 1995.

"Gulf Crisis." *The New Republic* (8/5/1996), 25.

Watson, Douglas. "Indigenous Peoples and the Global Economy." *Current History: A Journal of Contemporary World Affairs* 96/613 (November 1997): 389–391.

Weale, Albert. "Equality, Social Solidarity, and the Welfare State." *Ethics* 100 (April 1990): 473–488.

Weber, Max. *The Protestant Ethic and the Spirit of Capitalism.* Translated by Talcott Parsons. New York: Routledge, 1992 [1930, 1904/5].

Weigel, Van B. "The Basic Needs Approach: Overcoming the Poverty of *Homo oeconomicus.*" *World Development* 14/12 (December 1986): 1423–1434.

Weinberg, Daniel H. "A Brief Look at Postwar U.S. Income Inequality." *Current Population Reports – Household Economic Studies* P60–191. Washington: US Census Bureau, 1996.

Weinstein, Michael M. "How Low the Boom Can Go." *New York Times* (6/13/1999).

Weithman, Paul J. "Introduction: Religion and the Liberalism of Reasoned Respect." In *Religion and Contemporary Liberalism,* edited by Paul J. Weithman, 1–37. Notre Dame, IN: University of Notre Dame Press, 1997.

"Complementarity and Equality in the Political Thought of Aquinas," Society of Christian Ethics Annual Meeting, Atlanta, January 1998.

Weithman, Paul J., editor. *Religion and Contemporary Liberalism.* Notre Dame, IN: University of Notre Dame Press, 1997.

Wilkinson, Richard G. "Divided We Fall: The Poor Pay the Price of Increased Social Inequality with Their Health." *British Medical Journal* (4/30/1994): 1113–1114.

"The Epidemiological Transition: From Material Scarcity to Social Disadvantage?" *Daedalus* 123/4 (fall 1994): 61–77.

Will, George. "Healthy Inequality." *Newsweek* (10/28/1996), 92.

Wilson, William Julius. *When Work Disappears: The World of the New Urban Poor.* New York: Alfred A. Knopf, 1996.

Wolff, Edward N. *Top Heavy: The Increasing Inequality of Wealth in America and What Can Be Done about It.* New York: New Press, 1995.

Wolterstorff, Nicholas. *Until Justice and Peace Embrace.* Grand Rapids, MI: Eerdmans, 1983.

World Bank, *World Development Report 1993.* New York: Oxford University Press, 1993.

   World Development Report 1995. New York: Oxford University Press, 1995.

   World Development Report 1998/99. Oxford: Oxford University Press, 1999.

Yearley, Lee H. *Mencius and Aquinas: Theories of Virtue and Conceptions of Courage.* Albany, NY: SUNY Press, 1990.

Young, Iris Marion. *Justice and the Politics of Difference.* Princeton: Princeton University Press, 1990.

Index